THE ST. MARTIN'S
BIBLIOGRAPHY
OF
BUSINESS
AND
TECHNICAL
COMMUNICATION

Gerald J. Alred
University of Wisconsin–Milwaukee

St. Martin's Press
New York

TO JANICE

Sponsoring editor: Barbara A. Heinssen
Editorial assistant: Natalie Hart
Manager, Publishing services: Emily Berleth
Publishing services associate: Meryl Gross
Production supervisor: Joe Ford
Project management: Richard Steins
Cover design: Patricia McFadden

Library of Congress Catalog Card Number: 96-069583

For information, write:
St. Martin's Press, Inc.
175 Fifth Avenue
New York, NY 10010

ISBN: 0-312-13314-6

CONTENTS

PREFACE

The St. Martin's Bibliography of Business and Technical Communication is offered as a resource for a wide range of people involved with business and technical communication, including teachers, graduate students, program directors, and consultants. It will be particularly useful to those who are new to this field. With 376 annotated items in a variety of relevant subject areas, this bibliography offers a comprehensive framework for teaching, research, and professional development. It includes articles, journals, and books as well as listings of professional associations, conferences and meetings, and Internet discussion groups—all of which provide connections that can lead to the further study of important topics. The Subject Index is especially useful for those items that fall under more than one category.

The St. Martin's Bibliography of Business and Technical Communication was conceived in part because of the exponential increase in published works in business and technical communication during the past two decades. Even as this bibliography was in final production, many important books and articles were being published or were in press. In this context, the book is a work in progress. It is interesting to consider what the bibliography might look like when a future edition is published. To that end, suggestions are welcome; please direct any comments or suggestions to:

Editor, Business and Technical Communication
St. Martin's Press
345 Park Avenue South
New York, NY 10010

ACKNOWLEDGMENTS

When the second edition of *The Bedford Bibliography for Teachers of Writing* was published, I asked St. Martin's Press when something comparable would be published for teachers of business and technical communication. St. Martin's responded by saying, in effect: "Good idea. Why don't you do it?" Although the work has been daunting at times, we both realize the value of such a bibliographical resource for the field of business and technical communication, and we hope we have achieved our objectives.

This project has been challenging, and I have enjoyed reviewing many works with which I was unfamiliar. I have appreciated even more working with colleagues across the country. Indeed, this bibliography could not have been completed without the generous help of many people.

First, I owe an intellectual debt to the many colleagues who have influenced my thinking and given me encouragement over the years. I must also acknowledge the significant contributions of those who compiled the "Professional Resources" sections: Dave Clark and Clay Spinuzzi, Iowa State University, for the section "Professional Associations"; Michael J. Hassett, Boise State University, for the section "Professional Journals"; and Christianna White and Mark Zachry, Iowa State University, for the section "Conferences and Meetings." I want to thank especially Stuart A. Selber, Texas Tech University, who compiled the section "Internet Discussion Groups" and also helped in numerous ways as we regularly filled each other's email boxes.

I owe a debt that I can never fully repay to the following colleagues who contributed to this project at various stages of its development: Karen D. Austin, University of Wisconsin–Milwaukee; Rebecca E. Burnett, Iowa State University; Nancy Gaynor, University of Wisconsin–Milwaukee; William Hart-Davidson, Purdue University; Sandra E. Jones, University of Wisconsin–Milwaukee; Mohan R. Limaye, Boise State University; Kitty O. Locker, Ohio State University; Michelle L. Lublin, University of Wisconsin–Milwaukee; Mike Markel, Boise State University; Renee A. Meyers, University of Wisconsin–Milwaukee; Carolyn R. Miller, North Carolina State University; Tim Peeples, Purdue University; James E. Porter, Purdue University; Diana C. Reep, University of Akron; John Frederick Reynolds, City College of CUNY; William E. Rivers, University of South Carolina; Erin Sahlstein, University of Wisconsin–Milwaukee; Donald Samson, Radford University; Jack Selzer, Penn State University; Jackie M. Simon, University of Wisconsin–Milwaukee; James P. Soderholm, University of Wisconsin–Milwaukee; Christine M. Tutlewski, University of Wisconsin–Milwaukee; William V. Van Pelt, University of Wisconsin–Milwaukee; Debra Villa, University of Wisconsin–Milwaukee; Marsha Watson, University of Wisconsin–Milwaukee; Katherine Wikoff, Milwaukee School of Engineering; and Kristin Woolever, Northeastern University.

I would like to thank particularly Nancy Linh Karls, my research assistant and a contributor. Nancy's impressive abilities together with her cheerful optimism helped me believe I could finish the project by the deadline. Thanks to Anne Dempsey, my developmental editor at St. Martin's Press, who was a constant help and resource, and to Barbara Heinssen of St. Martin's Press for sustaining and enhancing this project. Finally, I give my heartfelt appreciation to Nancy Lyman for believing in me and giving life to this project.

INTRODUCTION

> Work can provide the opportunity for spiritual and personal, as well as financial, growth. If it doesn't, then we're wasting far too much of our lives on it.
>
> James A. Autry
> *Love and Profit*

The academy has traditionally viewed the workplace as something "out there," the "nonacademic," the "real world," the place students go "to enter." However, as we have come to understand better the nature of modern workplaces and to recognize academic institutions as organizational structures, the boundaries between the two have become more illusory than actual. Indeed, we can no longer view workplaces as "places" where individuals appear at an appointed time and spend a defined period with a limited group of coworkers. As communication technology continues to evolve and as organizational structures radically change in a global environment, such views are becoming anachronistic. Consider how one observer, Tom Peters, describes the business scene at the end of the twentieth century:

> Individuals are becoming more autonomous, with responsibility for creating projects and managing their careers, on or off corporate payrolls. And they are engaged in more partnering activities—depending more on each other as teammates, and on other members of an expansive network that invariably includes numerous "outsiders." (473)

What I find personally interesting about this statement is that it describes precisely the way this bibliography was prepared. At one point, I felt as though I had become part of a "virtual department" of colleagues geographically separated from one another but connected by the Internet. In fact, I had much more regular contact with my "virtual" colleagues than I did with colleagues in my own department.

Such workplaces are not inscribed by walls or even by single institutions. They exist anywhere reachable by cellular phone, near a fax machine, or connected to the Internet. In such an environment, the question "Where do you work?" has much less meaning than "What projects occupy your work?" Under these conditions, we begin to recognize that academic departments are workplaces as much as are such diverse sites as hospitals, law firms, offices in homes and apartments, and businesses both small and large.

WORK AND HUMAN COMMUNICATION

Regardless of how work is organized, the workplace is far more than technology and even structure: Work is an essential condition of human activity. The conditions are not always ideal, of course, and those with whom we share our workplaces are not always easy collaborators. Nevertheless, the workplace (virtual or otherwise) is where we live out much of our lives with other people. That's why James A. Autry (CEO, poet, and author of books on management) declares: "In fact, there is no business; there are only people. Business exists only *among* people and *for* people" (39). Indeed, even when we work in physical isolation, we can no longer work in social isolation. For this reason, I wrote a number of years ago that one goal of communication in the workplace should be to "help us conduct our business with some humanity toward our fellow human beings" (Alred, Reep, and Limaye 9). Certainly the scholar-authors of works published early in the twentieth century advocated high "moral ideals" because they understood that the workplace is where communication has significant human consequences.

This bibliography demonstrates that scholars today are similarly concerned with ethics and with issues of gender, culture, and collaboration—all those ways our communication affects those with whom we work and for whom we produce material goods. As many authors in this bibliography also suggest, the way we communicate technical information affects the application of technology for all of us. For this reason, Peter Drucker has observed that "specialists have to take responsibility for making both themselves and their specialty understood" (217). In the past, teachers of technical communication gave similar admonitions. For example, Sada Harbarger wrote in 1923:

> To be one of the best engineers [is] to explain, for example, the engine so that the uninformed, the disinterested will not only admire its mechanical perfection but also appreciate its possibilities as the engineer dreams them. . . . (254)

Many early teachers also understood that, when specialists communicate information, the well-being of their audiences is at stake. As numerous authors in this bibliography have suggested, the way technology is communicated affects us all for good or ill (cf. Sauer). But lest we see the specialist as the "other," Peter Drucker reminds us that in the future we will all be specialists at one time or the other (214). I agree. But I would add that the future is now.

INTERDISCIPLINARY ENTERPRISE

The teaching and study of writing and communication in the workplace have a long tradition in the American academy. Even so, finding a satisfactory name for this enterprise has always posed problems. Technical and business writing, English, or communication; professional writing or communication; management communication; writing in the workplace, nonacademic settings, or professions: None of these names is entirely descriptive, and critics have pointed out how some are even misleading (cf. Allen; and Dobrin). Many of these labels reflect the organizational structure of the academy, and others represent traditional associations. None of them is sufficiently ecumenical to make everyone comfortable. As a result, many of us have struggled with this problem in establishing our own professional identities.

A significant part of the difficulty in finding a name is the interdisciplinary character of our enterprise. This character is evident in the diversity of categories in this bibliography: visual and graphic design, rhetorical studies and audience, computer documentation, workplace and genre studies, ethics and gender, management and organizational theory, technology theory, and so on. Other fields are certainly interdisciplinary to one extent or the other, but this field is *necessarily* interdisciplinary. Because workplaces are not like classrooms or laboratories, we must study not only writing processes but also organizational theories, for example, that modulate those processes. We must be concerned not only with written texts but also with visual design that clarifies meaning and establishes the ethos of the organization. We must study not only the qualities of written texts but also the interactions of all forms of verbal and nonverbal communication as they function in the workplace simultaneously—and quite oblivious to academic boundaries.

To teach or to study such an interdisciplinary subject, even when it is rewarding, is also problematic (cf. Locker). For one thing, academic institutions are organized in ways that fragment such work methodologically, philosophically, and politically. However, working on this bibliography as well as seeing changes in the academy have reinforced my sense that the organizational and philosophical barriers to interdisciplinary work are not as rigid as in the past. At least I would like to hope that disciplinary boundaries are blurring, because I find that interdisciplinary work is not only challenging but also exciting—and even liberating.

THEORY, PRACTICE, AND PEDAGOGY

Finally, as I reviewed the works in this bibliography, I became acutely aware of why theory, practice, and pedagogy are inevitably connected. Essentially, the practice of writing and communicating in the workplace is both the object of our study and the goal of our pedagogy. Therefore, theory is necessary to prevent us from being overwhelmed by what is local, particular, and temporal. In turn, pedagogy both mediates practice and transforms our theory. Indeed, one reason I find this work rewarding is that I sense it puts me at the intersection of theory, practice, and pedagogy as they are involved with writing in the workplace. As academic institutions increasingly begin to recognize the value of cross-disciplinary research and the importance of making connections to what is "out there," perhaps the scholarly work represented in this bibliography will serve as a model for other disciplines in the twenty-first century.

METHODOLOGY

Because business and technical communication is so thoroughly interdisciplinary, I needed to find ways to compensate for my own limitations and scholarly prejudices. The first task was to gather titles as candidates for inclusion; my goal here was to collect them from as many diverse sources as possible. The result was a year-long search, during which I collected more than 800 titles from over 50 of the following sources:

- Published literature reviews and selected bibliographies
- Formal content and citation studies in a number of appropriate scholarly journals
- The works-cited sections from recent scholarly books and selected articles
- Standard lists used in graduate and undergraduate programs
- Lists of award-winning books and articles
- Published lists of "recommended" or "influential" books and articles from academic, nonacademic, and Internet sources.
- Personal lists and recommendations from both new and experienced teachers and scholars, many of whom are listed in the "Acknowledgments" section of the Preface
- My own lists gathered over the past 20 years

As I reviewed sources, each title was coded for every source in which it was listed. With this coding, then, I would know which and how many sources listed any particular title.

The next step was to determine the categories. My primary goal was to allow the categories to grow out of the subjects of the works themselves, as opposed to fitting titles into some sort of predetermined outline. I also wanted the categories to reflect the interdisciplinary nature of the field while recognizing its particular focus: What are the general categories that apply to any scholarly subject? What are the particular concerns of business and technical communication? For books, I considered the categories used by major libraries, such as at Harvard and MIT. Certainly it was important to make categories useful and balanced. Still, many categories overlap; for example, some "Workplace and Genre Studies" could easily fit under "Rhetorical Studies and Audience." To help compensate for such inevitable overlap, I have included a Subject Index. The Subject Index is a vital tool because many articles about specific topics appear within collections.

Practical reasons and publishing constraints made it clear that I could not include up to a thousand items. A huge list would not be useful in any case. One consideration, as suggested earlier, was the number and diversity of sources that listed any particular item. For example, when a title appeared in many diverse sources, I could be fairly certain that it was a strong candidate. However, I did not want to use a purely numerical count as the overriding criterion for including or excluding a title. So I considered as well the following criteria:

- Whether a work provides leads for further study (particularly in the "Interdisciplinary Connections" section)
- Whether a work introduces an important area of study unfamiliar to some readers, or an area in which fewer titles had been published
- Whether early publications had great historical importance
- Whether a work had been superseded by later publications (for example, I did not list bibliographies published before 1980 and thus included in the Alred, Reep, Limaye bibliography)
- Whether an item was readily available to readers through standard means, such as interlibrary loan

Although I used all these strategies and appealed to colleagues for help in areas less familiar to me, ultimately mine was the final judgment.

WORKS CITED

Allen, Jo. "The Case against Defining Technical Writing." *Journal of Business and Technical Communication* 4.2 (September 1990): 68–77.

Autry, James A. *Love and Profit: The Art of Caring Leadership.* New York: Morrow, 1991.

Alred, Gerald J., Diana C. Reep, and Mohan R. Limaye. *Business and Technical Writing: An Annotated Bibliography of Books, 1880–1980.* Metuchen, NJ: Scarecrow, 1981.

Dobrin, David N. *Writing and Technique.* Urbana: NCTE, 1989.

Drucker, Peter F. *Post-Capitalist Society.* New York: HarperCollins, 1993.

Harbarger, S. A. *English for Engineers.* New York: McGraw, 1923.

Locker, Kitty O. "The Challenge of Interdisciplinary Research." *Journal of Business Communication* 31.2 (April 1994): 137–49.

Peters, Tom. *Liberation Management: Necessary Disorganization for the Nanosecond Nineties.* New York: Knopf, 1992.

Sauer, Beverly A. "Sense and Sensibility in Technical Documentation: How Feminist Interpretation Strategies Can Save Lives in the Nation's Mines." *Journal of Business and Technical Communication* 7.1 (January 1993): 63–83.

PROFESSIONAL RESOURCES

The following lists provide information on professional associations, conferences, journals, and Internet discussion groups of interest to teachers of business and technical communication. The addresses and other details provided were accurate at the time this bibliography was published.

PROFESSIONAL ASSOCIATIONS

Compiled by Dave Clark and Clay Spinuzzi
Iowa State University

The following are professional associations of interest to business and technical communication teachers.

ACADEMY OF MANAGEMENT

The Academy of Management supports teaching and research in management. Its members include professors of management as well as businesspeople in industry who contribute to the literature of management and organizational theory and practice. The academy produces a number of publications, including a bimonthly journal, a newsletter, and a quarterly review.

Contact Information:
PACE University
P.O. Box 3020
Briarcliff Manor, NY 10510-8020
Phone: (914) 923-2607 Fax: (914) 923-2615
email: aom@academy.pace.edu
WWW: http://www.aom.pace.edu

ALLIANCE FOR COMPUTERS AND WRITING

The Alliance for Computers and Writing (ACW) promotes the use of computers in the teaching of writing. Its members include teachers and researchers in public schools and in two-year and four-year colleges and universities. Members of the organization collaborate on methods and technology using its email discussion list and World Wide Web pages.

Wired Style: Principles of English Usage in the Digital Age, by the editors of *Wired* magazine, recommends spelling *email* with a lower-case *e* and without a hyphen.

1

Contact Information:
Fred Kemp, Co-Director
Department of English
Texas Tech University
Lubbock, TX 79409
Phone: None at publication
email: alliance@ttacs.ttu.edu
WWW: http://english.ttu.edu/acw/

AMERICAN ASSOCIATION FOR THE ADVANCEMENT OF SCIENCE

The American Association for the Advancement of Science (AAAS) is the largest general scientific organization; its 143,000 members represent all the fields of science. The goals of the association are to promote the work of scientists by facilitating collaboration and advancing education and to improve the effectiveness of science in promoting human welfare. The association has established committees for many scientific specialties, from History and Philosophy of Science to Psychology to Physics, and it publishes *Science* magazine as well as numerous annual research reports and newsletters.

Contact Information:
1200 New York Avenue, Northwest
Washington, DC 20005
Phone: (202) 325-6400 Fax: (202) 371-9526
email: None at publication
WWW: http://www.aaas.org

AMERICAN SOCIETY FOR TRAINING AND DEVELOPMENT

The American Society for Training and Development (ASTD) is a professional association for those involved in the training and development of business, industry, education, and government employees. The society operates a 3,000-volume information center, performs and promotes research projects, and maintains a database of information from conferences and seminars. The society also produces books, collections, and periodicals on topics in training and development.

Contact Information:
Box 1443
1640 King Street
Alexandria, VA 22313

Phone: (703) 683-8100 Fax: (703) 683-1523
email: info@ASTD.org
WWW: http://www.astd.org

ASSOCIATION FOR BUSINESS COMMUNICATION

The Association for Business Communication (ABC) is an international organization dedicated to research and practice in business communication. Its members
include teachers and researchers from both educational and workplace settings
who are interested in promoting improvements in workplace communication. The
association publishes the *Business Communication Quarterly, Journal of Business
Communication,* and other special publications. ABC sponsors both national and
regional conferences.

Contact Information:
Baruch College, CUNY
Department of Speech
Box G1326
17 Lexington Avenue
New York, NY 10010
Phone: (212) 387-1340 Fax: (212) 387-1406
email: magabc@aol.com
WWW: http://www.cohums.ohio-state.edu/english/facstf/kol/abc/

THE ASSOCIATION OF COMPUTING MACHINERY SPECIAL INTEREST GROUP FOR DOCUMENTATION (SIGDOC)

SIGDOC encourages professional communicators to examine, discuss, and
improve documentation both for the computer industry and for other industries
using computers. Its members include documentation professionals, researchers,
system analysts, and program managers.

Contact Information:
ACM Member Service Department, Association for Computing Machinery
P.O. Box 12115
Church Street Station, NY 10249
Phone: (212) 626-0500 Fax: (212) 944-1318
email: acmhelp@acm.org
WWW: http://www.acm.org/sigdoc

ASSOCIATION OF PROFESSIONAL COMMUNICATION CONSULTANTS

The Association of Professional Communication Consultants (APCC) is a non-profit organization "dedicated to supporting and improving the communication consulting profession." Members include consultants who have their own consulting firms, who work for consulting firms, or who have full-time positions in business or in academic institutions and consult part time. The APCC maintains a listserv for discussion of consulting issues and produces a newsletter titled *Consulting Success*.

Contact Information:
Reva Daniel
Dynamic Business Writing
1301 Post Road
Clinton, MS 39056
Phone: (601) 924-2173
email: revadaniel@aol.com
WWW: http://www.iupui.edu/%7Ekdavis/apcc/home.html

ASSOCIATION OF TEACHERS OF TECHNICAL WRITING

The Association of Teachers of Technical Writing (ATTW) fosters the development of technical communication by encouraging technical communication teachers and professional communicators to promote the discipline, both inside and outside the classroom. The ATTW's international membership includes over one thousand teachers and professional communicators. The ATTW publishes materials on a wide variety of topics of interest to teachers of technical writing.

Contact Information:
Billie J. Wahlstrom, ATTW
Department of Rhetoric
201 Haecker Hall
1364 Eckles Avenue
University of Minnesota
St. Paul, MN 55108-6122
Phone: None at publication
email: See WWW page for officers' addresses.
WWW: http://english.ttu.edu/ATTW/

COUNCIL FOR PROGRAMS IN TECHNICAL AND SCIENTIFIC COMMUNICATION

The Council for Programs in Technical and Scientific Communication (CPTSC) includes administrators of programs in technical and scientific communication, service programs, and publication groups, as well as academics and professionals who plan to develop such programs. The CPTSC also produces a newsletter and an annual proceedings.

Contact Information:
Henrietta Shirk, CPTSC Treasurer
Department of English
Boise State University
698 North Heathstone Drive
Boise, ID 83702
Phone: (505) 646-2027 (Stephen A. Bernhardt)
email: sbernhar@nmsu.edu

IEEE PROFESSIONAL COMMUNICATION SOCIETY

The IEEE Professional Communication Society (PCS) encourages engineers and technical communicators to develop skills for presenting information in written and oral forms, using visual and digital media. The PCS encourages technical accuracy, user friendliness, and cross-cultural effectiveness.

Contact Information:
Membership, IEEE Service Center
P.O. Box 1331
Piscataway, NJ 08555
Phone: (800) 678-IEEE in U.S. or (908) 562-5501
email: member.services@ieee.org (Operations Center)
memservice.asia-pac@ieee.org (Asia/Pacific Customer Service Center)
memservice.europe@ieee.org (European Operations Center)
WWW: http://www.ieee.org/pcs/pcsindex.html

INTERNATIONAL ASSOCIATION OF BUSINESS COMMUNICATORS

The International Association of Business Communicators (IABC) is a world-wide organization of professionals in public relations, employee communication, marketing communication, public affairs, and other forms of communication. The IABC offers services that include *Communication World* magazine, an annual international conference, the Gold Quill awards program recognizing communication excellence, and an accreditation program.

Contact Information:
1 Hallidie Plaza
Suite 600
San Francisco, CA 94102
Phone: (415) 433-3400 Fax: (415) 362-8762
email: See WWW page for officers' addresses.
WWW: http://www.iabc.com/homepage.html

MODERN LANGUAGE ASSOCIATION

The Modern Language Association (MLA), founded in 1883, has over 32,000 members; nearly 4,000 are also members of its divisions dedicated to the history, theory, and teaching of rhetoric and composition.

Contact Information:
Membership Services, Modern Language Association
10 Astor Place
New York, NY 10003-6981
Phone: (212) 614-6378
email: member@mla.org
WWW: None at publication

NATIONAL COUNCIL OF TEACHERS OF ENGLISH

The National Council of Teachers of English (NCTE), with a membership of almost 100,000, has served English teachers since 1912. The NCTE offers various journals and publications for its members as well as three constituent organizations; for professional writing teachers, the most important of these organizations is the Conference on College Composition and Communication (CCCC)

Contact Information:
NCTE Order Fulfillment Department
1111 West Kenyon Road
Urbana, IL 61801-1096
Phone: (217) 328-3870 or (800) 369-6283 outside Illinois
Fax: (217) 328-9645
email: standards@ncte.org
WWW: http://www.ncte.org

RHETORIC SOCIETY OF AMERICA

According to its constitution, the Rhetoric Society of America (RSA) is dedicated to gathering knowledge of rhetoric from "all fields of study" and disseminating them. The RSA does so through meetings, newsletters, reports, and its journal.

Contact Information:
Membership Chair Cheryl Glenn
Department of English
Oregon State University
Corvallis, Oregon 97331
email: rsq@psu.edu
WWW: None at publication

SOCIETY FOR TECHNICAL COMMUNICATION

The Society for Technical Communication (STC) is the largest professional organization serving technical communicators, with more than 20,000 members and 144 chapters worldwide. About 20 percent of those members are either students or instructors. The STC's mission is "to improve the quality and effectiveness of technical communication for audiences worldwide," and its "Code for Communicators" provides an ethical guide for members. The STC publishes *Technical Communication* and *Intercom* as well as materials on a wide variety of topics concerning technical communication.

Contact Information:
901 North Stuart Street
Suite 904
Arlington, VA 22203-1854
Phone: (703) 522-4114 Fax: (703) 522-2075
email: stc@tmn.com
WWW: http://stc.org

PROFESSIONAL JOURNALS

Compiled by Michael J. Hassett
Boise State University

The following are professional journals of interest to business and technical communication teachers. Before submitting materials for publication, contributors should read the instructions for authors that these journals provide or should contact the editor for submission information.

ADMINISTRATIVE SCIENCE QUARTERLY

Administrative Science Quarterly (ASQ) publishes theoretical and empirical research dealing with all aspects of administration. Many of the articles published in *ASQ* deal with administrative communication, including organizational, management, and interpersonal communication. Each issue includes reviews of books dealing with administration issues.

Published four times per year. Ithaca, NY: Cornell University. Subscription information: *ASQ*, Cornell University, 20 Thornwood Drive, Suite 100, Ithaca, NY 14850. Submissions: Editor, *ASQ*, Cornell University, 20 Thornwood Drive, Suite 100, Ithaca, NY 14850.

BUSINESS COMMUNICATION QUARTERLY

Business Communication Quarterly (formerly *Bulletin of the Association for Business Communication*) is a refereed journal published for members of the ABC. Issues include articles on business communication practices and pedagogy with an emphasis on business communication education. The *Quarterly* also publishes book reviews and columns on classroom assignments and consulting issues.

Published four times per year. New York, NY: Association for Business Communication: Subscription information: ABC, Department of Speech, Baruch College—CUNY, 17 Lexington Avenue, New York, NY 10010. Submissions: Scott Ober, Editor, *Business Communication Quarterly*, College of Business–BEOA, Ball State University, Muncie, IN 47306-0335.

CPTSC NEWSLETTER

The *CPTSC Newsletter,* published by the Council for Programs in Technical and Scientific Communication, primarily contains notices and information relevant to members of the CPTSC. However, it also carries information about academic programs, hiring trends, and research resources and short articles on topics of interest to people involved in technical communication.

Published twice annually. Houghton, MI: Council for Programs in Technical and Scientific Communication. Subscription information: CPTSC membership (see Professional Associations). Submissions: Marilyn M. Cooper, Department of Humanities, Michigan Technological University, 1400 Townsend, Houghton, MI 49931.

COMMUNICATION ABSTRACTS

Communication Abstracts provides bibliographic entries and abstracts for articles, books, and reports published by a variety of international and national organizations, publishers, and institutions in areas such as general communication, mass communication, organizational communication, inter- and intrapersonal communication, communication theory, and public relations.

Published six times annually. Thousand Oaks, CA: Sage Publications, Inc. Subscription information: Sage Publications, Inc., 2455 Teller Road, Thousand Oaks, CA 91320. Submissions: none, since this is an abstracting service only.

IEEE TRANSACTIONS ON PROFESSIONAL COMMUNICATION

IEEE Transactions on Professional Communication provides articles of interest to practicing technical communicators, engineers, and scientists as well as to teachers of technical communication. *IEEE Transactions* publishes articles on a wide variety of topics, including oral, written, and visual communication, corporate communication, and communication technology; it also reviews books of interest to readers in these areas.

Published quarterly. New York, NY: The Institute of Electrical and Electronic Engineers, Inc. Subscription information: IEEE, 345 East 47th Street, New York, NY 10017-2394. Submissions: Mike Markel, Editor, *IEEE Transactions on Professional Communication,* Department of English, Boise State University, 1910 University Drive, Boise, ID 83725.

INFORMATION DESIGN JOURNAL

Information Design Journal (IDJ) publishes articles on all aspects of design, including both paper and on-line issues. The journal is designed for readers in a variety of disciplines and includes reports from a variety of theoretical and research approaches. *IDJ* publishes research reports, design evaluations, reviews, and theoretical discussions about such topics as desktop publishing, multimedia design, design methods and history, graphic user interface design, text design, and quantitative graphic displays.

Published three times per year. Reading, UK: *Information Design Journal* Ltd. Subscription information: *IDJ* Subscriptions, P.O. Box 2230, Reading, RG5 4FH, England. Submissions: Paul Stiff, Editor, Department of Typography & Graphic Communication, University of Reading, P.O. Box 239, Reading, RG6 6AU, England.

INTERCOM

Formerly a newsletter, *Intercom* is now the magazine for members of the Society for Technical Communication. It publishes feature articles dealing with practical applications of technical communication as well as letters to the editor and conference/convention information of interest to members of STC.

Published 10 times per year. Arlington, VA: Society for Technical Communication. Subscription information and submissions: *Intercom* Editor, 901 North Stuart Street, Suite 904, Arlington, VA 22203.

JOURNAL OF APPLIED COMMUNICATION RESEARCH

Journal of Applied Communication Research is one of six journals published by the Speech Communication Association. This journal focuses on practical applications of communications research from a variety of perspectives. It publishes interdisciplinary work as well as work focused specifically on speech communication. Articles include a variety of research methods.

Published quarterly. Annandale, VA: Speech Communication Association. Subscription information: Speech Communication Association, 5105 Backlick Road, Building E, Annandale, VA 22003. Submissions: Julia T. Wood, Editor, *Journal of Applied Communication Research*, CB #3285, Department of Communication Studies, University of North Carolina, Chapel Hill, NC 27599-3285.

JOURNAL OF BUSINESS COMMUNICATION

Journal of Business Communication (JBC) is the principal journal of the Association for Business Communication. It publishes articles from a variety of theoretical and research perspectives on issues pertinent to business communicators, including oral and written business communication, management communication, organizational communication, and information systems.

Published four times a year. New York: Association for Business Communication (ABC). Subscription information: ABC, Department of Speech, Baruch College–CUNY, 17 Lexington Avenue, New York, NY 10010. Submissions: John C. Sherblom, Editor, *Journal of Business Communication,* Communication and Journalism Department, University of Maine, 5724 Dunn Hall, Orono, ME 04469-5724.

JOURNAL OF BUSINESS AND TECHNICAL COMMUNICATION

Journal of Business and Technical Communication (JBTC) publishes a variety of articles of interest to technical and professional communicators. The journal seeks to bridge traditional dichotomies between the academy and industry; it publishes articles from a variety of research perspectives, including qualitative, quantitative, and theoretical approaches.

Published quarterly. Thousand Oaks, CA: Sage Publications, Inc. Subscription information: Sage Publications, Inc., 2455 Teller Road, Thousand Oaks, CA 91320. Submissions: Charles Kostelnick, Editor, *JBTC,* Department of English, Iowa State University, Ames, IA 50011-1201.

JOURNAL OF TECHNICAL WRITING AND COMMUNICATION

Journal of Technical Writing and Communication (JTWC) publishes articles covering all aspects of functional communication, including technical, scientific, business, organizational, intercultural, international, and visual communication. *JTWC* publishes research for both practicing technical communicators and teachers. Each issue includes articles and book reviews.

Published quarterly. Amityville, NY: Baywood Publishing Company. Subscription information: Baywood Publishing Company, Inc., 26 Austin Avenue, P.O. Box 337, Amityville, NY 11701. Submissions: Dr. Charles H. Sides, P.O. Box 546, Westminster, MA 01473.

MANAGEMENT COMMUNICATION QUARTERLY

Management Communication Quarterly publishes theoretical and empirical articles on management communication topics, including oral and written managerial communication, organizational communication, and interpersonal communication.

Published quarterly. Thousand Oaks, CA: Sage Publications, Inc. Subscription information: Sage Publications, Inc., 2455 Teller Road, Thousand Oaks, CA 91320. Submissions: Katherine Miller, Editor, *Management Communication Quarterly,* Department of Communication Studies, 3090 Wescoe Hall, University of Kansas, Lawrence, KS 66045-3633.

SCIENCE COMMUNICATION

Science Communication, formerly *Knowledge,* focuses on examinations of science and technology communication (both professional and public), the establishment of expertise, and the diffusion of knowledge in all disciplines. *Science Communication* gives preference to articles that represent interdisciplinary methods and bridge the gap between theory and practice. It also publishes reviews and scholarly commentaries.

Published quarterly. Thousand Oaks, CA: Sage Publications, Inc. Subscription information: Sage Publications, Inc., 2455 Teller Road, Thousand Oaks, CA 91320. Submissions: Marcle C. LaFollette, Editor, *Science Communication,* Center for International Science & Technology Policy, George Washington University, 2130 H Street Northwest, Room 714, Washington, DC 20052.

TECHNICAL COMMUNICATION QUARTERLY

Technical Communication Quarterly (TCQ) (formerly the *Technical Writing Teacher)* is the journal of the Association of Teachers of Technical Writing. It publishes articles on all facets of technical writing with a focus on pedagogical applications of technical writing principles and practices. Each issue also includes book reviews. Issue number 4 in each volume also includes a selected bibliography of articles and chapters of interest to teachers of technical writing published the preceding year in a variety of journals and books.

Published quarterly. St. Paul, Minnesota: Association of Teachers of Technical Writing (ATTW). Subscription information: Billie J. Wahlstron, ATTW, Department of Rhetoric, 202 Haecker Hall, 1364 Eckles Avenue, University of Minnesota, St. Paul, MN 55108-6122. Submissions: Mary M. Lay, *TCQ,* Department of Rhetoric, 202 Haecker Hall, 1364 Eckles Avenue, University of Minnesota, St. Paul, MN 55108-6122.

TECHNICAL COMMUNICATION

Technical Communication is the journal of the Society for Technical Communication (STC). It publishes articles written for technical writers, editors, artists, teachers, managers, and consultants. Each issue also provides book reviews and bibliographies of recent books and articles of interest to the intended audience.

Published quarterly. Arlington, VA: Society for Technical Communication. Subscription information: STC, 901 North Stuart Street, Suite 904, Arlington, VA 22203. Submissions: Dr. Roger A. Grice, Roger Grice Associates, Inc., 52 Doris Lane, Lake Katrine, NY 12449-5127.

VISIBLE LANGUAGE

Visible Language publishes articles on all aspects of the use of visual elements of written language. Articles provide theoretical, historical, and empirical research concerning elements of visual design that would be of interest to technical communicators working in a variety of genres.

Published quarterly. Providence, RI: Rhode Island School of Design. Subscription information: *Visible Language,* Rhode Island School of Design, Graphic Design Department, 2 College Street, Providence, Rhode Island 02903. Submissions: Prof. Sharon Helmer Poggenpohl, Editor, *Visible Language,* Institute of Design, IIT, 10 West 35th Street, Chicago, Illinois 60616.

Note: *The Bedford Bibliography for Teachers of Writing* provides descriptions of a number of periodicals devoted to composition, rhetoric, and communication—such as *College Composition and Communication, Journal of Advanced Composition,* and *Written Communication*—that might be of interest to teachers and researchers of technical communication. In addition, the periodicals listed there occasionally carry articles directly related to technical communication.

CONFERENCES AND MEETINGS

Compiled by Christianna White and Mark Zachry
Iowa State University

The following are professional meetings and conferences of interest to business and technical communication teachers.

ASSOCIATION FOR BUSINESS COMMUNICATION

The ABC annual meeting is held every autumn in a major city in North America. Both members and nonmembers of the association present research papers at the meeting. Presenters are encouraged to submit their papers for publication in the proceedings for the annual meeting.

The ABC is divided into six regions (East, Canada, Midwest, Southeast, Southwest, and West). These divisions of the ABC sponsor regional conferences or hold joint conferences. Announcements about the national and regional meetings appear regularly in *The Journal of Business Communication* and in *Business Communication Quarterly.*

For more information about the national or regional conferences, contact the program chair or the national office:
ABC National Office
Baruch College, Department of Speech
17 Lexington Avenue
New York, NY 10010

ASSOCIATION FOR COMPUTING MACHINERY

The ACM annually sponsors the Special Interest Group on Documentation (SIG-DOC) Conference. The conference is held in the autumn at different locations in the United States. Researchers are encouraged to submit proposals for papers, sessions, panels, tutorials, or poster presentations. Accepted papers and abstracts appear in the conference's proceedings.

For more information about SIGDOC, contact the program chair at:
ACM/SIGDOC
1515 Broadway, 17th Floor
New York, NY 10036
(212) 869-7440

CONFERENCE ON COLLEGE COMPOSITION AND COMMUNICATION (CCCC)

The CCCC holds a conference every spring in a major city in the United States. Both members and nonmembers present research papers at the conference. The CCCC does not publish proceedings.

During the conference several groups interested in professional communication sponsor a session. The groups include the Association for Business Communication, the Association of Teachers of Technical Writing, the Association of Professional Communication Consultants, the National Council of Teachers of English, and the NCTE's Technical and Scientific Communication group (periodic basis; not annual). A call for papers is distributed every spring after the conference to members of the National Council of Teachers of English.

For more information about the CCCC convention, contact the program chair or:
CCCC
National Council of Teachers of English
1111 West Kenyon Road
Urbana, IL 61801-1096

COUNCIL FOR PROGRAMS IN TECHNICAL AND SCIENTIFIC COMMUNICATION

The council holds a conference every autumn in different locations across the United States. Members of the CPTSC present papers related to educational program issues. Papers presented at the conference are eligible to be published in the conference proceedings. The deadline for proposal submissions is typically in early summer.

For more information about the conference, contact the program chair or:
CPTSC
Department of English
Case Western Reserve University
Cleveland, OH 44106
(216) 368-2340, ext. 2362

INTERNATIONAL ASSOCIATION OF BUSINESS COMMUNICATORS

The IABC sponsors an annual conference during the early summer in a major international city. The conference includes presentations, forums, and other types of sessions.

For more information about the conference, contact:
IABC
One Hallidie Plaza, Suite 600
San Francisco, CA 94102 USA
(800) 776-4222 (U.S. or Canada)

(415) 433-3400 (outside U.S. and Canada)
Fax: (415) 362-8762

INSTITUTE OF ELECTRICAL AND ELECTRONICS ENGINEERS (IEEE) PROFESSIONAL COMMUNICATION SOCIETY

The Professional Communication Society (PCS) is one of 37 technical groups in the IEEE. The group sponsors an annual International Professional Communication Conference (IPCC). The conference has been held in major international cities, though it typically is held in either the United States or Canada. The conference includes presentations, workshops, and panels.

For more information about the IPCC, contact the program chair or:
IEEE/PCS
194 Aberdeen Drive
Aiken, SC 29803-7100
(803) 642-2156
Fax: (803) 642-9325

LANGUAGES AND COMMUNICATION FOR WORLD BUSINESS AND THE PROFESSIONS

Every spring the World College at Eastern Michigan University in Ypsilanti, Michigan, sponsors the Languages and Communication for World Business and the Professions conference. The conference includes presentations and workshops, and selected presentations are published in the conference's proceedings. A call for papers is distributed to members of the Association for Business Communication and the International Association for Language and Business.

For more information about the conference, contact the program chair or:
The World College
307 Goodison Hall
Eastern Michigan University
Ypsilanti, MI 48197-2260

MODERN LANGUAGE ASSOCIATION

The annual MLA convention is held in a major city in the United States at the end of December. At the convention, the Association for Teachers of Technical Writing (ATTW), an affiliate organization of the MLA, sponsors two panels.

Presenters must be members of both the MLA and the ATTW, but membership is not required to submit a proposal. The MLA is also divided into several regions, such as the Midwest and Rocky Mountain regions. These divisions of the MLA sponsor regional conferences. The Rocky Mountain Modern Language Association has a Technical/Professional Communication Section in conjunction with the ATTW.

For more information about MLA conferences, contact the program chair or:
Modern Language Association
10 Astor Place
New York, NY 10003-6981

For information about ATTW sessions, contact:
Association of Teachers of Technical Writing
Department of English
Texas A&M University
College Station, TX 77843-4227

NATIONAL COUNCIL OF TEACHERS OF ENGLISH

The NCTE sponsors an annual conference focusing on college writing and rhetoric during the autumn in different major cities in the United States. During the conference, groups interested in professional communication hold special sessions. The Scientific and Technical Communication group holds full-day workshops at the NCTE conference on a periodic basis.

For more information about the NCTE conference, contact:
NCTE
1111 West Kenyon Road
Urbana, IL 61801
(800) 369-6283
(217) 328-3870
Fax: (217) 328-9645

SOCIETY FOR TECHNICAL COMMUNICATION

The STC annual conference is held every spring in a major city in the United States. Members of the society present research papers at the meeting. Approximately 2,000 technical communicators from around the world attend the educational programs, seminars, and workshops. Presenters are encouraged to submit their papers for publication in the proceedings of the annual meeting. The STC is divided into several regions, and these divisions sponsor regional conferences, as do some local chapters. Meeting times and locations vary. Some regional conferences also publish proceedings. Announcements about the national and regional meetings appear regularly in *Technical Communication* and in *Intercom*.

For more information about the national or regional conferences, contact the program chair or the national office:
901 North Stuart Street, Suite 904
Arlington, VA 22203-1854
(703) 522-2075
Fax: (703) 522-2075
email: stc@tmn.com

TECHNICAL WRITERS INSTITUTE

Rensselaer Polytechnic Institute sponsors an annual program in Troy, New York, for professional communicators. The program includes a variety of sessions.

For more information about the program, contact:
Department of Language, Literature & Communication
Rensselaer Polytechnic Institute
Troy, NY 12180-3590
(518) 276-2828

INTERNET DISCUSSION GROUPS

Compiled by Stuart A. Selber
Texas Tech University

The following Internet discussion groups are of interest to business and technical communication teachers. Messages generated from these discussions come directly to your electronic mailbox, either as they are distributed or in digest form (when available).

ACW-L (ALLIANCE FOR COMPUTERS AND WRITING)

Participants are primarily members of the Alliance for Computers and Writing, a national organization supporting technology-based writing instruction at college and secondary levels. Discussion topics include concerns of the profession, professional merit, gender issues, pedagogical alternatives, and technical questions related to the implementation of network and hypertext-based instruction. The ACW has a World Wide Web site at http://english.ttu.edu/acw.

To subscribe, send electronic mail to:
listproc@ttacs6.ttu.edu (no subject) with the following message:
subscribe ACW-L YourFirstName YourLastName

For more information, contact:
Fred Kemp (ykfok@ttacs.ttu.edu)

ATTW-L (ASSOCIATION OF TEACHERS OF TECHNICAL WRITING LIST)

Participants are primarily members of the Association of Teachers of Technical Writing, including both instructors and practicing professionals. Discussion topics include news of the association, issues of the discipline, calls for papers, job vacancies, and teaching practices. ATTW has a World Wide Web site at: http://english.ttu.edu/attw.

To subscribe, send electronic mail to:
listproc@ttacs6.ttu.edu (no subject) with the following message:
subscribe ACW-L YourFirstName YourLastName

For more information, contact:
Sam Dragga (ditsd@ttacs.ttu.edu)

BIZCOM (BUSINESS COMMUNICATIONS)

Participants are primarily members of the Association for Business Communication. Discussion topics include pedagogical issues related to business communications classes, teaching resources, business practices, writing practices in various professional settings, as well as related announcements, calls for papers, and requests for proposals.

To subscribe, send electronic mail to:
listproc@ebbs.english.vt.edu (no subject) with the following message:
subscribe BIZCOM YourFirstName YourLastName

For more information, contact:
Traci Gardner (traci@daedalus.com)

CAP-L (COMPUTER-AIDED PUBLISHING)

Participants are students and professionals interested in computer-aided publishing. Discussion topics include publishing software, ethics, preparing and finding publishing employment, gendered language, computer-aided publishing procedures in various technical communication departments, and the influences of computing and networking on the ways information is distributed.

To subscribe, send electronic mail to:
majordomo@mtu.edu (no subject) with the following message:
subscribe CAP-L YourFirstName YourLastName

For more information, contact:
Dickie Selfe (rselfe@mtu.edu)

CCCC-IP (CCCC INTELLECTUAL PROPERTY CAUCUS)

Participants include individuals affiliated with college composition and communication research, teaching, and publishing. The CCCC-IP is an extension of the CCCC Intellectual Property Caucus and provides a forum for conversations about intellectual property issues. Discussion topics include the fair use and distribution of text (both print and electronic), plagiarism, authorship, copyright, ethical uses of discourse, and uses of print and electronic materials in writing classes.

To subscribe, send electronic mail to:
listserv@vm1.spcs.umn.edu (no subject) with the following message:
subscribe CCCC-IP YourFirstName YourLastName

For more information, contact:
Laura J. Gurak (gurakL@epx.cis.umn.edu)

CPTSC-L (COUNCIL FOR PROGRAMS IN TECHNICAL AND SCIENTIFIC COMMUNICATION)

Participants are primarily members of the Council for Programs in Technical and Scientific Communication who are interested in programmatic and pedagogical issues related to scientific and technical communication instruction. Discussion topics include program promotion, pedagogical research, the exchange of ideas and information concerning programs, research and career opportunities, and the development of new programs.

To subscribe, send electronic mail to:
listserv@clvm.clarkson.edu (no subject) with the following message:
subscribe CPTSC-L YourFirstName YourLastName

For more information, contact:
Stuart A. Selber or Bill Karis (sselber@ttu.edu)

H-RHETOR (History of Rhetoric and Communication)

Participants are interested in rhetoric and composition, speech and communication, English, philosophy, classics, religious studies, and other disciplines. Discussion topics are wide ranging and include both classical and modern rhetorical issues, book reviews, notices, calls for papers, and job announcements.

To subscribe, send electronic mail to:
listserv@msu.edu (no subject) with the following message:
subscribe H-RHETOR YourFirstName YourLastName

For more information, contact:
Gary Hatch (gary_hatch@byu.edu)

MBU-L (Megabyte University)

Participants are primarily writing instructors at the college and secondary level interested in using computer technology to enhance their instruction. Discussion topics include concerns of the profession, professional merit, gender issues, pedagogical alternatives, and technical questions related to the implementation of network and hypertext-based instruction.

To subscribe, send electronic mail to:
listproc@ttacs6.ttu.edu (no subject) with the following message:
subscribe MBU-L YourFirstName YourLastName

For more information, contact:
Fred Kemp (ykfok@ttacs.ttu.edu)

PURTOPOI (RHETORIC, LANGUAGE, AND PROFESSIONAL WRITING)

Participants include teachers and students interested in a wide range of issues related to rhetoric, language, and professional writing. Discussion topics include poststructuralist approaches to rhetorical theory, the politics of composition instruction, the rhetorical nature of interface designs, the effect of computer networks on rhetorical theory and teaching, and revisionary histories of sophistic and classical rhetorical theories.

To subscribe, send electronic mail to:
listserv@vm.cc.purdue.edu (no subject) with the following message:
subscribe PURTOPOI YourFirstName YourLastName

For more information, contact:
Patricia Sullivan (nvo@omni.cc.purdue.edu)

TECHWR-L (TECHNICAL WRITING)

Participants include practicing professionals, teachers, and students interested in technical writing and communication issues. Discussion topics include the responsibilities of writers in the workplace, designing on-line documentation, usability metrics, working in development groups, and other issues directly related to technical communication.

To subscribe, send electronic mail to:
listserv@listserv.okstate.edu (no subject) with the following message:
subscribe TECHWR-L YourFirstName YourLastName

For more information, contact:
Eric J. Ray (ejray@galaxy.galstar.com)

TESP-L (TEACHERS OF ENGLISH FOR SPECIFIC PURPOSES)

Participants are teachers who design and deliver courses either for students in specific graduate and undergraduate disciplines or for learners working or preparing to work in science, medicine, law, business, industry, government, and other places of employment. Discussion topics include needs analyses, materials design, and methods of evaluation. TESP-L is a branch of TESL-L (Teachers of English as a Second Language). Additional information is available by Gopher at cunyvm.cuny.edu//CUNY Information and Resources//Teaching English as a Second/Foreign Language.

To subscribe, send electronic mail to:
listserv@cunyvm.cuny.edu (no subject) with the following message:
subscribe TESL-L YourFirstName YourLastName
subscribe TESP-L YourFirstName YourLastName
set TESL-L nomail

You must be a member of TESL-L to subscribe, but you can set the subscription for this list to nomail. If you want to subscribe to TESL-L, omit the "set TESL-L nomail" command.

For more information, contact:
Stephanie Stauffer (stauffes@guvax.georgetown.edu)
or Rick Rosenberg (rickpaul@earn.cvut.cz)

UTEST (Usability Testing Methodologies)

Participants include usability testing researchers and practitioners. Discussion topics include interface design, human factors, on-line documentation, methodological developments, professional communication theory, and user-design theory. Messages may not be archived or redistributed. Additional information is available on the World Wide Web at http://tigger.clemson.edu/utest.

To subscribe, send electronic mail to:
listproc@hubcap.clemson.edu (no subject) with the following message:
subscribe UTEST YourFirstName YourLastName

For more information, contact:
Tharon W. Howard (tharon@hubcap.clemson.edu)

WAC-L (Writing Across the Curriculum)

Participants include individuals involved in writing across the curriculum as teachers, researchers, and/or program administrators. Discussion topics include teaching strategies, useful texts, innovative courses, current research, funding sources, building writing across the curriculum programs, and problems that WAC programs encounter.

To subscribe, send electronic mail to:
listserv@postoffice.cso.uiuc.edu (no subject) with the following message:
subscribe WAC-L YourFirstName YourLastName

For more information, contact:
Gail E. Hawisher (hawisher@uiuc.edu)

RESEARCH AND HISTORY

BIBLIOGRAPHIC WORKS

1   **Alred, Gerald J., Diana C. Reep, and Mohan R. Limaye.** *Business and Technical Writing: An Annotated Bibliography of Books, 1880–1980.* **Metuchen, NJ: Scarecrow, 1981. Indexes. 240p.**

This bibliography identifies and annotates books that "deal significantly with writing or the analysis of writing, either for business or in technical and professional contexts" from 1880 to 1980 (vii). The nine-page introduction surveys and assesses the collected works, concluding that the products of technical and business writing are important to the extent that they "enlighten us about the complex and crucial issues of the day" and help us "conduct our business with some humanity toward our fellow human beings" (9). Each 100- to 250-word annotation describes the purpose of the book, its scope, primary and unusual topics covered, pedagogical materials, and historical interest. Included are 27 previous bibliographies (books and articles), 847 books in the main section, and 230 items in unannotated lists ("Industry and Society Style Guides"; "Government and Military Style Guides"; "Publishing"; "Oral Communication"; and "Style, Language, and Readability"). The book concludes with coauthor, title, and subject indexes.

2   **Felker, Daniel B., ed.** *Document Design: A Review of the Relevant Research.* **Washington, DC: American Institutes for Research, 1980. 171p.**

This publication is a product of the Document Design Project (DDP), begun in 1978 through the American institutes for Research (AIR). The purpose of the DDP was "to help make forms, regulations, brochures, and other written materials easier for people to read, to understand, and to use" (i). *Document Design: A Review of the Relevant Research* surveys the appropriate literature in the fields described in its first six, separately authored chapters: "Psycholinguistics," "Cognitive Psychology," "Instructional Research," "Readability," "Human Factors," and "Typography/Graphics." Chapter VII presents a case study which applies the principles of document design represented in the works reviewed earlier to IRS taxpayer instructions. The final section contains 42 pages of citations for the works discussed in the first six chapters.

This literature review served to underpin the work and other publications of the DDP and the AIR, which included *Guidelines for Document Designers* (1981) by Daniel B. Felker and others and *Writing in the Professions* (1981) by Dixie Goswami and others. The DDP, through its Document Design Center, also published two newsletters, *Simply Stated* and *Simply Stated for Business*, which reported results of research and addressed segments of the general public.

3   **Greene, Beth G. "International Business Communication: An Annotated Bibliography."** *Bulletin of the Association for Business Communication* **53.4 (December 1990): 76–79.**

This bibliography is based on an ERIC database search for international business communication or correspondence; many of the 23 items included are proceedings from the annual Eastern Michigan University conference on languages for business and the professions. Each entry provides the ERIC document number and is followed by an annotation of about 60 to 80 words. The 150-word introduction deals mostly with the methodology the author used in gathering the titles.

4   **Hull, Debra L. *Business and Technical Communication: A Bibliography, 1975–1985*. Metuchen, NJ: Scarecrow, 1987. Indexes. 229p.**

This bibliography includes 1,133 articles and proceedings published from 1975 to 1985. These items are divided into three main sections, "classroom," "aspects," and "new horizons," which contain 17 subsections that are further divided into smaller groups. The annotations range from short sentences to paragraphs of 50 or 60 words. The author includes two unannotated sections which list 56 books and 18 previous bibliographies. Author and subject indexes are included. The introduction discusses the methodology used to gather the titles and the rationale for the organization.

5   **Hutton, Clark. "A Selected Annotated Bibliography on Using Computers to Teach Technical and Business Writing (1984–90)." *Technical Writing Teacher* 18.3 (Fall 1991): 223–35.**

This bibliography lists and annotates 48 articles in order "to compile some of the significant research" from 1984 to 1990 and to arrange it "in such a way as to allow teachers to incorporate this research in their classrooms" (223). The list is divided into five sections: previous bibliographies and research, computers as a medium for writing instruction, integrating the word processor into the technical writing course, computers in collaborative writing, and the use of ancillary software. Each section is introduced with a paragraph describing its contents and offering perspectives. The conclusion provides a critique of past research and suggestions for future work.

6   **Jorn, Linda A. "A Selected Annotated Bibliography on Collaboration in Technical Communication." *Technical Communication Quarterly* 2.1 (Winter 1993): 105–15.**

This bibliography includes 32 items selected by the author as well as those noted when the editors for this special issue on collaboration "asked contributors to highlight the two most important citations in their manuscripts that they would like to have included here" (205). The bibliography is divided into two sections: "Issues," which includes items on "interactions, strategies, gender, theoretical perspectives, pedagogy, and research agendas"; and "Technology," which includes items on the emergence of technologies that support collaboration. The 50- to 150-word annotations are preceded by a brief introduction describing the author's methodology.

7   **Kolin, Philip C., and Ronald G. Marquardt. "Research on Legal Writing: A Bibliography." *Law Library Journal* 78 (1986): 493–517.**

This bibliography includes more than 400 books, book reviews, bibliographies, articles, government documents, and papers on legal writing published between 1931 and 1986 and collected from various legal and publishing reference sources. The authors state their "guiding principle has been to concentrate on materials dealing with legal writing skills in general rather than studies of drafting specific documents" (493). The unannotated items are divided into six categories: previous bibliographies; book-length works on rhetoric, language, and law; the "plain English" movement; legal writing courses; and legal writing for practicing attorneys. The lists are preceded by a 600-word introduction describing the importance of writing in legal areas and the methodology used to collect the items.

8   **Moran, Michael G., and Debra Journet, eds. *Research in Technical Communication: A Bibliographic Sourcebook*. Westport, CT: Greenwood, 1985. Indexes. 515p.**

In their preface, the editors of this collection state that the 18 bibliographic essays demonstrate "the vigorous and growing tradition of work done in technical and scientific communication" (ix). Each chapter-length essay surveys works published in an area and concludes with complete reference sections. The author of each essay begins by defining and framing the subject before moving on to classifying and evaluating the works included. The essays are divided into four thematic sections: a "theoretical examination," including relationships with the humanities, works on history, communication theory, and pedagogy; "rhetorical concerns," including invention, audience analysis, organization, and style; "specific types," including proposals, reports, and business genres; and "related concerns," including computers, oral presentation, legal writing, and writing for government. Three appendices follow and cover textbooks, style manuals, and professional technical writing. The book concludes with a 26-page author index and a 4-page subject index.

9   **Rivers, William E. "Studies in the History of Business and Technical Writing: A Bibliographical Essay." *Journal of Business and Technical Communication* 8.1 (January 1994): 6–57.**

The author assesses 178 items, including works on disciplinary history, genre studies from historical periods, and examinations of specific events, such as the *Challenger* disaster. The 51-page essay is divided into 13 sections that cover bibliographies; pedagogical application of historical material; history of teaching business and technical writing; literature from historical periods (including ancient and classical, medieval European, the Renaissance, seventeenth and eighteenth century, and nineteenth century); studies of practices across periods; studies of early American writers and practices; twentieth century writers; and studies focusing on specific events or issues, such as AIDS. The author concludes with a number of recommendations for further work, concluding that historical study should help us see that "no matter how technical or mundane the subject matter, all writing is still a matter of one human being trying to communicate with another" (57).

10   Scott, James Calvert. "An Annotated Reference List of Publications Relating to International Business Communication: Expanding Horizons beyond Traditional Business Communication Sources." *Bulletin of the Association for Business Communication* 53.4 (December 1990): 72–76.

As the editor suggests, this bibliography is useful because it includes studies on international business communication from an unusually wide range of sources. For example, articles are included from the *Modern Language Journal, Intercultural Training, Harvard Business Review,* and the *Journal of Language for International Business* as well as various proceedings, government documents, and books not often listed elsewhere. Arranged alphabetically, the list includes 79 items.

11   Sides, Charles H., ed. *Technical and Business Communication: Bibliographic Essays for Teachers and Corporate Trainers*. Urbana, IL: NCTE; Washington, DC: STC, 1989. 360p.

The editor states that this collection of 17 bibliographic essays "provides detailed information for instructors and researchers who wish to further their knowledge of particular areas within technical communication" (1). The authors of each essay define and review the literature on the topic and conclude with a thorough bibliography, thus helping achieve the editor's goal. Part I, "Issues and Abilities in Technical Communication," includes reviews of rhetoric, reading, ethics, editing, visual representation, interpersonal communication for the technical communicator, consulting, style, and presentations. Part II, "Genres in Technical Communication," covers annual reports and public relations documents, instructions and procedures, proposals, letters and memos, reports, computer documentation, and medical science and technology. The book concludes with profiles of the editor and contributors.

12   Speck, Bruce W., and Lynnette R. Porter. "Annotated Bibliography for Teaching Ethics in Professional Writing." *Bulletin of the Association for Business Communication* 53.3 (September 1990): 36–52.

This bibliography, containing 140 items on ethics, is divided into four sections that "comprise three important foci." The first section, "Theory Focus," includes philosophical and analytical studies; the second, "Teaching Focus," covers practical applications and classroom activities with subsections on general composition, journalism, speech, business writing, and technical writing; the third, "Teacher Focus," examines the teacher's role and ethical stance. The last section lists five "related bibliographies." Each item includes a one-paragraph annotation intended to "describe the substance of each source so that other researchers can make an informed decision about whether to read a source in its entirety" (36). The items are selected from a wide variety of sources, including *Journal of Business Ethics, Rhetoric Review, Journal of Business Communication, College English,* and *Technical Communication.*

13   Swales, John M. "Discourse Analysis in Professional Contexts." *Annual Review of Applied Linguistics* 11 (1990): 103–14.

The author suggests that the boundary for this bibliographic essay is difficult; however, it is of particular interest for its coverage of English for Special Purposes (ESP) and items of interest to "applied linguists interested in discourse in professional contexts" (109). The six-page essay begins with an analysis of this subject, then goes on to cover works related to "law and order," "health sciences," "professional genres in the academy," and "other professions." The author concludes with a discussion of "issues and opportunities" for linguistic studies of the professional world. Following the essay is an annotated bibliography of nine books and an unannotated list of 60 items, both books and articles.

RESEARCH METHODOLOGY AND SCHOLARSHIP

14   **Beard, John D., and David L. Williams. "A Professional Profile of Business Communication Educators and Their Research Preferences: Survey Results."** *Journal of Business Communication* **30.3 (July 1993): 269–95.**

Based on a survey of 507 members of the Association for Business Communication, the authors examine the kinds of research topics and methods found to be valuable to business communication educators. The research topics rated most highly were "Cross-national Communication" and "Communication Ethics," while the least popular were "Historical Evolution of Business Communication" and "Linguistic Analysis." Except for a call for more use of the "case study," the authors find wide differences over preferred methodologies, which "tells [the authors] that the discipline is far from reaching a consensus on the primary methodologies to be used by researchers in the field" (292). The authors conclude that the broad range of research interests and methodologies may be seen as either a strength or weakness of business communication as a discipline and that differences reflect "the particular institutional pressures coming to bear on individual members" (293).

15   **Campbell, Patty G., Thomas Housel, and Kitty O. Locker, eds.** *Conducting Research in Business Communication*. **Urbana, IL: ABC, 1988. 297p.**

Designed primarily for those new to the business communication field, this book "provides a framework that novice researchers can use in developing a basic understanding of how research is conducted within the field" (iii). Its 12 separately authored chapters examine both quantitative and qualitative research and provide specific examples applicable to business communication. The collection provides a useful overview, especially for those not familiar with such research methods as survey design and the analysis of numerical data.

16   **Cross, Geoffrey A. "Ethnographic Research in Business and Technical Writing: Between Extremes and Margins."** *Journal of Business and Technical Communication* **8.1 (January 1994): 118–34.**

This article examines various methodological perspectives that weaken the results of ethnographic research: views that are centered on the researcher, research community, data gathered, and the subjects. To avoid the "extremes" and "margins" these perspectives represent, the author calls for "ethnographic accounts" based largely on Clifford Geertz's notion of "thick description." The author describes ways in which ethnographic research can offer much to business and technical writing studies, concluding that ethnographic accounts "provide us our only meticulous, prolonged, reviewable, and fairly systematic observations of writing in its (mostly) natural habitat" (131).

17   **Greenbaum, Howard H., Phillip Clampitt, and Shirley Willihnganz. "Organizational Communication: An Examination of Four Instruments." _Management Communication Quarterly_ 2.2 (November 1988): 245–82.**

One aim of organizational communication research is to determine the efficiency of communication in an organization. The authors examine four types of instruments (questionnaires) intended to measure efficiency primarily by examining information flow, communication climate, message characteristics, and communication structure. Each specific type is examined for its validity, applicability, and limitations. The authors conclude by considering the general limitations and possible reductive results of all the instruments. They suggest that further research might point out deficiencies that should be remedied.

18   **Greenbaum, Howard H., Sue DeWine, and Cal W. Downs. "Management and Organizational Communication Measurement." _Management Communication Quarterly_ 1.1 (1987): 129–44.**

This article begins by examining the disciplinary boundaries of organizational communication from its divisional status within the International Communication Association (ICA) in 1969. The authors then describe the objectives of a review by an ICA task force assigned to investigate the instrumentation used in organizational communication research. Based on a search of communication journals and social science dissertations, they report on the topics examined ("communication constructs," such as anxiety, communication style, leadership, personality, self-concept, sex-role, and stress/burnout) and the number of instruments used to measure them. The authors conclude that "we can strengthen the discipline by improving the availability of measurement tools" (144).

19   **Halpern, Jeanne W. "Getting in Deep: Using Qualitative Research in Business and Technical Communication." _Journal of Business and Technical Communication_ 2.2 (September 1988): 22–43.**

The author sees a need for research in business and technical communication to use more qualitative research, which can include "case studies, informal surveys and interviews, historiography, life histories, observational studies, and textual and content analysis" (27). She focuses closely on ethnography because it "provides the most textured and complete representation of communication in action" (27). After an analysis of how ethnography has been and might be applied to communication in workplace settings, she stresses the benefits of qualitative research, concluding that it can "allow us to _construct the theoretical bases of business and technical communication_" (39).

20   Harrison, Teresa M. "Frameworks for the Study of Writing in Organizational Contexts." *Written Communication* 4.1 (January 1987): 3–23.

This article argues that "in a rhetorically based theory of composing, context plays an important role in the production and comprehension of discourse" (5). Viewing context as community, the author examines ways in which organizations might be considered contexts: as systems of knowledge or as patterns of symbolic discourse. The author concludes with several implications for the use of context in research.

21   Lay, Mary M. "The Value of Gender Studies to Professional Communication Research." *Journal of Business and Technical Communication* 8.1 (January 1994): 58–90.

Through a review of selected gender scholarship and articles on professional communication, the author demonstrates how "scholarship on gender difference offers a rich theoretical and research base with which to study professional communication in the workplace and in the classroom" (58). Areas examined in terms of their relationship to gender include communication, identity, writing, reading, speaking and language choice, visual communication, collaboration, content analysis, management, history, and case studies. The author concludes with questions involving gender that professional communication researchers might ask as they shape the direction of their research. The thorough section of references should be particularly useful to researchers who seek the answers to the questions the author raises.

22   Locker, Kitty O. "The Challenge of Interdisciplinary Research." *Journal of Business Communication* 31.2 (April 1994): 137–49.

Kent, Thomas. "Interdisciplinary Research and Disciplinary Toleration: A Reply to Kitty Locker." *Journal of Business Communication* 31.2 (April 1994): 153–55.

Smeltzer, Larry R. "Confessions of a Researcher: A Reply to Kitty Locker." *Journal of Business Communication* 31.2 (April 1994): 157–59.

In this expanded version of her 1993 ABC Outstanding Researcher Award Lecture, Locker points to the interdisciplinary nature of business communication. She then describes four difficulties of interdisciplinary research: it consumes more time and effort than traditional research in narrowly defined disciplines; it involves different paradigms, thus making research methodology and questions problematical; it invites conceptual and methodological mistakes by importing concepts and methods from other fields; it is less likely to be cumulative. Despite these difficulties, Locker describes many reasons why interdisciplinary research is valuable, including its potential for enabling us to make truly original and useful contributions to knowledge.

Thomas Kent describes the "political" as well as the "epistemological problems" of interdisciplinary research that Locker describes. He contends that the primary motivation for avoiding interdisciplinary research "is not epistemological; it is political" (154). While praising Locker for articulation of the benefits of interdisciplinary research, Kent concludes, "If we truly desire to promote an ecumenical disciplinary attitude in the area of business communication, we might begin by inspecting our motives for devaluing interdisciplinary research" (155).

Larry R. Smeltzer states, "While it is easy to support the notion of interdisciplinarity, application of it is much more difficult" (157). Smeltzer then "confesses" his own lack of interdisciplinary perspective and concludes: "I seriously question the extent to which we have much interdisciplinary research. Rather, what we have is individual research projects from various perspectives. And these perspectives are not integrated into one research project" (159).

23   **Miles, Matthew B., and A. Michael Huberman.** *Qualitative Data Analysis: An Expanded Sourcebook.* **2nd ed. Thousand Oaks, CA: 1994. Index. Bib. 338p.**

This book aims not only at the practicing and beginning researcher but also at "staff specialists and managers, who rely on qualitative information as a routine part of their work and who need practical methods for making the best use of it" (3). The authors view qualitative research very broadly to include fields that study "the ways people in particular settings come to understand, account for, take action, and otherwise manage their day-to-day situations" (7). Chapter 1, "Introduction," provides a broad overview of qualitative research, observing that the "paradigms for conducting social research seem to be shifting beneath our feet" (5). Nevertheless the book offers "orderly" standard methodologies, while advising the reader to "look behind any apparent formalism and seek out what will be useful in your own work" (5).

Chapters 2 and 3 cover the issues needed to begin research: building a conceptual framework, formulating research questions, and the general management of data. Chapters 4 through 9 cover various facets of research: creating ways to record data as well as developing and using matrix displays. Chapter 10 suggests ways of "making good sense" when drawing and verifying conclusions. Chapter 11 discusses ethical issues, and Chapter 12 describes the production of research reports. The final short chapter of "concluding remarks" is an informal series of suggestions that are intended to be provocative; for example, "Be open to invention"; "Seek formalization, and distrust it" (310). An appendix by Matthew B. Miles and Eben A. Weitzman discusses the selection of computer programs for qualitative data analysis.

24   **Rainey, Kenneth T., and Rebecca S. Kelly. "Doctoral Research in Technical Communication, 1965–1990."** *Technical Communication* **39.4 (November 1992): 552–70.**

This article is based on a survey of technical communication programs, searches of electronic databases, and content analyses of dissertation abstracts. The authors summarize their findings concerning research at the doctoral level, examine the institutions conducting doctoral research, describe the methodologies used, and catalog the topics of dissertations. They conclude their analysis with a bibliography that lists 155 (of the 170) dissertations produced from 1965 to 1990.

25   **Reinsch, N. Lamar, Jr., and Phillip V. Lewis. "Author and Citation Patterns for** *The Journal of Business Communication,* **1978–1992."** *Journal of Business Communication* **30.4 (October 1993): 435–62.**

Examining citations and author affiliations, these authors assess the trends in *JBC* articles regarding authorship, intellectual content, and the relationship between the *JBC* and other journals. Among other findings, the authors conclude that coauthorship has increased, but that the *JBC* has "not had the degree of impact on other fields that business communication professionals might wish" (455). The authors provide various tables that list such information as the most frequently cited journals and the topical categories represented by those journals.

26   **Reinsch, N. Lamar, Jr., and Janet W. Reinsch. "Some Assessments of Business Communication Scholarship from Social Science Citations."** *Journal of Business and Technical Communication* **10.1 (January 1996): 28–47.**

In an effort to determine the impact of business communication on other fields, the authors analyze the citation patterns of the Social Sciences Citation Index®*(SSCI)*, an influential "database that many tenure and promotion committees consult" (29). Among other findings, the authors conclude "the *SSCI* does not adequately sample the field of business communication . . . [so] scholars who are being considered for promotion or tenure, should not rely too heavily on the *SSCI*" (41). Further, business communication periodicals (especially compared with highly respected communication journals) "demonstrate favorable overall and own-field impact, suggesting that they effectively disseminate business communication scholarship" (42). This work complements an earlier work that studies author and citation patterns for the *Journal of Business Communication* by Lamar Reinsch and Phillip V. Lewis (*JBC* 30.4).

27   **Selzer, Jack. "Critical Inquiry in a Technical Writing Course."** *The Writing Teacher as Researcher: Essays in the Theory and Practice of Class-Based Research*. **Ed. Donald A. Daiker and Max Morenberg. Portsmouth, NH: Boynton/Cook, 1990.**

The author maintains that "when students are asked to pursue answers to substantial questions and to report their results to a teacher who is honestly interested . . . and when [those questions] relate explicitly to the subject matter of the course, both students and teachers benefit" (194). To illustrate this process, Selzer reproduces specific assignments and discusses student responses. One assignment asks students to uncover various rhetorical maneuvers used in two sets of instructions. As a result, students learn practical tactics for writing their own instructions, and teachers grow wiser about "the exigencies contained in the genre called 'instructions'" (198). Selzer concludes that "as a result of the assignment teacher and student can collaborate to generate new knowledge about technical writing" (198).

28   **Smeltzer, Larry R. "Emerging Questions and Research Paradigms in Business Communication Research."** *Journal of Business Communication* **30.2 (1993): 181–98.**

Suchan, Jim. "Why We Do Irrelevant Research." *Journal of Business Communication* **30.2 (1993): 202–03.**

Limaye, Mohan R. "Relevance Versus Significance in Business Communication Research [Letter to the Editor]." *Journal of Business Communication* 30.4 (1993): 463–71.

Suchan, Jim. "Response to Mohan Limaye: The Need for Contextually Based Research." *Journal of Business Communication* 30.4 (1993): 473–76.

Smeltzer, Larry R. "Relevance Is the Issue." *Journal of Business Communication* 30.4 (1993): 477–78.

"Emerging Questions," the 1992 ABC Outstanding Researcher Award Lecture by Larry R. Smeltzer, together with the responses by Jim Suchan and Mohan Limaye (and a concluding final response by Smeltzer) compose a useful conversation about research questions and methodology.

In his lecture, Smeltzer states, "it is my belief that relevant research adds credibility to an academic discipline" (181). He then reports on a survey that demonstrates differences in the importance of research topics as seen by business practitioners and academics. Citing a study of what constitutes significance in research and reporting his own analysis of research published in the *Journal of Business Communication,* he concludes that business communication researchers need to "bridge the worlds of business and academia" (196).

Suchan states that the view that "the direction or content of academic research should not be heavily influenced by practitioners' needs" is "politically naïve and, more importantly, negates the integrating role between knowledge and practice that professional schools . . . and academic areas such as business communication play" (202). He finds two reasons for the lack of connection: "we know little about the kind of communication that goes on in organizations" (202) and "many of us know very little about management theory and practice" (203).

Limaye argues that "there should be room for both basic research and applied (what Smeltzer and Suchan term 'relevant') research" (463). Limaye further asserts that "significance" is a broader concept than "relevance." He suggests several reasons "why academics need not worry too much" that there are differences between what practitioners and researchers consider important: academics and business practitioners differ in their use of terminology, their goals, and their priorities (467). Limaye ends with "a plea for balance," suggesting valuing of "diverse interests rather than one overly-emphasized interest" (470).

Suchan responds that Limaye misinterprets his position: "What I am advocating is an increase in *contextually based* business communication research," which he does not find prevalent in much of what has been published in *JBC*— that privileging "irrelevant" research is self-defeating to the field (473).

Smeltzer concludes, "my purpose is to point out that good research must be applied, theoretical, rigorous and relevant all at the same time" (477). He calls for "relevant research that develops and tests theoretical constructs that provide useful business knowledge" (478).

29   Thompson, Isabelle. "Competence and Critique in Technical Communication: A Qualitative Content Analysis of Journal Articles." *Journal of Business and Technical Communication* 10.1 (January 1996): 48–80.

According to the author, "the primary goal of the study is . . . to examine what has been written about pedagogy in technical communication and to discuss patterns of similarity and difference in the underlying assumptions of these journal articles" (50). To achieve this goal, the author examines all the issues of five journals from 1990 to 1994 for articles that "mentioned teaching in undergraduate technical communication courses" (53). The author discovered 98 such articles and divided them into four categories of "broad pedagogical perspectives": functional (69), rhetorical (14), ideological (4), and intercultural and feminist (9). Following an analysis of the works in each category, the author concludes that "we should value classroom research and encourage it as significant scholarship" (74). In revealing the direction and quantity of pedagogical research published in the relevant journals, this article provides potential authors both a register of what has been published and a heuristic for new work.

30   **Yin, Robert K. *Case Study Research: Design and Methods*. 2nd ed. Thousand Oaks, CA: Sage, 1994. Indexes. Bib. 170p.**

The author suggests that while critics have pointed to weaknesses in the case study, researchers continue to find this methodology worthwhile. The purpose of the book is "to guide investigators and students who are trying to do case studies as a rigorous method of research" (xiv). The first, introductory chapter describes when case studies should be used as well as what type is best suited to a research question, particularly in workplace settings. The remaining five chapters include "Designing Case Studies"; "Conducting Case Studies: Preparing for Data Collection"; "Conducting Case Studies: Collecting the Evidence"; "Analyzing Case Study Evidence"; and "Composing the Case Study 'Report.'" Boxed examples and commentaries appear throughout the chapters, which conclude with exercises, making the book useful for both those new to the case study method as well as graduate students in research methodology courses.

HISTORICAL STUDIES AND EARLY WORKS

31   **Adams, Katherine H. *A History of Professional Writing Instruction in American Colleges: Years of Acceptance, Growth, and Doubt*. Dallas: Southern Methodist UP, 1993. Index. Bib. 192p.**

This history examines curricular development of "professional writing" from the founding of American education. The eight chapters include a review of higher education's abandonment of traditional rhetoric training, the call for more English, and the development of a wide range of writing courses—from advanced composition to creative writing to journalism. The penultimate chapter examines "'Professional Writing' in Agriculture, Engineering, and Business." The book draws from primary sources, including teacher notes and student papers, to call attention to the divisions among departments of writing instruction and to the need to transform current writing curricula.

Acknowledging the challenges facing professional writing instruction, Adams writes, "the difficult effort of teaching students to write has not been furthered by characterizations of muddleheaded creative writers or one-column-of-fragments journalism teachers or form-letter business and technical writing teachers or grammar-fixated composition teachers or snooty, troublemaking rhetoricians. We need to recognize our common beginnings and talk about our respective strengths with the goal of training today's students to be writers" (xi).

32   **Alford, Elisabeth M. "Thucydides and the Plague in Athens: The Roots of Scientific Writing."** *Written Communication* **5.2 (April 1988): 131–53.**

Greek historian Thucydides wrote a history of the Peloponnesian War, within which is a section that describes a plague that devastated Athens in 430 B.C.E. This article discusses the controversy surrounding Thucydides' description and suggests that "examining the plague account as an early model of scientific writing shows the venerable age of some modern conventions in this genre" (133) and comparing the account with a funeral oration that precedes it "adds to our understanding of differences and similarities between epideictic and scientific writing" (134).

33   **Aydelotte, Frank, ed.** *English and Engineering: A Volume of Essays for English Classes in Engineering Schools.* **New York: McGraw-Hill, 1917. 390p.**

Frank Aydelotte was Professor of English at Massachusetts Institute of Technology. He states that this collection of essays is built on the theory that the function of English in technical education is not only to train students in writing but also "to furnish something of the liberal, humanizing, and broadening element which is more and more felt to be a necessary part of an engineering education" (xii). Among the 27 selections are "Writing and Thinking" by John Ruskin, "The Profession of Engineering" by George S. Morison, "Poetry and Science" by William Wordsworth, and "Science and Culture" by Thomas Henry Huxley. Other authors included are Matthew Arnold, Robert Louis Stevenson, and Thomas Carlyle. *English and Engineering* is typical of such collections of the period.

34   **Carbone, Mary T. "The History and Development of Business Communication Principles: 1776–1916."** *Journal of Business Communication* **31.3 (July 1994): 173–93.**

This article traces principles found in the works of British rhetoricians George Campbell, Hugh Blair, and Richard Whately through nineteenth-century rhetoric and etiquette manuals to the early business English textbook of George Burton Hotchkiss and Celia Anne Drew. The author includes a table that summarizes the evolution of those business communication principles.

35   **Connors, Robert J. "The Rise of Technical Writing Instruction in America."** *Journal of Technical Writing and Communication* **12.4 (1982): 329–52.**

As long as human beings "have used tools and have needed to communicate with each other about them," the author observes, "technical discourse has existed" (329). Before tracing the history of technical writing instruction during the period from 1900 to 1980, the author examines its origins in engineering education in the nineteenth century. He describes the key figures and their texts during the early years (1895–1939): T. A. Rickard, Samuel Chandler Earle, J. Raleigh Nelson, Frank Aydelotte, Sada A. Harbarger, and others. Several controversies are evident from the field's beginnings: vocationalism versus liberal arts, faculty status in English departments, and debates over the goals of courses. Surveying refinements from World War II until 1980, the author concludes "in general the prospect is excellent for both teachers and students of technical writing" (349).

36   **Douglas, George H., and Herbert W. Hildebrandt, eds.** *Studies in the History of Business Writing*. **Urbana, IL: ABC, 1985. 215p.**

In their introduction, the editors of this collection state that the essays are "a step toward providing a seminal statement on the history and practice of business writing" (v). Surveying its rhetorical heritage, they assert that although "the term 'business writing' is a modern term, what is taught today under that rubric is rooted in ideas as old as Western Civilization" (v).

The articles include "Business Writing and the Spread of Literacy in Late Medieval England" and "The First Century of English Business Writing, 1417–1525" by Malcolm Richardson; "'Sir, This Will Never Do': Model Dunning Letters, 1592–1873" and "The Earliest Correspondence of the British East India Company (1600–19)" by Kitty O. Locker; "'Elegant Simplicity': Lord Chesterfield's Ideal for Business Writing" by William E. Rivers; "The Communication Theory of Johann Carl May: Its Influence on Business Communication in Germany" by Herbert W. Hildebrandt and Iris Varner; "Business Writing in America in the Nineteenth Century" by George H. Douglas; and "The Teaching of Business Writing at the Collegiate Level 1900–1920" by Francis W. Weeks.

The articles, as the editors state, do not provide a linear history of business writing; rather, they provide a "hint" of the tradition of business writing. In fact, they provide a helpful starting point for further historical research.

37   **Earle, Samuel Chandler.** *The Theory and Practice of Technical Writing*. **New York: Macmillan, 1911. Index. 301p.**

In his preface, the author suggests that the textbooks published "of late" are collections of "specimens of technical writings," "dissertations on correct English," and "treatises on technical writing addressed, with 'a certain condescension,' to engineers, but in reality based on a study of literary exposition" (vi). Earle's theory is based in part on the following assertion: "Thought and verbal expression are practically inseparable, consequently the main purpose of a course in technical writing should be to train one in thinking and in expressing oneself accurately, completely, logically, and economically" (13). Part I, "A Study of the Principles of Logical Structure," includes chapters on "synopses" and "fundamental principles" as well as "descriptive exposition," "narrative exposition," "directions," and combinations of these three forms. Part II, "Practical Application of Principles," uses the principles in Part I to cover various aspects of technical documents, but it also devotes a chapter to "addressing general readers" and a chapter to "addressing specialists." A 58-page appendix provides examples of various technical documents which include text, diagrams, and photographs.

38   **Gardner, Edward Hall.** *Effective Business Letters: Their Requirements and Preparation, with Specific Directions for the Various Types of Letters Commonly Used in Business.* **New York: Ronald, 1915. Index. 376p.**

The content of this book was based on the author's classes at the University of Wisconsin; the organization, according to the author, is based on Professor Edwin C. Woolley's *Handbook of Composition.* Chapters 1 and 2 focus on general letter-writing principles, such as "sympathy, patience, genuine courtesy, and kindliness" (7). Chapters 3 through 5 treat mechanics and language, and Chapters 6 through 19 cover types of letters (credit, sales, inquiry, etc.) and job applications. Chapters 20 through 22 cover general composition, form letters, and filing methods. Two appendixes provide information about telegrams, cablegrams, and abbreviations and offer case problems for the chapters.

39   **Hagge, John. "The Spurious Paternity of Business Communication Principles."** *Journal of Business Communication* **26.1 (Winter 1989): 33–55.**

This article describes how current business communication principles, such as the "Seven Cs" and reader adaptation, were not developed in the early twentieth century by "a small, readily identifiable band of . . . 'pioneers'" (33). Rather, they grew out of a 2,000-year-old tradition of epistolographic writings. The author notes, as a particular example, how these principles were expounded in J. Willis Westlake's 1876 letter-writing guide. In his conclusion, the author calls for a reexamination of those principles that he sees as "essentially vacuous" (49).

40   **Harbarger, S. A.** *English for Engineers.* **New York: McGraw-Hill, 1923. Index. 266p.**

An important historical feature of this early textbook by Sada Harbarger of Ohio State University is the inclusion of "Collateral Reading" at the end of each chapter. These readings include references to Hotchkiss and Drew, Edward Hall Gardner, S. C. Earle, and other authors of books and articles on business and technical writing. The 26 chapters include coverage of various types of letters with a chapter devoted to the "you" attitude. Other chapters consider parts of reports, the book review, the editorial, and papers presented at professional meetings. The author stresses throughout both the practical and the "cultural" value of English to the engineer.

41   **Hotchkiss, George Burton, and Celia Anne Drew.** *Business English: Its Principles and Practice.* **New York: American Book Company, 1916. Index. 376p.**

Often cited as instrumental in the development of business communication practice and pedagogy, this textbook was aimed at giving students general principles, since "the student cannot be given a set of formulas for writing every conceivable type of business message" (iii). The 25 chapters are divided into four parts. Part I, "The Essentials of Business English," describes such principles as the "you attitude" ("The style of business English as well as the substance is governed by the principle of taking the reader's point of view" [8]). Part II covers "Business Forms and

Usages"; Part III, "Business Correspondence," treats letters in general and four types in particular; and Part IV, "Sales Letters and Advertising," includes reports and a two-week, day-by-day account of a businessman at work. The end-of-chapter exercises include cases, and the appendix includes a description of filing systems and "legal points" in correspondence.

42   **Locker, Kitty O. "'As *Per* Your Request': A History of Business Jargon."** *Iowa State Journal of Business and Technical Communication* **1.1 (January 1987): 27–47.**

Tracing the history of jargon in business letters, the author discusses how stock expressions originate and have proliferated as inexperienced business writers copy existing correspondence. Although the use of jargon has been criticized since at least 1914, it persists because many people think business letters "are *supposed* to use a special 'phraseology' or 'mode of expression' to be professional" (40). The author concludes, "Compared to some of the problems that afflict business and administrative writing—poor organization, obfuscation, and lack of consideration for the reader—phrases such as 'as per your request' are a minor ill" (42); nevertheless, Locker believes that students should be encouraged to avoid jargon. The article includes an extensive bibliography, noting the specific sources containing lists of phrases to be avoided.

43   **Menning, J. H. "A Half Century of Progress in Business Writing."** *ABWA Bulletin* **15.4 (January 1951): 4–11.**

This article reproduces an address on December 28, 1950, by J. H. Menning, then president of the American Business Writers Association (ABWA, now the Association for Business Communication). Menning traces not only the origins of the ABWA from its genesis in 1935 but also the development of key principles, including "'you' viewpoint presentation, conversational style, adaptation, positive suggestion, resale, appropriate tone and tempo" (8). With its citations from influential texts, this article is a useful resource for historical study.

44   **Nelson, J. Raleigh. *Writing the Technical Report*. New York: McGraw-Hill, 1940. 373p.**

Professor of English in the College of Engineering at the University of Michigan, the author aimed to give students and professionals "greater assurance based on a better understanding of their own mental processes and of the practical procedures involved in the preparation of a well-organized report" (vii). He suggests that technical people can be successful writers if they conceive of a report as analogous to an engineering project ("like any structure destined to carry its load" [vii]). Part I, "The Design of the Report," consists of 17 concise chapters covering theory and the function of reports and their parts, and Part II covers the mechanics of reports and includes a 100-page section of annotated reports. Part III, "The Criticism of the Report," includes "clinics" that examine the strengths and weaknesses of sample reports; the author observes that "the development of a consciously critical attitude toward one's own work and the work of others of similar sort is an important means

of self-education" (267). Part IV contains various classroom projects and assignments "for those who may wish to use the book as a textbook" (viii).

45   **Rickard, T. A.** *A Guide to Technical Writing*. **San Francisco: Mining and
Scientific, 1908. 127p.**

This book is of particular historical interest because it is the first published book on
technical writing for the professional. The author comments, "It has been said that
in this age the man of science appears to be the only one who has anything to say,
and he is the one that least knows how to say it" (7). "Write simply and clearly, be
accurate and careful; above all, put yourself in the other fellow's place. Remember
the reader" (13). Geared to the mining and metallurgical sciences, the 17 short,
unnumbered chapters cover matters of language, usage, grammar, and mechanics
slanted toward the needs of the technical writer.

   The book ends with a paper the author read before the American Association for
the Advancement of Science, at Denver on August 28, 1901: "A Plea for Greater
Simplicity in the Language of Science." "We must remember," the author suggests,
"that language in relation to ideas is a solvent, the purity and clearness of which
effect what it bears in solution" (126).

46   **Yates, JoAnne.** *Control through Communication: The Rise of System in
American Management*. **Baltimore: Johns Hopkins UP, 1989. Index. 339p.**

This book examines the relationship of communication systems to managerial
development during the period from 1850 to 1920. The first three chapters discuss
"Managerial Methods and the Functions of Internal Communication,"
"Communication Technology and the Growth of Internal Communication," and
"Genres of Internal Communication." The remaining five chapters examine three
specific organizations: The Illinois Central Railroad, Scovill Manufacturing
Company, and E. I. Du Pont de Nemours & Company. The book is richly illustrat-
ed with organizational documents, photographs, and other archival materials.

   One of the author's findings is that "new communication genres developed as a
product of organizational needs and available technologies. Circular letters, reports,
and manuals were shaped by the demands of their production and use. Older cus-
toms of form and style gave way in the face of a new desire to make documents
more efficient to create and to use. Thus, developments in managerial methods,
communication technologies, and communication genres fed on one another in the
evolution of the communication system" (xviii). This book not only provides historical insight but also offers a lens through which we might better understand the
impact of modern communication technologies.

GENERAL ANTHOLOGIES

47   **Anderson, Paul V., R. John Brockmann, and Carolyn R. Miller, eds.** *New
Essays in Technical and Scientific Communication: Research, Theory, Practice*.
Farmingdale, NY: Baywood, 1983. 254p.

The introduction to this anthology suggests some central characteristics of technical and scientific communication: its worthiness as an intellectual pursuit, its diversity and eclecticism, its value to the disciplines from which it borrows, and its need to be studied contextually.

Among the articles in this collection are "Studying Writing in Non-Academic Settings" by Lee Odell, Dixie Goswami, Anne Herrington, and Doris Quick; "A Cognitive Approach to Readability" by Thomas N. Huckin; "Revising Functional Documents: The Scenario Principle" by Linda Flower, John R. Hayes, and Heidi Swarts; "Scientific Writing as a Social Act: A Review of the Literature of the Sociology of Science" by Charles Bazerman; "The Role of Models in Technical and Scientific Writing" by Victoria M. Winkler; "A Rhetoric for Research in Sciences and Technologies" by James P. Zappen; and "Bacon, Linnaeus, and Lavoisier: Early Language Reform in the Sciences" by James Paradis. The final part of the collection is "What's Technical about Technical Writing?" by David N. Dobrin, who concludes that "technical writing is writing that accommodates technology to the user" (242).

The significance of this collection is evident not only in the frequency with which its articles have been cited but also in the influence of many articles on the direction of research.

48 **Bazerman, Charles, and James Paradis, eds.** *Textual Dynamics of the Professions: Historical and Contemporary Studies of Writing in Professional Communities.* **Madison: U of Wisconsin P, 1991. Index. 390p.**

The editors state that the 15 articles in this collection "concretely elucidate the broad abstraction that writing is social action" (3). Furthermore, by "studying texts within their contexts, we study as well the dynamics of context building. In particular, by understanding texts within the professions, we understand how the professions constitute themselves and carry out their work through texts" (3).

Part One, "Textual Construction of the Professions," examines the rhetorics of the sciences, management, and literary criticism. Part Two, "The Dynamics of Discourse Communities," examines how discourse communities are formed. Part Three, "The Operational Force of Texts," includes studies of particular texts in context: "Text and Action: The Operator's Manual in Context and in Court" by James Paradis; "Understanding Failures in Organizational Discourse: The Accident at Three Mile Island and the Shuttle *Challenger* Disaster" by Carl G. Herndl, Barbara A. Fennell, and Carolyn R. Miller; and "Creating a Text/Creating a Company: The Role of a Text in the Rise and Decline of a New Organization" by Stephen Doheny-Farina.

The editors conclude that the world "cannot be reduced to the rhetorical domination of a powerful monolithic discourse of science and technology, as is sometimes feared" (10). In fact, as this collection demonstrates, discourse communities "provide varied enough voices to maintain a robust rhetorical environment and keep the forces of reductionism at bay. And they provide enough of a rhetorical challenge to require our best efforts at understanding them" (10).

49   **Blyler, Nancy Roundy, and Charlotte Thralls, eds.** *Professional Communication: The Social Perspective*. Newbury Park, CA: Sage, 1993. Index. Bib. 292p.

In his foreword to this collection, Charles Bazerman suggests that "in the humanities we have a fear of the social. The humanities, we believe, constitute the place where the individual learns to express the self against compulsive society" (vii). Through the 14 essays, the authors present a diversity of issues that suggest the importance and value of the social perspective in embodying the "particularities that we live and to these particularities that we write" (x).

The collection is divided into two parts—Part I: "History, Theory, and Research"; and Part II: "Pedagogy and Practice"—each of which is subdivided into "Overviews" and "Interpretations." Hoping "to advance . . . conversations about a social paradigm in professional writing research and pedagogy" (xii), the editors include selections from a variety of areas, for example, "The Social Perspective and Professional Communication: Diversity and Directions in Research" by Charlotte Thralls and Nancy Roundy Blyler; "Rhetoric Unbound: Discourse, Community, and Design Practice" by Bruce Herzberg; "Ideology and the Map: Toward a Postmodern Visual Design Practice" by Ben F. Barton and Marthalee S. Barton; "You Are What You Cite: Novelty and Intertextuality in a Biologist's Experimental Article" by Carol Berkenkotter and Thomas Huckin; "The Role of Law, Policy, and Ethics in Corporate Composing: Toward a Practical Ethics for Professional Writing" by James E. Porter; and "Conflict in Collaborative Decision-Making" by Rebecca E. Burnett.

In their preface, the editors cite earlier works that anticipated the importance of social and contextual studies and suggest that these studies should continue to be central to research and pedagogy in business and technical communication.

50   **Fearing, Bertie E., and W. Keats Sparrow, eds.** *Technical Writing: Theory and Practice*. New York: MLA, 1989. Index. Bib. 176p.

Since this was the first technical writing collection published by the Modern Language Association, the editors aimed to include articles on theory and pedagogy that reflect the wide range of interests of technical writing specialists, particularly teachers, from across the nation and beyond. Acknowledging the great diversity of forms that technical writing and its teaching have assumed, the editors assert that the field remains one of great opportunity.

The editors divide the 13 articles into four parts on history and theory, the composing process, products of technical writing, and teaching technical writing. The collection includes "Teaching Technical Writing: A Retrospective Appraisal" by James W. Souther; "What's Practical about Technical Writing?" by Carolyn R. Miller; "Collaborative Writing in Industry" by Mary Beth Debs; "Composing Processes for Technical Discourse" by Jack Selzer; "Writing and Testing Instructions for Usability" by Janice C. Redish and David A. Schell; and "The Prescriptive versus the Heuristic Approach in Teaching Technical Communication" by John H. Mitchell and Marion K. Smith. While this book's articles are important contributions, its MLA publication makes it particularly significant historically.

51   **Gould, Jay R., ed. *Directions in Technical Writing and Communication*. Baywood's Technical Communications Series. Farmingdale, NY: Baywood, 1978. 152p.**

The 14 articles in this collection, originally published in the *Journal of Technical Writing and Communication*, examine the definitions, basic forms, and evaluation methods of technical communication. Articles include "External Examiners for Technical Writing Courses" by Thomas M. Sawyer; "The Persuasive Proposal" by Lois DeBakey; and "The Trouble with Technical Writing Is Freshman English" by W. Earl Britton.

52   **Kogen, Myra, ed. *Writing in the Business Professions*. Urbana, IL: NCTE and ABC, 1989. 300p.**

The editor of this collection of 14 articles observes that the "field of business writing has always been intensely multidisciplinary, and this has accounted for its strength and adaptability as well as for many of its problems" (xi). One problem is boundary, which this collection defines "very broadly to encompass all aspects of professional writing, including organizational communication, managerial communication, legal and other career writing, and even technical writing" (xiv). The word *business* in its title signifies any working situation, whether corporate, governmental, professional, industrial, or even academic.

Part I aims to define the circumstances and features of professional writing in such articles as "Rhetorical Problem-Solving: Cognition and Professional Writing" by Linda Flower; "What Classical Rhetoric Has to Offer the Teacher and the Student of Business and Professional Writing" by Edward P. J. Corbett; and "Interactive Writing on the Job: Definitions and Implications of 'Collaboration'" by Barbara Couture and Jone Rymer.

Part II describes characteristics and conventions of writing in several major fields and includes "Writing in Organizations" by Janice Redish; "Understanding the Writing Context in Organizations" by Linda Driskill; and "The State of Legal Writing: *Res Ipsa Loquitur*" by George D. Gopen.

Part III examines pedagogical implications and origins in such articles as "Use of the Case Method in Teaching Business Communication" by John L. DiGaetani and "The Teaching and Practice of 'Professional Writing'" by C. H. Knoblauch.

Part IV describes how business communication is currently categorized and defined by colleges and universities.

53   **Matalene, Carolyn B., ed. *Worlds of Writing: Teaching and Learning in Discourse Communities of Work*. New York: Random House, 1989. 399p.**

Writing on the job is thoroughly rhetorical since, as the editor states, "what finally appears on paper—as a memo, proposal, or report—is but the end result of a complex set of negotiations between the writer and the writer's real and imagined audiences; between the writer and the text's stated and unstated purposes; between the writer and the beliefs, practices, and constraints of the community" (v–vi).

The 23 articles in this collection are divided into eight sections. Part One compares academic and nonacademic writing and includes "Coming to Terms with Different Standards of Excellence for Written Communication" by Kristin R. Woolever; "Process and Genre" by Mary Ann Eiler; and "From the Garret to the

Fishbowl: Thoughts on the Transition from Literary to Technical Writing" by William E. Rivers.

Part Two includes "Adaptation: Business Writing as Catalyst in a Liberal Arts Curriculum" by Janette S. Lewis and "Rhetoric and the Discourse of Technology" by Theresa Enos.

Part Three examines the role of writing in different contexts and includes "Writers in Organizations and How They Learn the Image: Theory, Research, and Implications" by Jean Ann Lutz; "The Text and the Trade Association: A Story of Documents at Work" by Elisabeth M. Alford; and "The File Cabinet Has a Sex Life: Insights of a Professional Writing Consultant" by Lee Clark Johns.

Part Four contains articles on constraints unique to discourse communities in business and industry, such as "Storyboarding an Industrial Proposal: A Case Study of Teaching and Producing Writing" by Muriel Zimmerman and Hugh Marsh and "Written Communication: The Industrial Context" by J. C. Mathes.

Parts Five through Eight include articles by consultants concerning their work in four specific discourse communities: journalism, finance, computer technology, and the law. Among the articles are "How to Appear Reliable without Being Liable: C.P.A. Writing in Its Rhetorical Context" by Aletha S. Hendrickson and "Bridging the Gap: In Which the Author, an English Major, Recounts His Travels in the Land of the Techies" by Edward Gold.

In the introduction the editor states: "This volume is part of a growing effort to pay serious attention to the vast amount of writing in our culture and to the rich variety of contexts from which it arises" (xi).

54 **Odell, Lee, and Dixie Goswami, eds. *Writing in Nonacademic Settings*. New York: Guilford, 1985. Indexes. 553p.**

This collection of 14 articles intends to present some of the current scholarship on writing in nonacademic settings and "to suggest ways it might become the basis for teaching and for further research" (viii). The articles, which average about 40 pages, are divided into five parts. Part I is Paul V. Anderson's "What Survey Research Tells Us about Writing at Work." Part II includes "Perceiving Structure in Professional Prose: A Multiply Determined Experience" by Gregory G. Colomb and Joseph M. Williams and "Making Information Accessible to Readers" by Janice C. Redish, Robbin M. Battison, and Edward S. Gold. Part III treats the influence of new technologies in articles by Jeanne W. Halpern and Denise E. Murray.

Part IV begins with "Nonacademic Writing: The Social Perspective" by Lester Faigley and includes "Beyond the Text: Relations between Writing and Social Context" by Lee Odell; "Writing at Exxon ITD: Notes on the Writing Environment of an R&D Organization" by James Paradis, David Dobrin, and Richard Miller; and "Special Topics of Argument in Engineering Reports" by Carolyn R. Miller and Jack Selzer. Part V includes "The Writing Teacher in the Workplace: Some Questions and Answers about Consulting" by Dwight W. Stevenson in addition to two articles on building a professional writing program and courses in collaboration with those outside the academy. Part VI includes "Survey Methodology" by Paul V. Anderson and "Ethnographic Research on Writing: Assumptions and Methodology" by Stephen Doheny-Farina and Lee Odell. The collection ends with author and subject indexes.

55   **Spilka, Rachel, ed. *Writing in the Workplace: New Research Perspectives*. Carbondale: Southern Illinois UP, 1993. Index. Bib. 332p.**

"In many respects," according to the editor, "this book is a follow-up to the 1985 anthology *Writing in Nonacademic Settings*" (viii) (see 54). After commenting on the subsequent progress in the field, Spilka suggests that "before the discipline can mature further, it needs to determine where it has been and where it needs to go next" (vii). Accordingly, the 19 articles are divided into two parts—"Part One: Research Studies of Writing in the Workplace" and "Part Two: Implications of Recent Research Findings for Theory, Pedagogy and Practice, and Future Research."

Part One begins with "Situational Exigence: Composing Processes on the Job by Writer's Role and Task Value" in which Barbara Couture and Jone Rymer survey working professionals relative to writing processes, roles, and tasks. The nine other articles include studies of specific contexts, audiences, and genres by Barbara Mirel, Jamie MacKinnon, Susan Kleimann, Rachel Spilka, Judy Z. Segal, Jennie Dautermann, Anthony Paré, Graham Smart, and Geoffrey A. Cross.

Part Two begins with "Corporate Authority: Sponsoring Rhetorical Practice" by Mary Beth Debs, who examines the concept of authorship in the workplace. The following two articles provide overviews of intertextuality by Jack Selzer and research on discourse communities by Leslie A. Olsen. Patricia Sullivan and James E. Porter examine research methodology and suggest it should take place "with these perspectives—theory, practice, method—in dialectic tension" (237). Other contributors examining these various tensions include James A. Reither, Rachel Spilka, Mary Beth Debs, and Stephen Doheny-Farina. The collection concludes with an article by Tyler Bouldin and Lee Odell, who use a "systems theory perspective" to examine writing in the workplace.

THEORY AND RHETORIC

THEORIES AND MODELS

56   **Alred, Gerald J. "'We Regret to Inform You': Toward a New Theory of Negative Messages." *Studies in Technical Communication: Selected Papers from the 1992 CCCC and NCTE Meetings*. Ed. Brenda R. Sims. Denton: U of Texas and NCTE, 1993. 17–36.**

This paper discusses the dissatisfaction of students, teachers, and theorists with the classic paradigm for delivering negative messages: buffer–explanation–bad news–goodwill. To demonstrate how and why writers situate the negative information within a message, the author presents a number of examples that include Martin Luther King's "Letter from Birmingham Jail." To better understand why approaches differ, Alred develops a "negative message continuum" and suggests five "factors" that help explain the relative directness or indirectness of a negative message: (1) the writer's and/or reader's stakes in the message, (2) the expectations of the discourse community or culture, (3) the ethos or value the writer wishes to project, (4) the writer's anticipation of the reader's response, and (5) the writer's and/or reader's personality characteristics. The author concludes that the theory "allows us to situate and apply new theories whether they are based on speech acts, reader responses, gender, or some other area" (32).

57   **Campbell, Kim Sydow. "Explanations in Negative Messages: More Insights from Speech Act Theory."** *Journal of Business Communication* **27.4 (Fall 1990): 357–75.**

The author finds that professional writing textbooks, despite scarce research on the subject, are "amazingly uniform in the prescription" for using explanations in negative messages (358). Moreover, the principles underlying the need for such explanations are not always clear. The author argues that speech act theory provides a theoretical perspective which can help writers understand how and why explanations work to maintain goodwill in negative messages: "Speech Act Theory supports the use of an explanation in composing negative messages and also provides a useful classification of such explanations based on five universal strategies for politely refusing requests" (357). The five strategies for explaining bad news include the following: (1) denying that an item referred to in the request exists, (2) denying that the addressee is the agent of the requested action, (3) denying that the requested act is a future act, (4) citing reasons for the addressee's inability to perform the requested act, and (5) citing reasons that the requested action is actually not desired by the requester. "This classification, in turn, illuminates some problems which novice writers exhibit in 'inventing' explanations and has some specific pedagogical implications" (357).

58   **Dobrin, David N.** *Writing and Technique*. **Urbana: NCTE, 1989. Bib. 212p.**

In this collection "about writing and tools" (ix), Dobrin examines writing about tools (for example, instructions for operating a coffee mill), considers how writing itself is a tool, and concludes with an evaluation of tools and techniques used to aid writing. According to Dobrin, the aim of this book is "to study the interpenetration of writing and technology: in particular, how technology has affected writing" (ix). Furthermore, "the book cheerfully allies itself with a tradition of opposition to technology" (ix). In one chapter, computer applications such as text analyzers and invention aids are demonstrated to be useful but limited tools. Each of the book's nine previously published essays "takes up a specific idea, or even a phrase expressive of an idea, and examines it closely" (x). Chapters include "The Technology of Writing," "What's Technical about Technical Writing?" "Know Your Audience," and "What Makes a Paragraph Coherent?" Theoretical attempts to reduce writing to a technique are superficial and limiting, says the author (155). Dobrin concludes that "Technical writing is writing that accommodates technology to the user," a definition that "calls attention to the experience of technology, rather than to the technology of writing" (54).

59   **Driskill, L. P., and Jone Rymer Goldstein. "Uncertainty: Theory and Practice in Organizational Communication."** *Journal of Business Communication* **23.3 (Summer 1986): 41–56.**

The authors write that "complexity and change have been heralded as the most salient features of the business world today" (41). Using Jay Galbraith's formulation, the authors define uncertainty in organizational communication as "the perceived lack of information, knowledge, beliefs, and feelings—whatever is necessary for accomplishing the organizational task and the personal objectives of communicators in the organization" (45). Uncertainty may exist at corporate, departmental, and individual levels. It can be managed by coordinating informal and formal communications systems, that is, meeting with people face-to-face in conjunction with the issuance of official corporate documents.

60   **Harris, Elizabeth. "Applications of Kinneavy's Theory of Discourse to Technical Writing."** *College English* **40.6 (February 1979): 625–32.**

Harris writes that typical definitions of technical writing are both too restrictive and not restrictive enough. She uses James Kinneavy's work to propose a definition of technical writing as "mainly *reference discourse*—discourse the primary purpose of which is to represent reality (which is assumed, without proof, to preexist outside the writer or speaker)" (627). The author discusses discourse, types of referential writing, concepts of information conveyance in informative writing, components of exploratory discourse, and semantic components of style. She also uses Kinneavy's model to demonstrate the relevance of its application toward the teaching of writing.

61   **Kent, Thomas. "Schema Theory and Technical Communication."** *Journal of Technical Writing and Communication* **17.3 (1987): 243–52.**

The author states, "Three of the most important and far-reaching writing guidelines given to technical writing students are the following: 1. Move from information readers know to information they do not know in every segment of a written communication; 2. Move from the most general information to the most particular information in every segment of a written communication; 3. Employ formats and organizational strategies that the reader recognizes" (243). These guidelines are "not composing rules; instead, they are really descriptions of how readers read" and are derived from schema theory (249). They are powerful because "schemata" (preexisting patterns in readers' minds) "facilitate the communication process by serving as common ground between writer and reader" (248). Kent arranges this article into four sections: "Schema Theory," "The Category Effect," "Script Theory," and "Schema and Processing Information."

62   **Killingsworth, M. Jimmie, and Michael K. Gilbertson.** *Signs, Genres, and Communities in Technical Communication.* **Amityville, NY: Baywood, 1992.**

According to the foreword by Joe Chew, "the authors have searched for a philosophical basis for technical communication (applicable to other forms or genres of communication as well) and have found it in semiotics, the study of signs" (v). "In their blending of social theory and semiotics, Killingsworth and

Gilbertson provide a comprehensive and provocative theory of technical rhetoric" (vi). The authors' thesis is that "technical action is mediated by at least three major kinds of influences—signs, genres, and communities" (7). The book is divided into three corresponding sections which explore the body of theory behind each aspect of the authors' descriptive theory of technical writing: "Semiotics covers signs, rhetoric covers genres, and social theory covers communities of discourse" (7). Because technical writing genres "engage the reader in a world-shaping technology," the authors conclude, "Technical communication is thus an essential tool of *Homo faber*, the human doer or maker, the active technologist" (232). As a result, the three-part theory can be revised to add a fourth layer—culture and cultural studies—and practice. The authors conclude, "Each level affects all the others in the processes by which technical communicators represent and interpret thoughts, texts, and actions in the technological world" (233).

63   **Limaye, Mohan R., and Roger D. Cherry. "Pragmatics, 'Situated' Language, and Business Communication."** *Iowa State Journal of Business and Technical Communication* **1.1 (January 1987): 68–88.**

The authors divide this article into two parts. The first portion focuses on variables from speech act theory and conversation analysis that may be applied to business communication. The second portion analyzes business letters to determine "how principles derived from linguistic studies of politeness might advance the methodology used in business-communication research" (68). They find that the perceived relationships among participants of a certain rhetorical situation exert a significant influence on the representation of a problem. The authors conclude that pragmatics research supplies rigorous tools to examine such standard business communication concepts as goodwill, you-attitude, and bad-news letters.

64   **Miller, Carolyn R. "A Humanistic Rationale for Technical Writing."** *College English* **40.6 (February 1979): 610–17.**

In this article, perhaps the most-often-cited in technical writing, Miller argues that technical writing possesses significant humanistic value. What has worked against this view, she suggests, is the dominant positivist perspective of science and a "windowpane theory of language" that have essentially turned technical writing into a task of simple transmission of given information.

Viewing writing as participation in a community, she proposes, "We can improve the teaching and study of technical writing by trading our covert acceptance of positivism for an overt consensualist perspective" (616). Further, by understanding that science is participation in a community, "Good technical writing becomes, rather than the revelation of absolute reality, a persuasive version of experience" (616). Miller suggests that technical writing teachers revise their understanding of science in order to reconceptualize the discipline as a whole in more systematic terms, and she concludes, "If we do begin to talk about understanding, rather than only about skills, I believe we have a basis for considering technical writing a humanistic study" (617).

65   Miller, Thomas P. "Treating Professional Writing as Social *Praxis." Journal of Advanced Composition* 11.1 (1991): 57–72.

Miller uses classical rhetoric "to develop a philosophical justification for stressing the social and ethical dimensions of business and technical writing" (57). The author argues that classical rhetoric provides a "context in which to ask questions about values, questions that are too often ignored in professional writing classes" (57). Miller notes that Aristotle's three-part conceptualization of *theoria, praxis,* and *techne* is at odds with the tendency to teach practical writing as a mere technique. The author discusses phronesis, a practical wisdom which is "fundamental to Aristotle's basic idea that rhetoric is a social art integrally related to the traditional values of the community and the ethical development of the individual" (59). Subsequent discussion of hermeneutics and the limitations of artificial intelligence lead to Miller's conclusion that the social context of professional communications classrooms should include not only the specific organization or discipline but also the larger public context (69). "Such literacy," says Miller, "is a means of reflecting on one's self and acting on one's world, a means of self realization in social *praxis*" (69). He concludes, "We cannot be both technicians of the word and humanists because there is a basic contradiction between teaching writing as a technique of information processing and teaching writing as the negotiation of shared values and knowledge" (70).

66   Neel, Jasper. "Dichotomy, Consubstantiality, Technical Writing, Literary Theory: The Double Orthodox Curse." *Journal of Advanced Composition* 12.2 (Fall 1992): 305–20.

Using the work of a technical writer as well as that of an associate professor of literature as examples to establish opposite extremes of writing, Neel discusses several dichotomies which characterize the writing spectrum: classical versus sophistic rhetoric, theoretical work in technical writing versus literary theory, the value of clarity and closure in technical writing versus the celebration of ambiguity and ongoing dialectic in literary criticism. He then examines writings from Plato and Aristotle and compares them with those of more contemporary writers to investigate what these two "extreme" positions can tell us about the "middle ground" that may exist between them. Returning to the two writers introduced at the beginning, Neel contrasts the differing pedagogies for each field (technical writing and literary criticism) and illustrates the political implications resulting from the inability of those operating at the extremes to understand and appreciate each other. In conclusion, Neel asks: "Where are the departments that are truly strong at both extremes, yet have a Rogerian discussion of the differences going on?" (318)

67   Porter, James E. "Intertextuality and the Discourse Community." *Rhetoric Review* 5.1 (Fall 1986): 34–47.

Porter writes, "All texts are interdependent: We understand a text only insofar as we understand its precursors" (34). He continues, "By identifying and stressing the intertextual nature of discourse . . . we shift our attention away from the writer as individual and focus more on the sources and social contexts from which the writer's discourse arises. . . . Thus the intertext *constrains* writing" (34–35). Intertextuality provides rhetoric with a perspective that counters composition pedagogies that "cultivate the romantic image of writer as free, uninhibited spirit, as independent, creative genius" (34).   Using three sample texts, Porter shows the principles of intertextuality at work.

To illustrate the exclusionary power of discourse communities, Porter cites Gregor Mendel, whose work was ignored by biologists of his time, and Robert Frost, who had difficulty publishing in an era when the literary world preferred a style similar to Tennyson's. Porter concludes that "Writing is an attempt to exercise the will, to identify the self within the constraints of the discourse community . . . with our goal being to effect change and establish our identities within the discourse communities we choose to enter" (41). He proposes and describes a pedagogy of intertextuality which will "help students learn to write for the discourse communities they choose to join" (42). He includes an appendix with several sets of questions appropriate for a business or technical communication course.

68   **Richardson, Malcolm, and Sarah Liggett. "Power Relations, Technical Writing Theory, and Workplace Writing."** *Journal of Business and Technical Communication* **7.1 (January 1993): 112–37.**

"Although *power* is a buzzword in composition theory today," state the authors, "we have found little in textbooks that explains how power relations influence workplace communication on the macro level" (114). An examination of medieval letters reveals, within the *ars dictaminis* (rules governing the writing of letters), an unstated rhetorical purpose aimed at reinforcing "the power relations that underpinned the feudal system" (117). As letter writing became a tool of commerce, however, "elaborate social positioning . . . pointed needlessly at distinctions often best left unsaid in business life" (119). An examination of a contemporary example, specifically from the nuclear power industry, reveals that power relations purposely obscure writer and audience and that regulatory procedures dictate format and content. (Appendixes of actual company documents are included.) Although current pedagogical practices call for teachers to reduce their own power in the classroom in order to empower students with language, teachers must avoid misrepresenting workplace culture, "a culture in many cases where power relations shape, define, or even distort the rhetoric of technical writing" (130).

69   **Riley, Kathryn. "Speech Act Theory and Degrees of Directness in Professional Writing."** *Technical Writing Teacher* **15.1 (Winter 1988): 1–29.**

The author examines "the application of speech act theory to questions about indirectness in letter-writing style, especially letters of request" (26). The article includes figures which illustrate (1) an indirectness continuum, showing the correlation between indirectness and the weight of a request; and (2) a summary of principles and strategies for making requests. The weight of a request can be determined by considering how well the requesting party knows the addressee, how much power the addressee may have over the requesting party, and how much of an imposition the request places upon the addressee. The higher the weight of request, the more indirectly it should be written. Thus, while a customer's order may be direct, a request for information written by a newcomer to an authority in the field should be indirect and deferential. Riley suggests using speech act theory to augment textbook advice, concluding "linguistic theory should continue to be investigated as a source of information about the structure and use of business and technical writing" (27).

70   **Samuels, Marilyn Schauer. "Technical Writing and the Recreation of Reality."** *Journal of Technical Writing and Communication* **15.1 (1985): 3–13.**

Samuels suggests that technical writing is a type of creative writing and cites the growing tendencies in the sciences and humanities to view creativity as a logical or problem-solving process and, correspondingly, to view reality as more a creation than an objective truth. Samuels reviews several theories of reality (including the theories of Einstein, Popper, and Kuhn) along with several theories of creativity which "link the concept of creativity to the current scientific view of reality and its relation to the observer" (8). While, in its extreme, this blurring of the line between fiction and fact "could become a skeptical or reductivist approach in which everything and nothing is true," Samuels concludes that "handled responsibly, the reexamination of formerly rigid distinctions between external reality, the objective observer, and the creative imagination is an opportunity for the field of technical writing" (10–11).

71   **Shelby, Annette N. "The Theoretical Bases of Persuasion: A Critical Introduction."** *Journal of Business Communication* **23.1 (Winter 1986): 5–29.**

The author points out that most business communication textbooks limit their treatments of persuasion to "the classical rhetorical model, motive-goal theories, and psychological organizational structures" (5). Shelby suggests that we should look at contemporary persuasion theories developed since World War II by social psychologists and communication theorists. She then synthesizes four major contemporary approaches to persuasion and suggests their relevance to business communication.

She examines first and at greatest length the "learning approach to persuasion theory." She states, "Learning theory attempts to explain or predict the *relationship between a stimulus and a response*" (10). She turns next to "consistency theory" which "focuses on the *relationship between the stimulus and the receiver's frames of reference*" (16). Third, she examines the "perceptual approach," which is "an attitude-change model that focuses on *factors that affect how receivers perceive messages*" (18). Finally, she surveys the "functional theory" of persuasion which focuses on understanding the receiver's needs and identifies the "*means of activating them*" (20). According to the author, "The next step must be to integrate these findings [of the theories] with traditional persuasion models" (25). This article provides a useful starting point for studying theories of persuasion.

72   **Targowski, Andrew S., and Joel P. Bowman. "The Layer-Based, Pragmatic Model of the Communication Process."** *Journal of Business Communication* **25.1 (Winter 1988): 5–24.**

The authors assert that earlier communication models tend to oversimplify the communication process, while their model "isolates the various components for individual measurement and analysis, places the components into a unified whole, and places communication and its business component into a larger cultural context" (5). Their model is intended to demonstrate "the way in which multiple levels of information are exchanged among sender, receiver, and environment" (10).

The model accounts for numerous variables in the communications process, such as the physical link between sender and receiver via telephone, voice, paper, electronic, and the "session" link, which is concerned with matters of space and time (for example, real-time exchanges versus "store-and-forward" messages such as voice mail). Their "functions/role" link incorporates the function of the communication (for example, a hiring interview versus a problem-solving interview) as well as the role of the sender and receiver (for example, boss and subordinate or lover and friend). The article includes four figures which illustrate these and other aspects of the authors' communications model at work. The authors conclude that their model shifts the paradigm, particularly for business communication, from a straightforward transmission theory of communication to one that recognizes the greater complexity of various influences on the quality of the message.

73   **Witte, Stephen P. "Context, Text, Intertext: Toward a Constructivist Semiotic of Writing."** *Written Communication* **9.2 (April 1992): 237–308.**

The author states that the objective of this wide-ranging essay is "to outline a theoretical perspective that I believe is necessary in order to account for how . . . writing appears to get done, what it seems to be, and how it apparently functions in contemporary culture" (238). The essay has eight sections that adopt various perspectives on reconceptualizing writing. In the first section, Witte presents six cases of situated writing from workplaces (two are student models) to illustrate the "real-world" issues involved and to serve as examples for his discussion.

Witte's reconceptualization would "bring the concepts or terms *text*, *context*, and *intertext* closer to the Latin root they share with one another, namely, *texere*, which refers to weaving, interweaving, or plaiting and braiding without regard to the specific material on which the operation is or can be performed" (264). In fact, his examples of situated writing reveal highly complex interactions of "memorial" and "projected" texts behind, in one example, the construction of a single-sentence "text."

In his conclusion, Witte notes that "The probability of the context-text-intertext(s) configuration that informs a given writer's constructive semiosis matching exactly that of a given reader is fairly minimal" (288). Although this "approximate communication" may be negatively construed as misunderstanding (or miscommunication), it may also be seen as "a necessary—although not a sufficient—condition for the creation of new knowledge" (288). In "some after words," Witte suggests five ways in which his constructivist semiotic has relevance for the study of writing: (1) it provides a theoretic basis for dealing with "written texts" constructed from multiple symbol systems; (2) it implies that writing instruction should address situated writing and, in the process, reconstruct itself to view "writing" and "text" in this new way; (3) it "should yield insights into how learning and creativity occur, about how expertise develops, and about how differences between experts and novices can be understood"; (4) it bridges the gap between differing approaches to the study of writing, for example, anthropological versus psychological; and (5) it implies "that the current division of the field of writing research into textual, psychological, and social perspectives is itself not defensible, regardless of whether we seek to understand writing from the standpoint of processes or products, or both" (291–92).

RHETORICAL STUDIES AND AUDIENCE

74   Bocchi, Joseph S. "Forming Constructs of Audience: Convention, Conflict, and Conversation." *Journal of Business and Technical Communication* 5.2 (April 1991): 151–72.

According to the author, "this quasi-ethnographic study" examines how disciplinary and institutional conventions influence the way writers construct their audience and the textual strategies they use to address and invoke audience (152). The study is based on the author's observation of a group of construction engineers and a group of design architects who worked in the same department. He finds that "(1) writers' textual choices were based more on institutional conventions than on disciplinary norms or on specific rhetorical situations, (2) writers' attitudes toward situational audience analysis were influenced primarily by their perceptions of the importance of writing to the work of their disciplinary and institutional communities, (3) incongruities among contextual conventions restricted audience analysis, resulted in inappropriate textual features, and necessitated conversation during corporate training" (152–53). The author suggests that his findings support the position that "audiences are constructed through community conversation" (153). Thus he calls on those involved in the study of audience to "pay more attention to the multiple cultural, disciplinary, and institutional contexts for conversation" because conversation "is the juncture at which community knowledge and functions are formed and tested" (170–71).

75   Brown, Vincent J. "Facing Multiple Audiences in Engineering and R&D Writing: The Social Contexts of a Technical Report." *Journal of Technical Writing and Communication* 24.1 (1994): 67–75.

This article is based on an ethnographic case study of three authors of a 12-page report written for an agency of the federal government. Brown finds that the authors considered an audience not mentioned in other studies or textbook treatments of audience. Specifically, in addition to various intended audiences, external industry reviewers would examine the report for its accuracy and currency. While these reviewers had no decision-making power, as did the other audiences, they could influence the long-range reputation of the company. The author finds that "the external industry reviewers constituted what I call a *watchdog* audience—not quite a *primary* audience but certainly more powerful than an *immediate*, *gatekeeping*, or *secondary* audience" (71). He concludes that instructors "should lead students to recognize that some audiences are important in the short term, whereas other audiences, perhaps more difficult to identify, may be just as important in the long term" (74).

76   Fahnestock, Jeanne. "Accommodating Science: The Rhetorical Life of Scientific Facts." *Written Communication* 3.3 (July 1986): 275–96.

The author investigates the "accommodation" of science and scientific facts when a research report originally intended for a scientific audience is rewritten for an article aimed at a general audience. The author finds that the accommodations to the public audience "emphasize the uniqueness, rarity, originality of observations, removing hedges and qualifications and thus conferring greater certainty on the reported facts" (275). After examining the texts of the articles in some detail, the author suggests that a useful way to understand the process is through the classical rhetorical notion of stasis theory, which defined and ordered the kinds of questions that could be at issue in a criminal case (290). The author concludes that even if the scientific report were translated with minimum distortion of language, public readers would still ask very different questions than the scientific audience (292). In her conclusion, the author also suggests a pedagogical implication of her findings: Writing components added to discipline-specific courses cannot replace a full rhetorically based writing course because they "do not give students practice in addressing significantly different audiences" and "they do not teach the public dimensions and responsibilities of specialist knowledge" (293).

77   **Forsberg, L. Lee. "Who's Out There Anyway? Bringing Awareness of Multiple Audiences into the Business-Writing Class."** *Journal of Business and Technical Communication* **1.2 (September 1987): 45–69.**

The author demonstrates how audience assessment in business writing "requires awareness of the corporate community and its many audiences, an awareness that is difficult to provide in the classroom" (45). Forsberg first presents a case study he uses in his business writing classes to help students become aware of audience. After commenting on typical student responses, he presents three responses to the case written by experienced business writers (himself and two colleagues who have come from different professional backgrounds). He points out how each response reveals the differing organization experiences of the writers and the resulting varied approaches to their audiences.

To demonstrate what he terms the "context" that forms such responses, he presents a diagram of a three-staged "conceptual model of the business-writing context" (61). The first stage shows a variety of "attributes," such as professional/industry knowledge and verbal ability, that inform the writer's understanding of audience. The second section includes such "audience concerns" as corporate goals, specific readers, and reader functions (legal, personnel, etc.). The third section identifies such "actual audiences" as "addressed reader(s)," "copy list reader(s)," and the like. After pointing out the complexity of assessing corporate communities with which students may work, he concludes: "Rich reading of a community requires membership, and membership requires time. Transitions between discourse communities are not easily made, and we should not minimize the difficulty" (67). We can prepare students for this transition by helping them "to look for situational issues, allow them to adjust their expectations, and help them gain strategies for learning on the job" (67).

78   **Gates, Rosemary L. "Understanding Writing as an Art: Classical Rhetoric and the Corporate Context."** *Technical Writing Teacher* **17.1 (Winter 1990): 50–60.**

Two concepts from classical rhetoric, according to the author, could be useful in constructing a much-needed theory for technical writing: *kairos* and *aitia*. *Kairos*, or "appropriateness," seems obviously well suited to situational writing. *Aitia*, a lesser-known rhetorical concept, translates as "cause" and suggests for Aristotle that "we may investigate the 'causes of success' in speaking persuasively" (51). Since, as the author points out, all writing (like speaking) is an art, as an inquiry into causes of success, *aitia* has implications for studying business and technical writing. The author gives 10 "implications to *praxis*" that emerge from this classical theory. One suggestion is that a course establish "a situational environment permitting the student an opportunity to develop mastery of the art of timing and fitness while also learning the technical skills of writing" (55). Another implication is that "corporations would benefit from examining the 'causes' (explanatory factors) of successful writing in their companies, and move toward teaching these situational/cultural/contextual specific features" (56). The author concludes that "as a scientific method of inquiry used for centuries *aitia* is now valuable as a method of inquiry about the art of rhetoric" (59).

79 **Gross, Alan G. *The Rhetoric of Science*. Cambridge, MA: Harvard UP, 1990. Index. Bib. 248p.**

In his "Epilogue," the author states that "Traditionally, in the hegemony of knowledge, science has been the master, dialectic and rhetoric the servants" (206). In this book the author upsets this view by suggesting that dialectic and logic can be defined in terms of rhetoric. Under these conditions, dialectic is seen to generate the first principles of the sciences and logic to derive true statements from these principles; he thus views dialectic and logic as "rhetorics for special purposes" (206).

To reach these conclusions, in Part I Gross examines "The Relation of Rhetoric to Science" in four chapters that describe the components of his rhetorical analysis, examine analogy and language in science, and describe the rhetoric of the discovery of the structure of DNA. The six chapters in Part II, "Style, Arrangement, and Invention in Science," examine various examples of historical and contemporary scientific discovery and reporting. Part III, "Science and Society," examines in two chapters the social enterprise of scientific work.

80 **Halloran, S. Michael. *"Technical Writing and the Rhetoric of Science." Journal of Technical Writing and Communication* 8.2 (1978): 77–88.**

This article argues that "the traditional view of rhetoric and science as sharply distinct has helped reduce the technical writing course to mere vocational training" (77). The author then describes two important changes. First, the notion of science as an enterprise that directly addresses reality is giving way to an emphasis "more to winning the agreement of other scientists" (81). Second, the author points out that rhetoric is moving in a direction that "would understand a rhetorical dimension in all human discourse, including that among scientists" (81). He suggests the overlap of these two developments could be of "real interest to the teacher of technical writing" (81). He illustrates this point by examining the accounts of the discovery of the structure of DNA by James Watson and Francis Crick that demonstrate the rhetorical character of modern science. He concludes,

"Scientific discourse can be studied as an evolving human tradition, continually shaped by the conscious choices of working scientists and technical writers. So understood, the study of technical writing could become a central element of liberal education for a technological society" (87).

81   **Halloran, S. Michael, and Annette Norris Bradford. "Figures of Speech in the Rhetoric of Science and Technology."** *Essays on Classical Rhetoric and Modern Discourse*. **Ed. Robert J. Connors, Lisa S. Ede, and Andrea A. Lunsford. Carbondale: Southern Illinois UP, 1984. 179–92.**

After suggesting that "many, perhaps all scientific theories" have an "essentially metaphorical character," the authors state: "We hope in this essay to suggest that a judicious use of figures—both schemes and tropes—is warranted in scientific and technical writing" (180). They first describe the "antifigurist" tradition in scientific and technical writing. Next, they examine the role of metaphor in the formulation and communication of scientific ideas, finding as an example that the "standard model of DNA is in essence a metaphor, a figure of both thought and speech" (186). Then, they examine the role which schemes can play in enhancing the comprehensibility of scientific and technical prose. Finally, they argue that "the antifigurist tradition places unnecessary constraints on scientific invention and communication" (180). They conclude that technical writing students should be taught to understand rhetorical principles: "Indeed, if a student really understands rhetorical principles, he or she will inevitably question (but not necessarily disregard) some of the more mindless conventions that are enforced in certain fields" (192).

82   **Hays, Robert. "Political Realities in Reader/Situation Analysis."** *Technical Communication* **31.1 (1984): 16–20.**

The author suggests that little discussion of reader analysis has been concerned with politics. He states: "In this article 'politics' means 'any factor that disturbs the objective reading and use of a document.' These factors include stresses, preferences, biases, alliances, ambitions, conflicts, and friendships" (16). The author presents two examples in which politics affect the reader's reception of the writing. Then he presents various causes for similar problems—such timeless political issues as policy disagreements, personal relationships, personality problems, and organizational problems. He then gives various ways to avoid problems, including staying alert to people pressures, studying the likely results (both desired and undesired), deciding where loyalty really lies. Although he points out that "none of these approaches will solve all problems," he suggests that it helps to be aware of what can occur (19).

83   **Journet, Debra. "Interdisciplinary Discourse and 'Boundary Rhetoric': The Case of S. E. Jelliffe."** *Written Communication* **10.4 (October 1993): 510–41.**

The author states that "Interdisciplinary research is often described as the recasting of disciplinary boundaries, suggesting that interdisciplinary writing might require a 'boundary rhetoric'—one that negotiates the borders between the various disciplinary rhetorics involved" (510). Journet presents the work of S. E.

Jelliffe (1866–1945), a physician-writer who proposed a controversial theory of psychosomatic medicine that crossed the boundaries of neurology and Freudian psychoanalysis. Journet documents Jelliffe's theory, the competing modes of explanation in the disciplinary areas Jelliffe hoped to bridge, and the rhetorical methods he used to cross boundaries. Journet concludes that the success or failure of Jelliffe's work was based on his "ability to help the reader find a way into the discourse. His ability to make disciplinary connections or to connect new knowledge to established knowledge is thus related to his ability to connect his writing to established generic norms" (534).

84   **Kallendorf, Craig, and Carol Kallendorf. "The Figures of Speech, Ethos, and Aristotle: Notes toward a Rhetoric of Business Communication."** *Journal of Business Communication* **22.1 (Winter 1985): 35–50.**

In an effort to emphasize clarity, the authors point out that most business communication textbooks present figures of speech as "at best distracting and at worst confusing" (36). After examining the use of figures of speech in actual examples of business writing, the authors advocate the use of "figures of speech as an aid, not an alternative, to clarity" (40). In describing the value of figures of speech, the authors point to the rhetorical notion of *ethos*, "the image a writer or speaker projects to an audience" (42). They find that figures of speech can help develop an *ethos* that conveys intelligence, character, and goodwill—all elements that make business writing persuasive. In seeing classical rhetoric as important to business communication, they conclude "Aristotle would also remind us that in the final analysis, rhetoric is one of the liberal arts, and this includes the rhetoric of business as well" (46).

85   **Killingsworth, M. Jimmie, and Jacqueline S. Palmer.** *Ecospeak: Rhetoric and Environmental Politics in America.* **Carbondale, IL: Southern Illinois UP, 1992. Index. Bib. 312p.**

The authors believe that rhetorical analysis can and should be brought to bear on the issues surrounding the environment. In particular, Killingsworth and Palmer argue that the advocates on both sides of these issues use rhetorical techniques that inevitably result in a stalemate, or lack of sympathy. By "Ecospeak," the authors refer to the oversimplified dichotomy that reduces both sides in the debate to two stages of liberal consciousness, "a kind of allegory of good guys and bad guys, demanding of the observer a value judgment about the goodness or badness of each side" (9). In order to show the baleful, stultifying effects of this dichotomy, the authors present a genealogy of the varieties of environmentalism in Chapter 1, followed by six chapters presenting a series of rhetorical analyses of a number of scientific and ecological discourses, including the way the news media present the findings of specialists. A discussion of environmental novels is also included as a way of suggesting the role of utopian discourse in reformist politics. The authors worry that we may "find ourselves in a Babel of discourse communities" (21), but they pin their hopes on the idea that informed rhetorical criticism can teach us how better to cooperate in making the world a safer and healthier place to live.

86   **Mathes, J. C., and Dwight W. Stevenson.** *Designing Technical Reports: Writing for Audiences in Organizations.* **2nd ed. New York: Macmillan, 1991. Index. 506p.**

Developed in part through the authors' summer institutes at the University of Michigan, the original version of this textbook (Bobbs-Merrill, 1976) presented a systematic procedure with which engineers could "design" reports. The second edition addresses "a wider range of subject matters . . . drawn from business, banking, health care, social service, criminal justice, and insurance as well as engineering" (viii). One of the most notable elements in both editions is their "egocentric organization chart for audience analysis" as graphic representation of various layers of audiences at increasing distance from the writer (33). In the second edition, charts are developed for the various audiences the authors describe in their preface. This notion of audience has contributed to a general understanding of complex, multiple audiences.

87   **McCloskey, Donald N.** *The Rhetoric of Economics.* **Madison: U of Wisconsin P, 1985. Index. Bib. 209p.**

According to the author, this book explores "a rhetoric of inquiry in economics" (xx). Through an explication of specific economics texts, the author finds that economic discourse employs such rhetorical methods as metaphor, authority, symmetry, and other means of persuasion. Among the ten chapters are "The Literary Character of Economic Science," "Figures of Economic Speech," "The Problem of Audience in Historical Economics," and "The Unexamined Rhetoric of Economic Quantification." The last chapter, "The Good of Rhetoric in Economics," argues that rhetoric can improve economic prose, teaching, relations with other disciplines, economic argument, and even the temper of economists.

88   **Nelson, John S., Allan Megill, and Donald N. McCloskey, eds.** *The Rhetoric of the Human Sciences: Language and Argument in Scholarship and Public Affairs.* **Madison: U of Wisconsin P, 1987. Index. 445p.**

The 22 essays in this collection result from the 1984 University of Iowa Humanities Symposium on the Rhetoric of the Human Sciences. Its editors state that the essays "explore an emerging field of interdisciplinary research on rhetoric of inquiry, a new field that stems from increased attention to language and argument in scholarship and public affairs. It examines how scholars communicate among themselves and with people outside the academy, and it investigates the interaction of communication with inquiry" (ix). One example of this inquiry is Charles Bazerman's "Codifying the Social Science Scientific Style: The APA *Publication Manual* as a Behaviorist Rhetoric." Bazerman describes how the *Publication Manual* reinforces the view of those "social scientists who believe that the behaviorists' positivist program creates an accurate picture of the human world and provides the surest (if not the only) path to knowledge" (141). Other contributors examine the rhetoric of such areas as mathematics, psychology, anthropology, economics, and history. Contributors include Richard Rorty, "Science as Solidarity"; Gerald L. Bruns, "On the Weakness of Language in the Human Sciences"; and Jean Bethke Elshtain,

"Feminist Political Rhetoric and Women's Studies." The editors conclude that the essays explore the thesis (quoting a report on the symposium) that "elements of rhetoric . . . are so thoroughly ingrained in scholarly research as to affect every step of the enterprise" (xiii).

89   **Ong, Walter J. "The Writer's Audience Is Always a Fiction."** *PMLA* **90.1 (January 1975): 9–21.**

This seminal essay about audience compares writing to speaking, not only through fiction but also through letters and other types of documents. Ong observes, "For the speaker, the audience is in front of him. For the writer, the audience is simply further away, in time or space or both" (10). According to Ong, the "fiction" of the audience involves two stages: "the writer must construct in his imagination, clearly or vaguely, an audience cast in some sort of role" and "the audience must correspondingly fictionalize itself" (12). For example, "the historian, the scholar or scientist, and the simple letter writer all fictionalize their audiences, casting them in a made-up role and calling on them to play the role assigned" (17). Ong concludes, "No matter what pitch of frankness, directness, or authenticity he may strive for, the writer's mask and the reader's mask are less removable than those of the oral communicator and his hearer. . . . Direct communication by script is impossible" (20).

90   **Porter, James E.** *Audience and Rhetoric: An Archaeological Composition of the Discourse Community.* **Englewood Cliffs, NJ: Prentice Hall, 1992. Index. Bib. 185p.**

The author states, "This study is partly a deconstruction of the conventional conceptions of audience, a deconstruction aimed at liberating the concept from its fixed position at the end of the assembly line of discourse production and from the east point of the communication triangle" (xi). After introducing the "problem of audience" in the first chapter, in the next five chapters the author traces the notion of audience through the development of rhetoric and composition. The final two chapters conclude with the author's attempt "to *reconstruct* a notion of audience for the discipline—by attempting to articulate a social vision of audience, and by attempting to compose the discourse community" (xii).

Of most significance for this bibliography is Appendix I, "Audience in Professional Writing" (127–36). As the author states, "Audience has been an important concern in professional writing research and textbooks for some time" (127). He points out that "in some interestingly distinct ways, rhetoric and composition have been influenced by professional writing" in such areas as research in readability, usability, and organizational communication (127). He then briefly summarizes the development of these and other notions of audience in professional writing. This appendix is followed by a guide to "Teaching a Community View of Audience" and a bibliography with over 300 citations relating to audience.

91   **Schriver, Karen A. "Teaching Writers to Anticipate Readers' Needs: A Classroom-Evaluated Pedagogy."** *Written Communication* **9.2 (April 1992): 179–208.**

This article details the results of the author's classroom study of 117 college juniors and seniors from 10 classes in "writing in the professions" regarding how to best teach writers to anticipate readers' comprehension needs. Her protocol teaching method, which critiqued poorly written texts through the use of a think-aloud reading protocol, was more successful than traditional audience analysis or collaborative peer-response techniques to help writers understand potential reader comprehension problems. This method, Schriver believes, may also offer other ways for instructors to teach the process of imagining a reader, to detect and diagnose textual problems, to expand student critique beyond sentence level analysis, and to teach revision. Schriver found that "the results of this study provide strong empirical evidence that the reader-protocol method helped increase writers' perceptual knowledge by teaching them to see and hear the audience as readers" (204).

92   **Selzer, Jack, ed.** *Understanding Scientific Prose: Rhetoric and the Human Sciences*. **Madison: U of Wisconsin P, 1993.**

Part of a general series, "Rhetoric of the Human Sciences," this collection of 13 essays examines a single scientific essay (which is reproduced in an appendix), "The Spandrels of San Marco and the Panglossian Paradigm: A Critique of the Adaptationist Programme," by Stephen Jay Gould and Richard C. Lewontin.

The essays include the following: Charles Bazerman's "Intertextual Self-Fashioning: Gould and Lewontin's Representations of the Literature"; Susan Wells's "'Spandrels,' Narration, and Modernity"; Carl G. Herndl's "Cultural Studies and Critical Science"; Mary Rosner and Georgia Rhoades's "Science, Gender, and 'The Spandrels of San Marco and the Panglossian Paradigm'"; Carolyn R. Miller and S. Michael Halloran's "Reading Darwin, Reading Nature; or, On the Ethos of Historical Science"; Dorothy A. Winsor's "Constructing Scientific Knowledge in Gould and Lewontin's 'The Spandrels of San Marco'"; John Lyne's "Angels in the Architecture: A Burkean Inventional Perspective on 'Spandrels'"; Jeanne Fahnestock's "Tactics of Evaluation in Gould and Lewontin's 'The Spandrels of San Marco'"; Gay Gragson and Jack Selzer's "The Reader in the Text of 'The Spandrels of San Marco'"; Davida Charney's "A Study in Rhetorical Reading: How Evolutionists Read 'The Spandrels of San Marco'"; Debra Journet's "Deconstructing 'The Spandrels of San Marco'"; Greg Myers's "Making Enemies: How Gould and Lewontin Criticize"; Barbara Couture's "Provocative Architecture: A Structural Analysis of Gould and Lewontin's 'The Spandrels of San Marco'"; and Stephen Jay Gould's "Fulfilling the Spandrels of World and Mind." According to the editor, the essays "demonstrate how various new methodologies can profitably be brought to bear on the rhetoric of science" (17).

93   **Spilka, Rachel. "Orality and Literacy in the Workplace: Process- and Text-Based Strategies for Multiple Audience Adaptation."** *Journal of Business and Technical Communication* **4.1 (January 1990): 44–67.**

This qualitative study of seven engineers addresses two questions: "What is the role of orality in the composing processes of corporate writers?" and "How does orality relate to literacy in the evolution of corporate documents?" (45). The author uses "orality" to mean the process of transmitting ideas via speech, including written forms such as email that resemble speech (45). As a result of her detailed study, the author observes that orality was the central means of analyzing multiple audiences, adapting discourse to multiple audiences, fulfilling rhetorical goals, and fulfilling social goals as well as building and sustaining the corporate culture (45). During the process of evaluating the data, the author graphically presents "an audience-adaptation model" to illustrate the strategies used by five of the engineers in the study who were rhetorically successful (53). The author concludes that we need to broaden our approach to multiple-audience analysis in the workplace in a way that considers the social features of a rhetorical situation. Further, we need to "develop a fuller appreciation of the multiple roles of orality in fulfilling rhetorical and social goals" (66).

94   **Stoddard, Eve Walsh. "The Role of Ethos in the Theory of Technical Writing."** *Technical Writing Teacher* **11.3 (Spring 1985): 229–41.**

The author states that her research confirms that ethos is an important component in the effectiveness of technical writing, even in manuals and reports. After defining the classical notion of *ethos* (a speaker "worthy of belief"), the author describes two experiments she conducted to test her hypothesis that *ethos* affects the reception of technical writing. In the first study, she found that students trusted and found clear and helpful a manual they assumed to be written by someone with great expertise who had high regard for them as users of a manual. In the second study, students found a report more persuasive when they understood that the writer was an expert in the subject area. She concludes that "high initial *ethos* will command the attention of the audience. Now we need to look into the components of derived *ethos*. Should there be more of a personality present in a technical text? How do style and format affect the audience's perception of the company behind the document?" (239)

95   **Suchan, James, and Ron Dulek. "Toward a Better Understanding of Reader Analysis."** *Journal of Business Communication* **25.2 (Spring 1988): 29–45.**

The authors suggest that reader analysis in business communication lacks much-needed "new critical thinking." They find four reasons for this problem. First, they find confusion over critical terminology, specifically clear distinctions between *reader* and *audience*. Second, they find "poor heuristics for assessing readers," particularly the demographic approaches (age, education, etc.) that imply readers are easy-to-categorize types. Another problem they find is oversimplified textbook cases that do not account for the complexity of readers. Finally, they see as a problem the "classification of business messages" (e.g., goodwill, sales, and sensitive) that ignore the "myriad psychological factors that affect a reader" (38).

To work toward a better understanding of readers, the authors adapt the term *perceptual set* from cognitive psychology "to describe a structure of integrated personal and professional experiences that shape a businessperson's perception of or reaction to language, people, and problems" (39). They focus specifically on three areas that affect the way readers perceive messages: the corporate image and culture, the various corporate subcultures, and position and power between the writer and reader. The authors conclude that instructors should acknowledge such complexities, offer students useful advice about situational variables (such as the relative power positions of writers and readers), and use cases from actual business settings. As a result, "students will begin to see that reader analysis, like management, is a complex, open-ended, problem-solving process that never can be mastered but can be managed more intelligently" (44).

96   **Witte, Stephen P., Neil Nakadate, and Roger D. Cherry, eds.** *A Rhetoric of Doing: Essays on Written Discourse in Honor of James L. Kinneavy.* **Carbondale: Southern Illinois UP, 1992. 376p.**

Although only one of the five parts of this collection of 18 essays is nominally aimed at "nonschool settings," many of the essays are of particular significance to the rhetoric of the workplace. The editors suggest that "the essays in this book reflect 'a rhetoric of doing,' a sort of implied rhetoric by which people get things done, by which they effect change in a larger social order" (1).

Following an introduction, Part One ("Rhetoric in Historical Contexts") treats classical rhetoric from a variety of points of view. Part Two, "Discourse, Discourse Communities, and the Social Construction of Knowledge," includes five essays, among them "Theories That Help Us Read and Write Better" by Charles Bazerman, "When Reference Discourse No Longer Refers" by George L. Dillon, and "More Meanings of *Audience*" by Jack Selzer. Part Three includes four essays on "Discourse in School Settings." Part Four, "Discourse in Nonschool Settings," comprises three essays: "The Individual, the Organization, and *Kairos*: Making Transitions from College to Careers" by Stephen Doheny-Farina, "*Kairos* in the Rhetoric of Science" by Carolyn R. Miller, and "Noun Phrases and the Style of Scientific Discourse" by William J. Vande Kopple. Part Five is a bibliographic essay by Timothy W. Crusius on the works of James L. Kinneavy.

ETHICS AND GENDER

97   **Allen, Jo. "Gender Issues in Technical Communication Studies: An Overview of the Implications for the Profession, Research, and Pedagogy."** *Journal of Business and Technical Communication* **5.4 (October 1991): 371–92.**

The author raises questions about "failures to address gender issues" in technical communication (372). In order to "highlight the kinds of changes we practitioners, researchers, and teachers should anticipate," the author sees a need for more and better (and unbiased) gender research on technical communication (372). She also sees a need for a better understanding, through research, of the devaluation of the technical writing profession as a result of its "feminization." She cites STC surveys that reveal more women entering the profession and corresponding slower salary growth when compared with similar professions. She asks, "What does it really mean to have women in the field?" She also examines the situation of women academics in technical communication, and, finally, she suggests that the communication styles (oral and written) of men and women would lead to "more informed teaching of technical communication principles" in order not to "perpetuate gendercentric views of communication" (385). A fairly extensive reference section is included.

98   **Brockmann, R. John, and Fern Rook, eds.** *Technical Communication and Ethics.* **Washington, DC: Society for Technical Communication, 1989. Bib. 119p.**

According to the editors, "because the discussion is controversial and because the problem of ethics crosses many professional boundaries, this anthology goes beyond the traditional STC anthology" (v). In addition to an extensive bibliography, five different ethical codes are reprinted in full—including the STC Code for Communicators. The collection of 16 previously published articles is intended for teachers in college classrooms as well as practicing professional technical communicators. Part 1 includes four articles on the foundation of ethics and ethical reasoning. Part 2 includes four papers from proceedings on the influence of business, technical, and medical contexts on ethics. Part 3 includes an article and a paper on the connection between ethics and rhetoric. Part 4 includes three articles on teaching ethics; Part 5 reprints five codes of ethics; and Part 6, titled "Afterword," includes two articles that examine the reasons for codes and a historical survey of codes for technical writers from the 1880s to the 1980s. To help achieve their goal of stimulating discussion, the editors include a list of issues at the begining of the first four parts.

99   **Burrell, Nancy A., Patrice M. Buzzanell, and Jill J. McMillan. "Feminine Tensions in Conflict Situations as Revealed by Metaphoric Analyses."** *Management Communication Quarterly* **6.2 (November 1992): 115–49.**

This article combines "interpretive and quantitative metaphoric analyses to examine conflict images of women in government" (115). The authors employ as their theoretical framework "feminist standpoint theory" which "argues that women do not share the same life experiences and social realities and, therefore, one woman cannot speak for all women" (117). The authors focus their analysis of this group on "conflict metaphors," explaining that the "study does not attempt to analyze conflict strategies and outcomes but uncovers how a group of women characterize their conflict experiences in government" (119). "Metaphoric analysis" is used in this investigation because it "enables researchers to uncover perceptions of how people approach and manage conflict" (121). The authors explain in detail their research method as well as the quantitative and interpretive results. They conclude that "although this investigation cannot be generalized to all professional women, it does provide a rich account of bureaucratic women's conflict images" (142–43).

100   **Clark, Gregory. "Ethics in Technical Communication: A Rhetorical Perspective."** *IEEE Transactions on Professional Communication* **30.3 (1987): 190–95.**

The author sees a distinction between the professional technical communicators' and the academicians' perspectives on ethics in technical communication. Using the STC Code for Communicators and citing various articles, the author suggests that professional technical communicators value most "the well-being of their profession and the organizations in which they work" (190), while academicians value most "the well-being of the larger society in which all technology is situated" (190). Based on these differing values, the author describes "points of conflict" and suggests that "classical rhetoric offers a perspective on ethics in communication that is both practical and responsible" (193). He sees a "rhetorical ethic," one which is based on the notion that communication is "a process of negotiation and compromise that values both the well-being of the persons who contribute to that process and the well-being of the cooperating community which they make up" (193). Using various examples, the author demonstrates how "ethical technical communication functions as a cooperative exchange between the people who can provide information and the people who need to use it" (195).

101 **Coletta, W. John. "The Ideologically Biased Use of Language in Scientific and Technical Writing."** *Technical Communication Quarterly* **1.1 (Winter 1992): 59–70.**

The author demonstrates how instructors can illustrate to students with examples from technical writing textbooks and elsewhere that the language in scientific and technical texts is not value free. Using the work of Michel Foucault, he shows students how "every 'description' of a thing or 'object' is an assertion or 'proposition' about that thing; there is no purely objective description" (60). He then demonstrates ideologically biased use of language in three examples: a technical report, a visual illustration from biology, and a technical description from physics. He concludes that "ideology must become an explicit part of technical writing courses because it is always already an implicit part of technical discourse" (69).

102 **Dombrowski, Paul M., ed.** *Humanistic Aspects of Technical Communication.* **Amityville, NY: Baywood, 1994. Index. 239p.**

According to its editor, this book's five chapters focus on the "human" side of technical communication rather than on the more technical side of information and objects. Written for two audiences—graduate teaching assistants and their instructors as well as "a general readership of scholars and professionals"—the collection posits that technical communication links the sciences and the humanities (iii).

In his introductory chapter, "Humanism and Technical Communication," Dombrowski states that "the basic thrust of this volume is to challenge the interrelated dualities of fact versus opinion and the sciences versus the humanities, dualities which seem to critics to dehumanize science while they disempower the humanities" (11). The eight remaining essays are grouped under the headings "Rhetoric of Science," "Social Constructionism," "Feminist Critiques of Science and Gender Issues," and "Ethics." Among the articles included are "Some Perspectives on Rhetoric, Science, and History" by Carolyn R. Miller, "Feminist Theory and the Redefinition of Technical Communication" by Mary M. Lay, and "A Basic Unit on Ethics for Technical Communication" by Mike Markel.

103 **Hall, Dean G., and Bonnie A. Nelson. "Sex-Biased Language and the Technical-Writing Teacher's Responsibility."** *Journal of Business and Technical Communication* **4.1 (January 1990): 69–79.**

The authors' survey of 82 female engineering graduates "indicates that sexist language persists in the workplace, that women react to it in various ways, and that such language can engender sexist attitudes which often have deleterious effects on the company and its employees" (69). Citing several of the women's responses, the authors maintain that "technical writing teachers have some of the responsibility to sensitize students to exclusionary language" and to show how certain language practices violate professional ethics (69). They also contend that technical writing textbooks frequently dismiss such problems and recommend textbooks that do address the issue. The authors divide the remainder of the essay into general guidelines for classroom activities: "Sensitize students to the presence of sex-biased language," "Discuss negative effects of sex-biased language," "Provide revising and editing exercises where eliminating sex-biased language is primary," "Make eliminating sex-biased language a standard editing procedure," "Train students to recognize sexism in oral communication," and "Teach students to be aware of the damaging effects of sexist nonverbal communication."

104   **Katz, Steven B. "The Ethic of Expediency: Classical Rhetoric, Technology, and the Holocaust."** *College English* **54.3 (March 1992): 255–75.**

The author begins this article by reproducing an actual memo requesting improvements for Nazi extermination vans. He writes, "Here, as in most technical writing and, I will argue, in most deliberative rhetoric, the focus is on expediency, on technical criteria as a means to an end" (257). Katz contends that Aristotle's "ethic of expediency" was "rhetorically embraced by the Nazi regime and combined with science and technology to form the 'moral basis' of the holocaust" (258). Suggesting that Hitler justified mass extermination through a rhetoric of technology, the author cautions against "a rationality taken to such extremes that it becomes madness" (267). He then discusses the use of propaganda and concludes that we should "question whether expediency should be the primary ethical standard in deliberative discourse, including scientific and technical communication" (272).

105   **McCord, Elizabeth A. "The Business Writer, the Law, and Routine Business Communication: A Legal and Rhetorical Analysis."** *Journal of Business and Technical Communication* **5.2 (April 1991): 173-99.**

McCord writes, "Business communicators today risk legal liability as courts are increasingly holding writers and their employing organizations responsible for reasonable—although often unintended—interpretations of their routine writing" (173). Stating that research and pedagogy have failed to recognize the implications of this change, she suggests, "Rhetorical theory, particularly a social perspective, provides a useful foundation for understanding judicial resolution of claims arising out of writing" (173). In a section titled "Teaching Our Students," McCord calls for writing instruction that provides specific strategies to avoid questionable prose. She concludes, "I am suggesting a fusion between writing and the law that I hope expands our current understanding of social rhetorical theory" (196).

106   **Nielsen, Elizabeth. "Linguistic Sexism in Business Writing Textbooks."** *Journal of Advanced Composition* **8 (1988): 55–65.**

Using the NCTE's *Guidelines for Nonsexist Use of Language in NCTE Publications* as her standard, Nielsen examines both blatant and less obvious linguistic sexism in 14 business and professional writing textbooks. She asks three questions of each text: "1) Is the concept of sexist language important enough to be indexed? 2) What problems related to linguistic sexism are identified? 3) How complete is the instruction given for correcting these problems?" (56). Nielsen finds that while most texts "acknowledge *some aspects* of linguistic sexism as problematic," their efforts to deal with the issue are too frequently only cursory, or at worst patronizing and biased (62). Indeed, she writes: "Many of these texts are instrumental in maintaining and perpetuating linguistic discrimination—even if inadvertently or unconsciously—by ignoring, patronizing or marginalizing the instruction they give for avoiding sexist language" (63). She observes that business writing textbooks can be viewed as a cultural barometer that reflect both current attitudes about women and changes that are taking place. She provides six steps authors of business writing texts could take to improve their coverage of sexist language, and she concludes "the texts themselves should be models of nonsexist language" (63).

107 **Reinsch, N. L., Jr. "Ethics Research in Business Communication: The State of the Art."** *Journal of Business Communication* **27.3 (Summer 1990): 251–72.**

The author examines the treatment of ethics in the publications of the Association for Business Communication (ABC) for a 30-year period. Grouping the publications into "pedagogical papers" and "nonpedagogical papers," he finds that business communication scholars have demonstrated a persistent interest in ethics. He sees two reasons business communication scholars "must" study ethics: "business communication is inherently moral and neglect of ethics will necessarily result in an incomplete treatment of the subject matter" and ethics is necessary "to improve the quality of educational efforts" (267). The article concludes with references that provide useful leads for historical study of the subject.

108 **Rentz, Kathryn C., and Mary Beth Debs. "Language and Corporate Values: Teaching Ethics in Business Writing Courses."** *Journal of Business Communication* **24.3 (Summer 1987): 37–48.**

The authors suggest that few discussions of ethics have directly addressed the use of language and values. They demonstrate through a sales letter and a letter requesting donations to Boy Scouts of America how language posits values and uses those values to influence readers. The authors assert that "the influence of language is everywhere, and students need to be alerted to its repercussions" (42). After examining how corporate values may be in conflict with a writer's value system, they conclude, "We are not taking a prescriptive stand on the ethics of the business community in general or of particular organizations, nor are we advocating that students become suspicious of every request to write something on the job. We are prescribing a more comprehensive approach to ethics in business communication courses than those currently being advocated" (46). One way to achieve that goal, they suggest, is to acknowledge the power of language to represent values.

109 **Rogers, Priscilla S., and John M. Swales. "We the People? An Analysis of the Dana Corporation Policies Document."** *Journal of Business Communication* **27.3 (Summer 1990): 293–313.**

This article presents "a close but selective discourse analysis of an admired corporation's policy statement" (306). Specifically, *The Philosophy and Policies of Dana,* an ethics code produced by "The Policy Committee" at Dana Corporation, is examined for the way in which it uses *we* as a reference. Using the standard linguistic technique of substitution, the authors demonstrate that the pronoun reference is not as stable as a superficial reading might suggest. Further, they find that the pronoun selection is a rhetorical choice with implications beyond mere expression of the content. In addition to reproducing the document itself, the authors include the Dana Corporation Organization Chart. The authors conclude that "the kind of analysis we have presented here may have a potential role to play as input for those engaged in designing or redesigning corporate codes" (307).

110 Russell, David R. "The Ethics of Teaching Ethics in Professional Communication: The Case of Engineering Publicity at MIT in the 1920s." *Journal of Business and Technical Communication* 7.1 (January 1993): 84–111.

The author states, "I want to point out some potential difficulties—what are essentially ethical difficulties—in literature-trained faculty teaching ethics in professional communication courses" (85). As one illustration of the dilemma he finds, he speculates how a teacher might apply Kathryn C. Rentz and Mary Beth Debs's critique in "Language and Corporate Values: Teaching Ethics in Business Writing Courses" (annotated earlier in this section) to literary criticism in a course for English majors. Describing his own experience teaching engineering students, he states that "for me, the first ethical question is, How can I, as a professional teacher of writing—and as a human being—best respect a student in her life choice and help her in her struggle?" He suggests that "we ought to consider what might be called the *kairos* of critique. When is the moment ripe for critiquing the structures and values of the community that an individual student is struggling to enter?" (105) He suggests that teachers of business and technical writing learn the historical, professional, and curricular contexts of the professions their students are preparing to enter. He concludes with a "rule of thumb" for teaching ethics to students who are from science, technology, and business: "Teach ethics to these students as you would have instructors from other disciplines teach ethics to English majors" (106).

111 Sauer, Beverly A. "Sense and Sensibility in Technical Documentation: How Feminist Interpretation Strategies Can Save Lives in the Nation's Mines." *Journal of Business and Technical Communication* 7.1 (January 1993): 63–83.

This article uses a feminist analysis to examine the rhetoric of a coal-mining accident report in the context of mine safety in general. The author quotes transcripts from the report as well as testimony from women at a 1982 hearing on the accident. Through this analysis, the author shows "how (1) the conventions of public discourse privilege the rational (male) objective voice and silence human suffering; (2) the notion of expertise excludes women's experiential knowledge; (3) the conventions of public discourse sanction the exclusion of alternative voices and thus perpetuate salient and silent power structures; and (4) interpretation strategies that fail to consider unstated assumptions about gender, power, authority, and expertise seriously compromise the health, safety, and lives of miners and, in a broader sense, of all those who are dependent on technology for their personal safety" (64–65). The author concludes that a feminist analysis "demands that technical writers acknowledge the silent power structures that govern public discourse, not because we are interested in theoretical constructs about language but because those power structures affect the fabric of technology on which we all depend" (79).

112   **Sims, Brenda R. "Linking Ethics and Language in the Technical Communication Classroom."** *Technical Communication Quarterly* **2.3 (Summer 1993): 285–99.**

Sims writes that students "may not understand that they have considerable control over how a reader perceives the writer, the message, or the context of the message" (285). She argues for greater discussion of such issues in the technical communication classroom to enable students to understand their ethical responsibilities. She states, "This essay discusses current research on ethics and technical communication, examines specific methods that writers may use to manipulate language and to present information unethically, and suggests questions designed to teach students how to analyze situations that may involve such manipulation and misrepresentation" (285). Sims presents students with a number of ways writers manipulate information: giving false impressions, using imprecise language, omitting information, presenting false or inaccurate information, deemphasizing or suppressing important information, emphasizing misleading or incorrect information, and using "no-fault" writing. The essay includes two case studies for analyzing ethical decisions in written communication.

113   **Sterkl, Karen S. "The Relationship between Gender and Writing Style in Business Communication."** *Journal of Business Communication* **25.4 (Fall 1988): 17–38.**

In a study at Colorado State University of 108 undergraduate business communication students (57 male and 51 female), the author sought to determine whether significant differences in writing style could be found based on gender. The author cites a number of studies in which significant differences have been found in oral and nonverbal forms of communication. The only previous study of business writing style and gender found no significant differences in a more limited test group (Smeltzer and Werbal, *JBC* 23.2). Sterkl's study examined 20 dimensions of style, such as directness, passive verbs, courtesy words, action demanded/requested, and tag questions. The author found "no significant differences between males and females on each of the 20 dimensions of writing style tested in this study" (34). She notes this study's discrepancy with comparable studies of other forms of communication and speculates that, among other reasons for it, "women may be changing their style of communication in a business writing situation to gain more power" (35). The author suggests that this area is clearly in its infancy and deserves further study, particularly in business environments.

114   **Walzer, Arthur E. "The Ethics of False** *Implicature* **in Technical and Professional Writing Courses."** *Journal of Technical Writing and Communication* **19.2 (1989): 149–60.**

The author suggests that technical and professional writing courses are most appropriate for the discussion of ethics, since they teach writing in the context of current practice. However, that focus risks leaving students with the impression that "whatever is done and is rhetorically effective is right" (149). To counter that impression, Walzer asks students to examine the unethical practice of implying something to an audience in order to mislead them, but without technically lying. Walzer draws on the work of H. Paul Grice, who referred generally to statements (or utterances) that are intended to imply as "implicatures." Walzer explains the four "categories of maxims" Grice uses to describe how speakers and listeners might "unlock what is implied" in an implicature: Quantity, Quality, Relation, and Manner (152). Walzer then provides examples of false implicatures, including a classroom case, and demonstrates how Grice's maxims can be used to evaluate their deception. The author concludes that "raising questions of the ethical implications of particular rhetorical means would increase our students' awareness of the power and complexity of language and sharpen their critical intelligence, thus giving to professional writing classes the critical detachment that distinguishes genuine education from vocational training" (159).

PROFESSION AND CURRICULUM

DISCIPLINARY AND CURRICULAR BOUNDARIES

115   **Allen, Jo. "Bridge over Troubled Waters? Conducting Research and Pedagogy in Composition and Business/Technical Communication."** *Technical Communication Quarterly* **1.4 (Fall 1992): 5–26.**

In this article, Allen suggests pedagogical and research connections between composition and business/technical communication "would allow students to move more readily from one course to the next, while clarifying for them that writing is primarily a system of options based on analyses of situations, readers, obstacles, and goals" (5). Directed toward both instructors and researchers, the article underscores "the value of connections in pedagogy and research between composition and professional communication studies" (5). Allen divides the article into three sections that compare publications in composition with professional communication, examine areas for more crossover in pedagogy, and suggest areas for more crossover research.

116   **Allen, Jo. "The Case against Defining Technical Writing."** *Journal of Business and Technical Communication* **4.2 (September 1990): 68–77.**

The author begins by suggesting why a definition of technical writing might be quite useful, for example, "in clarifying the bounds of our academic programs and our research" (69). After a review of previous definitions of technical writing and their limitations, Allen examines various problems with defining *technical writing*—trouble with the term itself, definitions that are limited to specific features, and definitions that try to identify subject matter. The author concludes that there are disadvantages in defining the field; for example, definitions draw lines that include or exclude forms of writing, and definitions foster divisional splits among those in technical writing. She states, "At the risk of being called a naysayer, I must contend that no definition will adequately describe what we do" (76). She concludes, "It would be far better to keep our field intact—with our impressionistic, experience-based ideas of what technical writing encompasses—than to succumb to simplistic or exclusionary definitions that separate us from one another" (76).

117 Blyler, Nancy Roundy. "Theory and Curriculum: Reexamining the Curricular Separation of Business and Technical Communication." *Journal of Business and Technical Communication* **7.2 (April 1993): 218–45.**

The author states that "past bases for distinguishing business and technical communication, such as aim, style, subject matter, and type of writing, no longer have their old validity—and yet our curricular separation persists" (221). To demonstrate the practical deficiency of this separation, the author examines a memo and a report, finding that neither form supports such a distinction. She then examines these documents using social construction and paralogic hermeneutics, finding that both theories "undercut our current separation between business and technical communication while positing provocative alternatives for a curricular dialogue" (237). After examining the pressures both outside and inside academe to maintain this separation, she concludes that we need a dialogue to help the profession "reexamine our conventional separation between business and technical communication so that rhetorical theory and a curriculum in workplace writing can be better aligned" (242).

118 Buchholz, William J., ed. *Communication Training and Consulting in Business, Industry, and Government.* **Urbana, IL: ABCA, 1983. Bib. 290p.**

In the foreword, Francis W. Weeks states that "this book has been needed for a long time—since 1935, at least, when ABCA was founded" (iii). The 29 articles are divided into six sections, each of which begins with a commentary on the topic and articles included. The sections are "Communication Consulting: The Present and Beyond," "Toward Increased Productivity," "The Consulting Business," "Needs Assessment and Communication Auditing," "Common Problems: From Strategies to Ethics," and "Program Deliveries" (which includes a variety of course outlines and program descriptions). The last section ends with a selected bibliography.

119 Couture, Barbara. "Categorizing Professional Discourse: Engineering, Administrative, and Technical/Professional Writing." *Journal of Business and Technical Communication* **6.1 (January 1992): 5–37.**

"In this article," the author states, "I present an argument for categorizing writing in the workplace as it reflects rhetorical constraints associated with three professions—engineering, administration, and technical/professional writing" (6). She then examines how values held within professions constrain the ways discourse is interpreted in organizational settings. For example, engineering writing responds to the professional values of scientific objectivity and professional judgment as well as to corporate interests. Administrative writing centers on decision-making authority and the promotion of institutional identity. Technical/professional writing (which includes "career writers") aims to accommodate audience needs through complying with professional readability standards. The author concludes, "These descriptions explain how writing comes to express both the unique ideas of an individual and the common aspirations of a social group" (34). She suggests that the descriptions will also be useful in research, teaching, and practice.

120   **Dulek, Ronald E. "Models of Development: Business Schools and Business Communication."** *Journal of Business Communication* **30.3 (July 1993): 315–31.**

This article appears in a special issue of *JBC* that examines "Business Communication as a Discipline" (see also 126). In the opening editorial and introduction to the issue, Kathryn Rentz poses basic questions about the identity of the discipline (233). Dulek responds by examining two models business schools followed in their development. The first is the academic (or "vertical") model, which stressed scientific examination and the development of the Ph.D. The second is the professional (or "horizontal") model, which stressed breadth and the development of the MBA. Next, he examines the advantages and disadvantages of both models, for example, the "vertical" bringing academic recognition and the "horizontal" appealing to the business community. He suggests that "the same horizontal/vertical forces influencing the development of business schools are also at work within this field [business communication]" (323). He then asks several "key questions": Who is our customer? How can we best serve our customers? What kind of academic credentials should faculty in business communication have? Rather that answering these questions himself, Dulek considers how proponents of the vertical and horizontal models might respond. He points out that now is a good time to consider these questions, since the AACSB "has made written and oral communication a vital, legitimate part of a business program" (329).

121   **Hagge, John. "The Process Religion and Business Communication."** *Journal of Business Communication* **24.1 (Winter 1987): 89–120.**

The author begins, "Not having its own specialized body of knowledge as do other disciplines, business communication traditionally has latched onto the findings of other fields to legitimize itself" (89). The field he examines in this article is composition studies—in particular, the process approach to writing. In Section 1, he finds problems with the assumption that "writing occurs as a recursive process rather than in linear stages" (91). Citing Selzer and Broadhead and Freed, who "sympathize with the general thrust of the process movement" (97) but who discover far more linear approaches in the workplace, he sees weaknesses in the basic claims of the process approach. Section 2 argues that the "process instruction just dresses up traditional techniques or, worse, leads to contentless courses full of solipsistic students" (91). Section 3 "argues that a major misconceptualization of the nature of language and mind lies behind the emphasis in process pedagogy on creativity, self-exploration, and self-expression rather than on the social nature of communication" (91). Section 4 finds that "The process approach may be an inappropriate model in the business writing classroom for reasons having to do with culturally shared textual norms, with 'textuality'" (110). The title of this article is based on the author's assertion that "The process movement in composition theory and instruction rests on a questionable methodology, rather vacuous pedagogical precepts, and mysticism about human linguistic communication. It is more an ideology than an enterprise backed by intellectual and empirical rigor; those who practice its tenets must take them largely on faith" (108).

122 **Mathes, J. C., Dwight W. Stevenson, and Peter Klaver. "Technical Writing: The Engineering Educator's Responsibility."** *Engineering Education* **69 (January 1979): 331–34.**

The authors see three possibilities for the teaching of technical writing: "1) Let the English department teach technical writing; 2) Contract with the English department to teach technical writing, but with control remaining in the engineering college; and 3) Have engineering educators undertake the task themselves" (331). They favor the third alternative and base their argument on a number of assertions. First, English departments tend to view technical writing as being in conflict with their traditional goals and, second, "some of the basic writing principles taught in English Composition courses are antithetical to basic principles of technical writing" (331). Finally, they suggest, most professors of English are trained to teach literature, not composition. The authors conclude by suggesting that English departments and engineering colleges are better served by their proposal and that because "technical writing is a professional discipline with its own role in education and in society, it should not be regarded as an extension of English Composition" (334).

123 **Ober, Scot, and Alan P. Wunsch. "The Status of Postsecondary Business Communication Instruction: A Longitudinal Study."** *Delta Pi Epsilon Journal* **33.3 (Fall 1991): 146–57.**

Similar to two earlier studies (*JBC*: 10.2 and 24.3), this study considered several questions: "What is the status of postsecondary business communication instruction in 1990? What differences exist in postsecondary business communication instruction between four-year and two-year institutions? What changes have occurred in postsecondary business communication instruction during the time periods 1982, 1986, and 1990?" (147). The authors surveyed instructors for various factors, such as administrative unit, student enrollment, textbooks used, and subject-matter emphasis. They conclude that "the field of business communication appears to be thriving at postsecondary institutions in the United States" (156). Specifically, they find the basic course is "more often a required course for most business majors than in the past," "enrollments are holding constant," and "class sizes are decreasing" (156). They find no major changes in course content since the previous study, except that more computers are used for out-of-class assignments and institutions are offering a wider variety of business communication courses. They also conclude that the academic job market is healthy, based on the increase in number of courses, decrease in class size, and variety of courses.

124 **Pickett, Nell Ann. "Teaching Technical Communication in Two-Year Colleges: The Courses and the Teachers."** *Technical Writing Teacher* **17.1 (Winter 1990): 76–85.**

This article presents the major findings of two previously published survey studies about the teaching of technical communication in two-year colleges across the United States. Among the findings on the nature of the courses are that 71 percent of the institutions require as a prerequisite an English course and that in 72 percent of the institutions the technical communication courses transfer readily to four-year institutions (79). The author concludes that the survey points to "a broad spectrum of courses from pre-college level applied writing to sophisticated programs offering an associate degree in technical communication" (80). Most of the teachers, she finds, report "heavy work loads, with a mean per term of 101 students, 4.6 classes, 15.7 hours, 3.2 preparations, and, for some, considerable non-teaching duties" (83). Nevertheless, she concludes, "Our studies point to the emergence in the nineties of a new wave of more informed, better formally prepared, more theoretically-based . . . teachers of technical communication in two-year colleges" (84).

125 **Rivers, William E. "The Current Status of Business and Technical Writing Courses in English Departments."** *ADE Bulletin* **82 (Winter 1985): 50–54.**

Based on a survey in April 1984, the author reports on the attitude of English faculty, the qualifications of teachers, and the advice that should be given to graduate students interested in the teaching of business and technical writing (50). In his analysis of the data, he finds, "Although some English faculty members do not think business or technical writing should be taught in English departments, most seem to accept these courses as important parts of our academic mission" (52). Among his other conclusions are (1) "the enrollments in business and technical writing have increased dramatically in the past five years and are likely to continue to increase in the next few years"; (2) most faculty have traditional literature degrees and departments are looking for "flexible new colleagues who are qualified and willing to teach a wide variety of composition and literature courses"; and (3) the job outlook "for PhD graduates in English who have training in business and technical writing" is good (53). As a mark at this point in time, the survey is a paradigm for future research.

126 **Shelby, Annette Nevin. "Organizational, Business, Management, and Corporate Communication: An Analysis of Boundaries and Relationships."** *Journal of Business Communication* **30.3 (July 1993): 241–67.**

Although the distinctions among the four fields named in this article's title are difficult to define, the author states, "We define the forms operationally through specifying what we do in our teaching and research" (241). The article examines in some depth the functions and parameters of each of the four areas and includes graphic matrices in terms of system, process, and product. The author finds that organizational communication in its "broadest sense" is "the most comprehensive of the disciplines, embracing and providing a theoretical framework for the other communication types" (258). The final figure is a Venn diagram showing the relationship of the four areas, with organizational communication (in its broad sense) as the most encompassing circle (261). Only business communication resides "both within and outside organizational communication" because "businesses sometimes operate outside formal organizations; an entrepreneur writing to a potential client, for example" (261). Shelby states that this "boundary analysis should help to provide a defensible rationale and focus (though not prescription) for course content, pedagogy, and scholarly research" (243).

---

127 **Sullivan, Dale L. "Political-Ethical Implications of Defining Technical Communication as a Practice."** *Journal of Advanced Composition* **10.2 (1990): 375–86.**

The author states, "Though technical communication shares classical rhetoric's orientation toward the professions, those of us who teach technical communication don't often think of ourselves as carrying on the rhetorical tradition. Indeed, it is rather hard to do so, since we teach thought forms and discourse forms demanded by the workplace, and we often find ourselves representing the military-industrial complex instead of the humanistic tradition" (375). To demonstrate this conflict, the author traces three articles by Carolyn Miller that lead to "a point of stasis: if we enculturate students in the technical writing classroom, at least in part by teaching technical genres that reinforce the dominance of the technological system, how can we call them to responsible social action?" (377) Sullivan finds a solution to this apparent paradox by defining *technical writing* as "practice": "When rhetoric, of whatever type, is defined as a practice, it is linked with virtue" (378). Sullivan demonstrates how the course is organized into a two-part "apprenticeship model" that "at once teaches the discourse appropriate for the technological world and makes students aware of the values embedded in such discourse and the dehumanizing effects of it" (379).

---

128 **Sullivan, Patricia A., and James E. Porter. "Remapping Curricular Geography: Professional Writing in/and English."** *Journal of Business and Technical Communication* **7.4 (October 1993): 389–422.**

The authors state that in this article they "are attempting to map the academic terrain that is and that ought to be professional writing" (390). The authors explore "the problem of defining *professional writing*" and consider the implications of "department geography," i.e., the traditionally "secondary status" of writing and writing instruction in English departments (390, 392–93). The authors note that "now common" but unsatisfactory alternatives to traditional department geography "subordinates" professional writing to rhetoric/composition or business and technical writing. The authors argue that professional writing "can occupy a new space" in English departments as a major and as a research field (405). The article examines several issues relating to the institution of these new "spaces," including sources of authority, design of curriculum, characteristics of professional writing as an academic field distinct from other fields, and whose interests a professional writing curriculum would serve. Whether or not this vision of professional writing will "comfortably inhabit the department of English," the authors predict, "will depend on the ability and willingness of English departments to grant professional writing full and equal status as a type of English major" (416).

129   Tebeaux, Elizabeth. "The Trouble with Employees' Writing May Be
Freshman Composition." *Teaching English in the Two-Year College* 15.1
(February 1988): 9–19.

From her experience as a consultant, Tebeaux finds a number of common workplace writing problems: "lack of clearly revealed organization; lack of deductive presentation strategy that gives the reader the main information first; lack
of visual presentation techniques for revealing organization and content; and
lack of analysis of the reader's needs concerning the topic being discussed"
(11). After surveying participants and based on her other experiences, the
author concludes that the employees are "applying techniques learned in freshman composition to the kinds of writing they are required to do on the job"
(14). She states, "Basic composition theory, in its emphasis on expressive discourse, continues to foster the traditional goals of writing as learning and writing as thinking, with little attention to ways by which these competencies can
be sustained and applied in nonacademic writing environments" (18). While
she is "not suggesting that freshman composition be replaced by courses in
technical or business writing," she nonetheless recommends a number of
changes to make composition courses "more relevant to students after they
leave school without damaging the basic mission of freshman composition"
(17). These include adding visual design strategies, using deductive reader-
based prose, de-emphasizing the essay, stressing the introductory nature of the
course, and integrating the paradigm in freshman composition with the paradigm in technical writing (17–18).

130   Tebeaux, Elizabeth. "Let's Not Ruin Technical Writing, Too: A Comment on
the Essays of Carolyn Miller and Elizabeth Harris." *College English* 41
(1980): 822–29.

This exchange from the "Comment and Response" section of *College English*
represents an essential theory-practice tension in technical writing. In commenting on the essays of Harris and Miller (see 60 and 64), Tebeaux states,
"While such theoretical and philosophical approaches as Miller and Harris suggest might be useful in advanced courses in technical communication, they are
unsatisfactory in the basic technical writing course because they ignore the
purely pragmatic topics and problems that must be emphasized in the course"
(823). She criticizes Miller specifically for the "position that technical writing
should be taught against a background of communality and enculturation"
(822), and she suggests that "real writing of the real industrial world" has little to do with "being able to apply Kinneavy's theory of discourse" (824).
Miller responds, "If Professor Tebeaux had understood the point of my original essay, she could not have said that 'the real writing of the real industrial
world [has] little to do with enculturation.' The culture that technical writing
students must become acquainted with consists of the values, aims, and methods of the professional community they intend to enter" (826). Harris responds
that "the test of a good theory is its usefulness" (828). Harris also suggests that
Tebeaux "has usefully drawn attention to the dangers of an overly theoretical,
inadequately practical approach to the basic undergraduate technical writing
course" (827).

131 Zappen, James P. "Rhetoric and Technical Communication: An Argument for Historical and Political Pluralism." *Journal of Business and Technical Communication* 1.2 (September 1987): 29–44.

The author describes how rhetoric has been traditionally "associated with philosophy and politics, with social and institutional good," while "scientific and technical communication was originally so associated in the works of Francis Bacon but became disassociated from politics for historical reasons reflected in the works of Herbert Spencer and John Dewey" (29). The author suggests that, with Einstein and modern physics, science itself has become more political, which calls for forms of technical communication to be commensurate with that change. Zappen states, "These forms of communication must be pluralistic in the sense that they will accommodate historical diversity, from the reasonable presumption of consensus in industrial organizations characteristic of Dewey's theory of communication, on the one hand, to the expectation of disagreement and even controversy about science and technology in the public arena in the wake of changes in modern physical science, on the other" (39). Such an approach, he suggests, will "require that scientists, engineers, and technical communicators possess an extraordinary set of social and rhetorical skills" (40).

TEACHING ANTHOLOGIES

132 Brockmann, R. John, ed. *The Case Method in Technical Communication: Theory and Models*. St. Paul, MN: Association of Teachers of Technical Writing, 1984. 204p.

The introduction states that the "case method is based on the assumption that writing is best learned by students performing in as real a situation as possible. A typical case encompasses a professional writing situation (complete with data, characters, politics, and a writer's role) whose communication solution is omitted from the published case and must be developed by the students themselves" (iv). The 18 sections in this collection are divided into three parts. The first part, "Case Method Theory," contains a "Case Method Annotated Bibliography" by R. John Brockmann and "Procedures for Developing a Technical Communication Case" by Barbara Couture and Jone Rymer Goldstein as well as six other articles on general principles. The second part, "Cases for Writing," includes eight cases, most of which include documents, illustrations, and dialogue. The third part is composed of two cases by Debra Journet and Alan Journet that involve the student with graphics.

133 Cunningham, Donald H., and Herman A. Estrin, eds. *The Teaching of Technical Writing*. Urbana: NCTE, 1975. Bib. 221p.

This anthology was designed for English teachers who must teach technical writing for the first time. It is divided into eight parts with 24 articles, including definitions of technical writing, the use of metaphor in technical writing, and general discussions of the differences between teaching technical writing and teaching freshman English. There is a bibliography of journals in the field, a list of bibliographies, and a list of articles published at the time the collection was prepared.

134 Douglas, George H., ed. *The Teaching of Business Communication.* **Champaign, IL: ABCA, 1978. 238p.**

This collection of 40 articles from the *ABCA Bulletin* (1972–1977) was aimed primarily at new instructors as well as directors of programs, as suggested by such articles as "What of the Inexperienced Instructor" by L. W. Denton, "The Basic Technical and Business Writing Course at Georgia Tech" by Karl M. Murphy, and "Teaching Writing in a College of Engineering" by Thomas M. Sawyer. Part I, "The Beginning Teacher," covers approaching the classroom for the first time. Part II, "Course Curricula and Content" includes course outlines as well as articles about content. Part III, "Teaching Methods and Techniques," provides pedagogical strategies. Part IV, "Grading Practices," focuses on methods for grading and evaluation assignments and includes "The Meaning of Grades" by Francis W. Weeks. Part V, "Teaching Aids," includes the use of media as well as Francis W. Weeks's "How to Write Problems."

135 Douglas, George H., ed. *Teaching Business Communication Two.* **Urbana, IL: ABC, 1987. 291p.**

This collection, as in the earlier collection, contains articles originally published in the *ABC Bulletin.* The 38 articles are divided into five parts. Part I, "A Word to the Teacher," includes five articles on general principles and includes "Making Business Communication Courses Academically Respectable" by Kitty Locker. Part II, "Course Curricula and Content," includes among the eight articles "Business Communication: A Community College Approach" by Marilyn B. Silver and "An Analysis of Communication Course Content for MBA Students" by Larry Smeltzer. Part III, "Teaching Methods and Techniques," includes 15 articles on various pedagogical concerns. Part IV, "Grading Practices," includes three articles on the pros and cons of checkmark grading systems by Michael J. Rossi, Kathryn C. Rentz, and Ruth Lupul. Part V, "Teaching Aids," covers various mechanical and electronic aids to teaching.

136 Halpern, Jeanne W., ed. *Teaching Business Writing: Approaches, Plans, Pedagogy, Research.* **Urbana, IL: ABCA, 1983. Bib. 224p.**

The 13 chapters are divided into four parts. The first part, "Approaches," includes "Emphasizing Rhetorical Principles in Business Writing" by Jack Selzer and "Teaching the Process of Business Writing" by Jeanne W. Halpern. The second part, "Plans," includes four articles related to course development, such as "Selecting a Textbook: A Structured Approach" by Melissa E. Barth. The third part, "Pedagogy," contains four articles including "Teaching a Rhetorical Case" by Linda S. Flower. The fourth part, "Research," provides an overview of current and needed research at the time of publication.

137 Sawyer, Thomas M., ed. *Technical and Professional Communication: Teaching in the Two-Year College, Four-Year College, Professional School.* **Ann Arbor: Professional Communication, 1977. 204p.**

In his introduction, the editor suggests that this collection aims to help the beginning instructor of technical communication. He asserts that English departments have for the most part failed to assist in the "gigantic task" of helping engineers and scientists make important information understandable to decision makers in society. The scope of the 20 articles is broad, covering not only standard pedagogical approaches but also teacher preparation, publishing, and internships. One article, by Carolyn M. Blackman, provides a bibliography for beginning teachers; another, by Roger E. Masse and Patrick M. Kelley, discusses teaching the tradition of scientific and technical writing.

138   **Sparrow, W. Keats, and Nell Ann Pickett, eds.** *Technical and Business Communication in Two-Year Programs*. **Urbana, IL: NCTE, 1983. Bib. 205p.**

The 25 chapters in this collection are divided into seven parts: (1) preparation for teaching, (2) design of the basic course, (3) enhancements to the basic course, (4) classroom strategies, (5) assignment preparation, (6) report writing, and (7) resources and titles of related works. Among many useful articles are "Establishing a Technical Communication Program at the Two-Year College" by Charles E. Albrecht and Leigh S. Barker, "Using Toulmin Logic in Business and Technical Writing Classes" by Kitty O. Locker and Michael L. Keene, and "The Importance of Summaries and Their Use in the Applied Writing Class" by William E. Rivers.

139   **Stevenson, Dwight W., ed.** *Courses, Components, and Exercises in Technical Communication.* **Urbana: NCTE, 1981.**

According to the editor, the articles were written specifically for this book, as opposed to being submitted in response to a call for papers. Special efforts were made "to advise teachers on how to make classroom activities directly relevant to writing done in the world beyond the classroom" (ix). The 21 articles are divided into three parts. Part One, "Courses," includes seven articles, such as "A Professional Scenario for the Technical Writing Classroom" by Lawrence J. Johnson and "A New Approach to Teaching a Course in Writing for Publication" by David L. Carson. Part Two, "Components," includes eight articles ranging from "*Scientific American* in the Technical Writing Course" by Wayne A. Losano to "Engineering Students Write Books for Children" by Herman A. Estrin. Part Three, "Exercises," consists of six articles, which include "Organizing Is Not Enough!" by Paul V. Anderson. A list of titles for "supplementary reading" is provided.

TEACHING METHODS

140   **Baker, Tracey. "Collaborating the Course: Organized Flexibility in Professional Writing."** *Journal of Business and Technical Communication* **5.3 (July 1991): 275–84.**

This article "describes how one professional writing course is entirely and success-fully organized around collaborative writing" using "organized flexibility" (275). By *organized flexibility* the author means that, although there is a "fixed structure and schedule," in every other way the course remains flexible, for example, as students decide on the group structure (277). In the course "students produce a series of shared documents based on one body of research, with shared problem solving and decision making demanding constant interaction among group members" (276). The author provides details about the course, including the students; how work groups are formed; the different ways work groups typically compose, revise, and edit their work; and the two methods of evaluation employed. The author concludes that "organizing a class carefully enough to allow for flexibility provides an environment for success by granting students important control and responsibilities about forming groups, working together, and evaluating the assignments" (283).

141   **Bishop, Wendy. "Revising the Technical Writing Class: Peer Critiques, Self-Evaluation, and Portfolio Grading."** *Technical Writing Teacher* **16.1 (Winter 1989): 13–25.**

The "form orientation" of many technical writing classes, where the central focus is on teaching "certain 'types' of papers," the author argues, "often results in a product oriented syllabus and an overemphasis on writing structure at the expense of writing content and writers' growth and development" (13). This article suggests several methods to overcome such problems and therefore increase "writing fluency" (14). These methods include "literacy autobiographies" (in which students analyze their own writing processes), professional interviews, writing peer groups, multiple drafts, and course portfolios (14). The author gives detailed suggestions for continuous course assessment, including a system of "critique sheets" for teacher and peer evaluations, a sample cycle for preparing course portfolios, and a method for student self-evaluation. Detailed appendixes are included.

142   **Butler, Douglas R. "Government Projects and Teaching the Technical Proposal."** *Technical Writing Teacher* **14.1 (Winter 1987): 44–51.**

The author states, "Student proposals are often awkward and unconvincing: we get a half-baked solution for an unsubstantiated problem" (44). The author "offers an approach to teaching technical proposals that argue and do not merely assert" (44). The first section of the article discusses the need for students to better substantiate the problem they are addressing in their proposals. The second section offers a paradigm of the proposal process used by government agencies. Based on this paradigm, the author outlines, in the final section, "a four-week unit on proposal writing that includes submission of prospectuses and proposals with two student-teacher conferences" (44). While this process "does not duplicate the conditions that our students will find in the real world" (50), the author is "more concerned that they recognize the intellectual process that lies behind the product" (51).

143   **Dragga, Sam. "Responding to Technical Writing."** *Technical Writing Teacher* **18.3 (Fall 1991): 202–21.**

In this article, the author suggests that "technical writing teachers might improve the usability of their commentary by adapting the responding techniques of technical editors and supervisors, including explicit and systematic usage of directives, questions, and suggestions" (202). The author presents findings of a study of commentary from 17 technical writing teachers and "forty-nine technical writers, editors, and supervisors at six companies" (206). Theoretically based on J. L. Austin's *How to Do Things with Words*, the author's study, which he terms "preliminary" and "tentative," includes an investigation of the "Structures of Commentary" (What types of comments are made?); "Sources of Commentary" (Who gives commentary on the job? In the classroom?); "Media of Commentary" (Is commentary oral or written? What is the relationship of the two?); and "Focus of Commentary" (What is the dominant subject addressed?) (204).

From the instructors he "solicited the commentary" on five samples of student writing (205). An appendix to the article includes the descriptions of the writing assignments and guidelines for the teachers which accompanied the writing samples. Information from the editors and supervisors was obtained through personal interviews and from copies of technical documentation that "displayed the commentary of editors and supervisors" (206). The article includes tables that break down, numerically, the types of comments (compliments, criticisms, directives, etc.) made by teachers. Similar numerical analysis is not provided for the editors and supervisors. The author claims that "the responding style of technical writing teachers is the likely consequence of their academic perspective and their teaching experience" and, therefore, "potentially inappropriate" (218).

144 **Elliot, Norbert, Margaret Kilduff, and Robert Lynch. "The Assessment of Technical Writing: A Case Study."** *Journal of Technical Writing and Communication* **24.1 (1994): 19–36.**

Containing the results of a three-year study by the authors, the article "describes the design and evaluation of a formal writing assessment program within a technical writing course" (19). The authors outline their efforts to evaluate student writing while addressing "fundamental issues of sound assessment: reliability and validity" (19). The authors explain their implementation of a program of portfolio assessment which proved both reliable and valid. Statistical data which support these claims are included in the section "Results and Discussion." The authors also provide tables and discussion of score variation across semesters, student performance in selected academic majors, and the possible "evidence of bias found in the analysis of culture/ethnicity" (32). As a result of their study, the authors conclude that "it is possible to achieve reliability through cluster scoring" and that "evidence of validity is both qualitative and quantitative" (33). However, they do not feel that "this type of assessment should be used to interrupt student progress in the undergraduate curriculum" (33). Assessment guidelines and a fairly extensive list of references are included.

145 **Elliot, Norbert, and Paul Zelhart. "Hermeneutics and the Teaching of Technical Writing."** *Technical Writing Teacher* **17.2 (Spring 1990): 150–64.**

"This essay," the authors state, is "a call for technical writing instructors to investigate the usefulness of a hermeneutic orientation through which they might . . . discover a meaningful sense of themselves and their students within the specific institutional site" (162). Using the hermeneutics theory of Martin Heidegger, the authors develop "a hermeneutic paradigm for technical writing" which they argue will allow technical writing programs to begin "to bridge the gap between the world of global industrialization and the world of the academic classroom" (157). In the final section, the authors present "a classroom project that exemplifies a hermeneutic approach to classroom instruction" (158). Extensive references are included.

146   **Ewald, Helen Rothschild, and Donna Stine. "Speech Act Theory and Business Communication Conventions."** *Journal of Business Communication* **20.3 (1983): 13–25.**

According to the authors, "This article applies speech act theory to business communication principles in order to determine why certain messages succeed while others fail. Specifically, it shows how H. P. Grice's maxims of quantity, quality, relation, and manner illuminate the writing process in business communication" (13). Using several letters and memos as examples, the authors illustrate how speech act theory can help students understand the success of certain nonconventional business writing strategies and the failure of other communication.

147   **Feyerherm, Joel. "Applications of Kenneth Burke's Theories to Teaching Technical Writing."** *Technical Writing Teacher* **17.1 (Winter 1990): 41–49.**

In this article, the author describes how teachers can use Kenneth Burke's "chief dialectic tool," the *Pentad* (Agent, Act, Agency, Scene, and Purpose), "to analyze the writing situations they present to their students" (41). Also, the author explains, "writers can use Burke's concept of *identification* as a strategy for analyzing and creating their audiences" (41). The author then shows how teachers might apply both the Pentad and "identification" to specific textbook exercises and examples.

148   **Hagge, John. "Presenting the Teacher-Based Case: Discourse Analysis in the Business Communication Class."** *Bulletin of the Association for Business Communication* **51.1 (March 1988): 5–9.**

This article focuses on the pedagogical uses of the "teacher-based case," which is described as a "piece of business writing" the teacher supplies, "usually one with egregious faults," as well as one which allows students to "infer the details of the situational context" through questions (5). The author argues that using teacher-based case assignments in business communications classes can "ameliorate some of the problems caused by cases and 'real-world' [writing] assignments," by forcing students to gather information through questions and by rectifying problems of "audience consideration" typical in case studies or "real-world assignments" (5). Through an example of a teacher-based case, the author demonstrates how such assignments can help students take on the role of "discourse analyst," i.e., study the ways "discourse participants use mutual contextual knowledge to make inferences that allow meaningful verbal interchanges to take place" (5). A table detailing "types of mutual contextual knowledge shared by discourse participants" and a list of suggestions for presenting teacher-based cases are included (6). Appended to the article is an entire assignment package.

149 **Harris, John S.** *Teaching Technical Writing: A Pragmatic Approach*. **St. Paul, MN: ATTW, 1989. Bib. 205p.**

In his foreword to this book, Donald H. Cunningham describes some of the changes that have occurred in technical writing over 25 years. In a somewhat personal style, Harris gives sage advice to new teachers of technical writing on nearly every facet of what that person might encounter both in the classroom and professionally. Among the 21 chapters are "The Politics of Establishing a Technical Writing Course," "Syllabi and Course Outlines," "Teaching Graphics," "Technical Writing Textbooks," "Teaching Technical Reading," and "How to Get Promoted." The closing chapter offers a final lecture to technical writing students, giving advice about continuing the process of learning to write.

150 **Haynes, Kathleen J. M., and Linda K. Robertson. "An Application of Usability Criteria in the Classroom."** *Technical Writing Teacher* **18.3 (Fall 1991): 236–42.**

The authors describe their modification of three studies of usability (the relative ability to use written technical documentation) in order "to develop a classroom approach for assessing usability that was appropriate for beginning technical writing students" (238). The studies incorporated are those of Patricia Wright on "contextual factors" (factors related to who is using the document and why), F. J. Bethke et al. on "Ease-of-Use Factors," and Daniel B. Felker on "Document Design Principles" (238–39). In developing a practical classroom application, the authors sought "to determine if novice technical writers would include certain contextual and ease-of-use factors in their material," to learn whether "they understood the effect these have on the way users interpret text," and "to help them understand and apply the principles of good document design" (238). The authors provide guidelines for selection of material and classroom procedure. Potential classroom problems are identified.

151 **Herndl, Carl G. "Teaching Discourse and Reproducing Culture: A Critique of Research and Pedagogy in Professional and Non-Academic Writing."** *College Composition and Communication* **44.3 (October 1993): 349–63.**

Noting that "research and teaching in professional writing" does not "go far enough," the author argues that recognizing and exploring "the challenge presented by the relationship between discourse, teaching, and social reproduction" will enable teachers and researchers "to discover ways to intervene and initiate cultural critique within our research and pedagogical practice" (350). The author warns that if "we are uncritical in our research and teaching," the culture of professional writing "will produce students who are ignorant of the ideological development of discourse and who cannot perceive the cultural consequences of a dominant discourse or the alternate understandings it excludes" (350). The author surveys the theoretical basis of research and teaching in the field, finding that the "largely descriptive focus of professional writing research" results in teaching which "may be merely reproducing the social structures, ideologies, and subjectivities of the various communities we study" (353).

The author acknowledges that, in practice, "radical pedagogy" (or teaching which shows "how discourse and the reality it constructs are shaped by the political, economic, and material interests of professions and the institutions they create" [354]) often creates numerous problems, including courses structured "as a confrontation between oversimplified positions" (359). The author concludes that collaborative learning will "allow students to recognize the ideological conditions and consequences" of different discourses and will provide "a practical mode of resistance" without condemning "professional or technical discourse as ideologically incorrect" (361).

152 **LaDuc, Linda. "Infusing Practical Wisdom into Persuasive Performance: Hermeneutics and the Teaching of Sales Proposal Writing."** *Journal of Technical Writing and Communication* **21.2 (1991): 155–64.**

The author states that the article has two purposes: "to urge teachers of technical communication to broach the subjects of ethics in sales proposal writing with their students" and "to explore the intersections of hermeneutics and rhetoric with their ethical practice in proposal writing and performance" (156). The author argues that since "ethical know-how," defined as the "practical wisdom a writer brings to bear in the preparation and performance of effective sales proposals" (156), is essential for students of technical communication, hermeneutic theory "is another way to incorporate ethical conduct into sales proposal writing" (159). The article assesses the connections between hermeneutic and rhetorical theory, finding that hermeneutic theory offers "a different conceptual relationship between means and ends than even new rhetoric suggests" (155). The article also briefly considers the benefits of hermeneutic theory for teaching. The author observes that, in the end, "teacher intervention may make the difference between well-conceived, ethical proposals and poorly conceived, unsavory practices" (162).

153 **Mascolini, Marcia, and Roberta Supnick. "Preparing Students for the Behavioral Job Interview."** *Journal of Business and Technical Communication* **7.4 (October 1993): 482–88.**

This article focuses on "preparing students to respond to interview questions, especially to behaviorally based questions" (482). The article defines the *behavioral interview* as an interview where "applicants are asked to solve situational dilemmas that they are likely to encounter on the job," and it defines *behavioral questions* as interview strategies that force the applicant to "recall and describe specific activities or behaviors" (483). A brief survey of "leading business communications textbooks" reveals that they emphasize primarily preparation for the standard interview. The authors offer suggestions for preparing students for behavioral interviews in the classroom, including an example of a classroom activity which "translates" "common questions" into "behavioral translations" (487). The authors argue that "in a competitive job market, the behavioral response to a targeted question may provide the applicant with the critical edge needed to land the job" (488).

154 **Mendelson, Michael. "The Rhetorical Case: Its Roman Precedent and the Current Debate."** *Journal of Technical Writing and Communication* **19.3 (1989): 203–26.**

Business and technical writing (BTW) courses "seek to contextualize composition," the author asserts in this article, and so they have "embraced the case-study assignment" because it "introduce[s] writers to the contextual features of audience, purpose, and situation" (203). The author observes that the present debate over the case study method has its origins in a Roman debate over declamations, and finds that "both exercises evince a desire to practice communication within the context of a fully developed rhetorical situation" (204). The author considers three important issues related to the pedagogical use of case studies in BTW courses: first, various arguments "against the efficacy of cases" (212), stemming from over-emphasis on problem-solving analysis and the possibility that students bring an unsatisfactory "amount of organizational knowledge" to the BTW case (213). Second, the question "about how much detail is appropriate for the case narrative and how it ought to be organized" is addressed (214). Third, the author assesses arguments concerned with the "place of audience and persona in the case situation and the role of the teacher in guiding the process" (217). The author concludes that "increased scrutiny is a positive trend for case study; for in the end, our recognition of problems and our response to them will serve to strengthen the case's viability as a pedagogical tool" (221–22).

155   **Montgomery, Tracy T. "Negotiating Corporate Culture: An Exercise in Documentation." *Technical Writing Teacher* 18.1 (Winter 1991): 75–80.**

This article describes a classroom exercise, the goals of which are, according to the author, "1) to give students experience in documenting a problem, and 2) to enhance students' awareness of their own writing choices by asking them to provide a separate rationale that justifies both the content and the form of their choices" (76). In addition to an overview of the assignment, the author provides criteria for the evaluation of students' writing. The author believes this exercise teaches students "the necessity and value of documenting problems" as well as how "to look at these problems from a useful paradigm of production/political/ethical difficulties" (80).

156   **Moore, Patrick. "Using Case Studies to Teach Courtesy Strategies." *Technical Writing Teacher* 17.1 (Winter 1990): 8–25.**

In this article, the author describes a method "teachers can use to show their students how to cope with interpersonal problems that arise in writing situations in their jobs" (9). In the first three sections, titled "Evaluating Face Threatening Actions," "Redressing Threats to Positive Face," and "Redressing Threats to Negative Face," the author uses "the work of Penelope Brown and Stephen Levinson (see 316) to explain some courtesy techniques for dealing with interpersonal situations that technical professionals face" (9). In the final major section, "Using the Cases," the author explains his use of case studies in the classroom, provides three cases, and analyzes sample responses.

157   **Parker, Anne. "Problem Solving Applied to Teaching Technical Writing." *Technical Writing Teacher* 17.2 (Spring 1990): 95–103.**

The author describes a four-step problem-solving approach "implemented in a first-year technical communication course in the Faculty of Engineering, University of

Manitoba, Canada" (95). The author believes that by "showing that both engineering design and communication rely on problem solving, this approach helps students become better communicators while at the same time introducing them to the world of engineering" (95). A list of references on "engineering problem solving" is included.

158   **Reynolds, John Frederick. "Classical Rhetoric and the Teaching of Technical Writing."** *Technical Communication Quarterly* **1.2 (Spring 1992): 63–76.**

This article's survey of current technical writing textbooks reveals that "the rhetorical theory underlying most technical writing textbooks is implicit rather than explicit, scattered rather than systemic, imbedded rather than openly frameworked" (64). The author contends not only that classical rhetorical theory "offers a flexible theoretical framework" but also that classical and contemporary "contexts are surprisingly similar, perhaps even analogous" (65). However, "classical rhetoric's ability to inform and empower technical communication studies has been for the most part ignored in our technical writing textbooks" (66). The author argues that a "basic framework for incorporating classical rhetorical theory into contemporary technical writing studies" can be established with three "key concepts": "rhetoric and dialectic"; "ethos, pathos, and logos"; and the "Five Canons" (content, arrangement, style, memory, and presentation) (68). The author concludes that "classical rhetoric and technical writing can readily come together in a powerful theoretical alliance from which all can benefit" (72).

159   **Ryan, Charlton. "Using Environmental Impact Statements as an Introduction to Technical Writing."** *Technical Communication Quarterly* **2.2 (Spring 1993): 205–13.**

This article focuses on the pedagogical uses of "Environmental Impact Statements (EISs)," which the author argues can "provide college students with hands-on experience working with genuine technical documents from the working world, an overview of the writing process, and the strategies and tasks encountered in technical writing" (205). The article outlines the author's approach to introducing technical writing students to EISs, noting both the "benefits gained and the problems encountered" (206). The author observes that many benefits "evolved" from using EISs in technical writing classrooms, including affording "an overview of [the] many tasks required in technical writing," an awareness of "the roles of alternatives and criteria in decision-making processes," and "fostering collaborative work among students with a minimum of teacher-imposed guidelines" (211).

160   **Samson, Donald C., Jr. "Technical Writing Situations in the Workplace."** *Technical Writing Teacher* **17.2 (Spring 1990): 114–18.**

This article, under "Exercise Exchange," outlines a classroom exercise which addresses "the many interpersonal or political challenges related to writing in professional settings" (114). The author states that the exercise "focuses on ten 'mini-cases'" (using ethical and political multiple-choice responses) and uses "individual analysis, collaborative work, and class discussion to help students see some of the problems in the dynamics of report writing in business and government" (114). The assignment and "possible responses" to the "mini-cases" are included.

---

161 **Smith, Herb. "The Company Profile Case Study: A Multipurpose Assignment with an Industrial Slant."** *Technical Writing Teacher* **17.2 (Spring 1990): 119–23.**

The article describes an assignment which the author states "generates students' interest," "has a *real world* dimension," and "covers a variety of technical and professional communication skills" (119). "The assignment," the author says, "gives students practice in research, provides group work, and includes an oral presentation and an individual written report" (122). The article includes a description of the assignment, a case description, and a three-step teaching approach.

---

162 **Speck, Bruce W. "The Professional Writing Teacher as Author's Editor."** *Technical Communication Quarterly* **1.3 (Summer 1992): 37–57.**

The author argues that "the editor-author relationship is quite similar to the teacher-student relationship and that both relationships are problematic" (39). As an alternative, the author suggests that teachers consider a new model of the author's editor: an editor whose focus is on collaborating with the author rather than on acting as a gatekeeper. The author presents "evidence in this essay" which, he believes, "should help allay the very real concerns that professional writing teachers may have about the author's-editor model" (52). This evidence comes from the author's answers to the following questions: "What is the connection between editors and teachers?" (38); "What is an author's editor?" (39); How might the professional writing teacher use the author's editor as a teaching model?" (41); and, finally, "What obstacles would keep teachers from using the author's-editor model in the professional writing classroom?" (45). An extensive reference list is included.

---

163 **Tebeaux, Elizabeth. "Redesigning Professional Writing Courses to Meet the Communication Needs of Writers in Business and Industry."** *College Composition and Communication* **36.4 (December 1985): 419–28.**

This article observes that "surveys on communication skills needed by employees strongly indicate" that current "conventional approaches" to course design in technical, business, and science writing "is outmoded" (421). According to the article, this situation indicates that "several curricular changes are clearly mandated" (422), including bringing together in the same classroom students from diverse majors, broadening the range of writing tasks, emphasizing the "common rhetorical principles that underlie the design and development of all writing" (423), developing case studies that force students "to engage in writing that responds to realistic problems in organizations" (424), and adopting "an integrated approach to communication" (425). Considering the "results of a decade of surveys and the growing influence of technology in communication and in industry," the author asks "why many pragmatic writing courses are still neatly packaged in curricula dictated by texts that teach writing having little resemblance to communication as it is actually done on the job" (427). The author concludes that teachers of professional writing can "move away from text-dictated courses" and teach professional writing in ways which will prepare their students for the tasks they will actually face in business and industry (427).

164 **Thralls, Charlotte, and Nancy Roundy Blyler. "The Social Perspective and Pedagogy in Technical Communication."** *Technical Communication Quarterly* **2.3 (Summer 1993): 249–70.**

Observing that there is "an emerging menu of socially based pedagogies rather than a single social paradigm for writing instruction," the authors focus in this article on describing four such pedagogies in terms of technical writing classrooms, including "the social constructionist, the ideologic, the social cognitive, and the paralogic hermeneutic" pedagogies (250). In addition, the authors show that "although all share a belief in the connections between writing and culture, each subscribes to a different pedagogic aim and recommends different practices for the technical communication classroom" (250). After considering some of the implications of these four socially based pedagogies for technical writing instruction, the authors "urge the profession" to "debate the impact of socially based pedagogies and to clarify competing visions of the social perspective for technical communication" (266).

165 **Wong, Irene B. "Teacher-Student Talk in Technical Writing Conferences."** *Written Communication* **5.4 (October 1988): 444–60.**

This article focuses on one-to-one technical writing conferences, where typically "only students had familiarity with the technical content in the texts, as well as knowledge about the products, processes, and contexts" for "specific writing tasks" (444). Through a "naturalistic case study" involving a school of engineering in a four-year university, the article attempts to address the following question by examining teacher-student talk in technical writing conferences: "If knowledge relevant to improving students' writing were more evenly distributed between teachers and students, would genuine exchange result in conference talk?" (446). The article describes in detail the conditions of the study and the type and method of data collection. The author argues that the study "shows that conference talk can be interactive and less teacher-dominated" in technical writing conferences (458). In conclusion, however, the author warns that "statistical generalizability" is not the study's purpose; rather, the "ultimate goal is to develop a more complete theory of conferencing for guiding instruction" (459).

COLLABORATION

166 **Allen, Nancy, et al. "What Experienced Collaborators Say about Collaborative Writing."** *Journal of Business and Technical Communication* **1.2 (September 1987): 70–90.**

This article presents a study of 20 writers who were involved in 14 separate collaborative projects. The subjects were involved in one variety of interactive writing, "shared-document collaboration," for which the authors note three distinguishing characteristics: "production of a shared document, substantive interaction among members, and shared decision-making power over and responsibility for the document" (84). The authors make particular note of group interaction. For example, concerning group conflict they note, "Our respondents indicated a range of tolerance for group conflict, referring to it in terms that went from the 'least satisfying' aspect of collaboration or 'painful but necessary' to 'exhilarating'" (80). The authors suggest that conflict contributed to the groups' creativity. The article ends with the authors' recommendations for future research in areas such as a systematic investigation of "failed" collaborations and a study of leadership techniques that might prove most productive (87–88).

167 **Battalio, John. "The Formal Report Project as Shared-Document Collaboration: A Plan for Co-Authorship."** *Technical Communication Quarterly* **2.2 (Spring 1993): 147–60.**

"Given the reality of co-authorship," this article contends, "business and technical writing instructors need to find ways to include collaborative projects in their own writing courses" (148). The article offers a "four-phase plan for a team formal report project" in business and technical writing courses (148). The phases of the plan include "methods for team organization," "the proposal submission," the "individual discussion chapter component," and "group components and team editing" (147). The article also describes an evaluation plan, which includes "instructor evaluation of the collaborative formal report" and "student evaluation of the project" (153–54; an example of a student evaluation form is included). The article concludes that "team projects place students in a context mirroring more closely their future work environment than do more traditional approaches" (157).

168 **Burnett, Rebecca E. "Benefits of Collaborative Planning in the Business Communication Classroom."** *Bulletin of the Association for Business Communication* **53.2 (June 1990): 9–17.**

In their introduction to this special issue of the *Bulletin*, John D. Beard and Jone Rymer note that "collaborative writing has become a central concern for business communication" primarily because "scholars and researchers currently studying collaboration are concerned with the social nature of discourse and of the construction of knowledge" (1). Rebecca Burnett's focus of this article is the technique of collaborative planning, which helps students to be actively engaged in considering rhetorical elements at the beginning of the writing process (9). The article's purpose is not only to define collaborative planning but also to "identify its benefits, discuss its implementation in upper-level business communication courses, and present a series of examples of students dealing with rhetorical elements during the collaborative planning of a coauthored document" (9). The author presents several useful examples, including instructions and questions that will help students understand the "roles and responsibilities of collaborative planners and supporters" (11), and short, sample classroom dialogues which the author explains are "excerpts from coauthors in a collaborative planning session" (13). The author concludes that collaborative planning gives students "the opportunity to explore and elaborate their plans for writing by identifying and then discussing various rhetorical elements and their relationship to each other, including the context in which the document is used," and gives teachers the "opportunity to hear our students work through the problem of planning a document," allowing teachers to collect "data that we can use to refine and improve our teaching" (16).

169   **Burnett, Rebecca E. "Substantive Conflict in a Cooperative Context: A Way to Improve the Collaborative Planning of Workplace Documents."** *Technical Communication* **38.4 (November 1991): 532–39.**

This article, according to the author, focuses on particular characteristics of successful "collaboration—deferring consensus, engaging in substantive conflict, and working cooperatively" (533). In the first section, the author discusses "what researchers know about conflict and consensus in a collaborative context" (533). In the second section, she begins "by arguing for a change in the way collaboration is approached" (535). She then suggests "specific moves that writers can use to defer consensus and stimulate substantive conflict in cooperative context" (535). Excerpts from a transcribed tape of a planning session help to illustrate her points.

170   **Cross, Geoffrey A. "A Bakhtinian Exploration of Factors Affecting the Collaborative Writing of an Executive Letter of an Annual Report."** *Research in the Teaching of English* **24.2 (1990): 173–203.**

Although many studies have presented the results of successful collaborative work, this article examines the influence of various factors on a "largely unsuccessful" collaborative writing project and is "the first detailed description of the editing of the executive letter of an annual report" (197). Using Bakhtin's language theory to explain the relationships among factors affecting the project, Cross illustrates how problems in production and credibility may occur, and he proposes solutions for resolving them. He concludes by emphasizing that collaboration entails a great deal of negotiation and that group writers must understand the politics behind such work. The final draft of the actual executive letter is included in an appendix.

171   **Forman, Janis. "Collaborative Business Writing: A Burkean Perspective for Future Research."** *Journal of Business Communication* **28.3 (Summer 1991): 233–57.**

The article "begins with a review of the research and scholarship on collaborative writing by composition and business and by technical communication specialists" (233). The author then employs a "Burkean framework that identifies key areas for future investigation and provides categories for conducting research" (233). In her conclusion, the author recommends that "qualitative and exploratory field studies [should be] undertaken by interdisciplinary teams" and that these should be "followed by quantitative studies" (252). With such research, the author proposes, we should be more able to develop curricula to teach collaborative business writing. An extensive list of references is included.

172   Forman, Janis, ed. *New Visions of Collaborative Writing.* Portsmouth, NH:
       Boynton/Cook, 1992.

Forman believes that the essays in this collection "capture the movement in our
profession's thinking about collaborative writing" (xi). "Considered sequential-
ly, the focus of these essays shifts from history to diverse sites for collaboration,
then on to conceptual frameworks for understanding collaboration, and to the
interplay between collaboration and technology" (xiv). Of the first eight essays,
some, according to the editor, "challenge earlier definitions of collaboration"
(xv), or "continue the healthy skepticism and reevaluation of collaborative concepts begun in the eighties" (xvi). Others address the "political and ethical
dimensions of collaboration" (xvi). Still others, the editor says, "explore previously uninvestigated or inadequately investigated sites for collaborative writing—women's clubs, a research lab, a government agency, . . . and on-line computer conferences" (xvii). A ninth section consists of a review essay which
"offers a critical 're-vision' of the essays" and "a series of letter exchanges
between the essayists" (170).

173   **Forman, Janis, and Patricia Katsky. "The Group Report: A Problem in Small
       Group or Writing Processes?"** *Journal of Business Communication* **23.4 (Fall
       1986): 23–35.**

In this article, the authors argue that "to teach the group report successfully, . . .
instructors need to attend to both the small group and writing processes involved in
the task" (23). Following a discussion of problems in both small group and writing
processes, the authors provide solutions "derived directly from [their] analysis of
problems and from the broader perspective of management education" (31). Among
the issues addressed are poor conflict management, poor division of labor, and mis-
conceptions about the writing process.

174   **Goldstein, Jone Rymer, and Elizabeth L. Malone. "Using Journals to
       Strengthen Collaborative Writing."** *Bulletin of the Association for Business
       Communication* **48.3 (September 1985): 24–28.**

In this article the authors "explain how instructors can use a journal assignment to
facilitate and monitor student groups without directly participating in them" (24).
The authors first offer a description of the journal assignment. Then, the authors
give examples of how the journal can aid instructors in dealing with individual
issues, dyadic conflicts, and group interaction issues. They conclude with a case
study of one group's journal process. The authors believe that "as the instructor
facilitates groups by responding to individual journal entries, students learn experi-
entially how to run groups that succeed, thus solving many of the problems in teaching group projects" (28).

175   **Kleimann, Susan D. "The Complexity of Workplace Review."** *Technical
       Communication* **38.4 (November 1991): 520–31.**

The author describes "previous models of review available and present[s] a model of the review process at the mid-sized government agency [she] studied that incorporates both multiple readers and document cycling among those readers" (521). Using flowcharts to help illustrate her points, the author presents older models of "document cycling" and multiple audiences, as well as her own initial attempt to diagram the approval process of a document. She then presents a workplace model which shows the magnitude of what the workplace means by "multiple readers" and "document cycling" by incorporating the "primary measurable factors that complicate review in the workplace" (525). These include "the number of drafts, the individuals involved, the time frame, and the movement" (524–25).

176   **Lay, Mary M. "Interpersonal Conflict in Collaborative Writing: What We Can Learn from Gender Studies."** *Journal of Business and Technical Communication* **3.2 (September 1989): 5–28.**

Drawing on the work of Nancy Chodorow and Carol Gilligan, the author examines how gender studies can help explain and perhaps remedy some interpersonal conflicts among collaborative writers. Interpersonal conflict, defined as "dislike of another's personal style of communicating," often springs from gender-based communication behaviors and differs from substantive conflict over ideas (5). Lay directs her article toward business and technical writing instructors, pointing out seven central issues that frequently arise in collaborative groups: self-disclosure, control, trust, perception of group, perception of conflict, congruence between experience and behavior, and expectation of reward. She offers aids to help students overcome these differences, looking "to a time when collaborators will bring androgynous personalities to the writing process, and team members will be flexible enough to handle conflict as well as form a strong and sensitive web of collaboration" (26).

177   **Lay, Mary M., and William M. Karis, eds.** *Collaborative Writing in Industry: Investigations in Theory and Practice.* **Amityville, NY: Baywood, 1991. Index. Bib. 284p.**

Collaboration is appropriately a central concern for business and technical communication since, as many of the authors in this collection suggest, it has always been an essential part of the fabric of workplace writing. According to the editors, this collection is intended to help teachers and technical communicators in industry "better understand each other's concerns and needs. . . . As Van Pelt and Gillam argue, "while collaboration in industry aims at a timely and usable product, collaborative activities in the classroom should focus on the intellectual and interpersonal development of students" (7). These objectives, the editors maintain, "should be recognized as complementary, not contradictory" (7).

The 12 articles in this collection are divided into four parts. Part I examines the theory of collaboration and includes "Bruffee, the Bakhtin Circle, and the Concept of Collaboration" by Timothy Weiss, in which the author concludes with revisions of Bruffee's theory that are particularly appropriate to workplace writing. Part II presents two case studies of collaboration, including an often overlooked type of collaboration in "Discourse Interaction between Writer and Supervisor: A Primary Collaboration in Workplace Writing" by Barbara Couture and Jone Rymer. Part III suggests implications for the classroom and includes "Peer Collaboration and the Computer-Assisted Classroom: Bridging the Gap between Academia and the Workplace" by William Van Pelt and Alice Gillam. Part IV discusses current industrial concerns about handling information and concludes with a useful "Selected, Annotated Bibliography on Collaborative Writing" by Margaret Batschelet, William M. Karis, and Thomas Trzyna.

178 **Louth, Richard, and Ann Martin Scott, eds.** *Collaborative Technical Writing: Theory and Practice*. **Minneapolis: ATTW, 1989.**

The editors have "divided this anthology into two major parts: 1) articles concerning approaches to design, management and evaluation of collaborative activities and projects and 2) actual ready-to-use assignments with accompanying explanatory material for instructors" (i). Essays in Part One include an introduction to collaborative writing and an annotated bibliography. Also covered are "various methods of course design," an inside look into the corporate writing process, and "classroom management and evaluation of collaborative writing" (ii). "Part Two," the editors state, "contains sixteen ready-to-use, carefully prepared and tested assignments for students. Each assignment has two parts: 1) notes to the instructor describing how to implement the assignment and 2) handouts for students" (iii). The preface includes a brief description of the articles and assignments as an aid to readers in "locating materials most applicable to their classroom situations" (i).

179 **Morgan, Meg, et al. "Collaborative Writing in the Classroom."** *Bulletin of the Association for Business Communication* **50.3 (September 1987): 20–26.**

In this article, the authors "describe the structure [they] use for collaborative projects, discuss the complexities such projects create, and suggest some solutions to problems that can arise" (20). "In describing the collaborative report project," the authors "focus on three aspects crucial to incorporating collaborative writing into the classroom successfully": "the nature and sequencing of the writing assignments, the formation, development, and performance of collaborative writing groups, and the evaluation of students' performance" (20). The authors believe that by writing in groups students "become more aware of and involved in the planning, writing, and revising stages of the writing process," "improve their problem-solving ability," and "develop a tolerance for others' opinions and styles" (25). Appendixes include a "Memo Describing Logs to Students" (25) and an "Assessment Sheet Designed as a Memo to the Instructor from the Student" (26).

WORKPLACES, GENRES, AND LANGUAGE

WORKPLACE AND GENRE STUDIES

180   Anson, Chris M., and L. Lee Forsberg. "Moving beyond the Academic Community: Transitional Stages in Professional Writing." *Written Communication* 7.2 (April 1990): 200–31.

Using qualitative research methodology (e.g., journals, logs, taped interviews, workplace texts), the authors studied the "transitions" of six university seniors moving from academic to professional discourse communities. The students were enrolled in a special 12-week writing internship course in which they discussed and analyzed the writing they were doing at corporations, small businesses, and public service agencies. The article describes the students' experiences through excerpts from their journals as well as interview statements and their own analyses.

The authors identify three stages in the students' transitions: expectation, disorientation, and transition and resolution (208). In describing the students' disorientation, the authors observe, "Much of the disorientation expressed by the interns soon after they began writing on the job . . . originated not only from the disappointment of generally held expectations, but from collision of what they saw in their new reality and what they had learned from previous experience in other discourse settings" (211). Among other findings, they observe, "Our study . . . suggests that the writer must first become a 'reader' of a context before he or she can be 'literate' within it" (225). They conclude that in searching for answers to the questions this study raises, "we may well discover some useful ways in which to extend our current pedagogy of professional writing beyond its primarily textual or 'composing process' orientation and into the realms of territoriality, initiation and membership, ritual, and dialect—concepts that would seem to lie at the heart of writing as cultural adaptation" (228).

181   Atkinson, Dwight. "The Evolution of Medical Research Writing from 1735 to 1985: The Case of the *Edinburgh Medical Journal*." *Applied Linguistics* 13.4 (1992): 337–74.

The study examines the *Edinburgh Medical Journal*, the oldest continuing medical journal in English, in terms of broad rhetorical issues and more narrow linguistic analysis of register. The article describes in detail the methodology used and includes a number of charts that reveal changes which the author ascribes to "changing epistemological norms of medical knowledge, the growth of a professional medical community, and the periodic redefinition of medicine vis-à-vis the non-medical sciences" (337). In addition to many specific conclusions, the author finds that "the linguistic and rhetorical analyses complement each other in suggesting that the evolution of medical research writing has been a gradual and continuous process, rather than a series of changes based on revolutionary and drastic 'paradigm shifts.' This view differs substantially from that taken by numerous historians on the development of modern science and medicine in general; it stands, as well, in contrast to at least some scholarly assumptions concerning the development of scientific/medical prose" (363).

182 **Barabas, Christine.** *Technical Writing in a Corporate Culture: A Study of the Nature of Information.* **Norwood, NJ: Ablex, 1990. Index. Bib. 313p.**

This study of reports in an organization is part of a series, "Writing Research: Multidisciplinary Inquiries into the Nature of Writing." According to the author, the audience includes "those in academe who are interested in either studying or teaching technical writing and . . . those in R&D organizations who either write or read technical reports" (xxxix). In the introduction, the author observes "a shortcoming in most composition research and instruction: our traditional emphasis upon the structure rather than the substance of texts, upon their form and expression rather than their content and function" (xxi–xxii). The 12 chapters are divided into three parts: Part I (107 pages) is a general examination of academic versus "real-world" writing. Part II (56 pages) looks at scientific and technical writing in theoretical terms and lays a conceptual framework for the author's study.

Part III (121 pages) describes the study itself and the conclusions of the author. Using surveys, interviews, and a variety of other means, the author studied a single genre, the progress report, from a wide variety of perspectives in an R&D organization. This focus allows the author to examine in detail and with precision the writing process of writers and the context of the organization. Barabas suggests that "this study demonstrates how researchers can use a combination of methods in order to conduct integrative, context-based studies. This study, for example, is partially descriptive and partially experimental" (286). As a result of her study, Barabas also recommends that teachers use real-world problems and samples of technical writing in the classroom, invite guest speakers from R&D organizations, provide students with firsthand experience through work-study arrangements, and treat topics of primary importance to real-world writers and readers (281).

183 **Bazerman, Charles.** *Shaping Written Knowledge: The Genre and Activity of the Experimental Article in Science.* **Madison: U of Wisconsin P, 1988. Index. Bib. 356p.**

As the author prepared to teach writing to students in a variety of disciplines, he found that he "could not understand what constituted an appropriate text in any discipline without considering the social and intellectual activity which the text was part of" (4). This book is an effort to make such an evaluation and in the process trace the emergence of the experimental article in science. The author states, "In the attempt to understand what scientific language has become in practice, this book consists of a series of case studies" (16). What this modest appraisal does not suggest is the author's important observations about the social and rhetorical nature of science as he examines these cases.

The 12 chapters of this book are divided into five parts. Part I includes an introductory chapter that defines the problem of assessing scientific texts and a chapter that examines three articles, two from the sciences and one from literary studies. Part II reviews the emergence of the experimental article. Part III looks at the genre of the experimental article in physics, and Part IV examines the experimental report in the social sciences, including an analysis of the rhetoric of the APA *Publication Manual.*

The final part examines how language realizes the work of science and suggests some strategies for writers of science and their teachers. Although scientists do not need to become expert rhetoricians, Bazerman concludes, one result of the author's study is a clear recognition that writing in the sciences is thoroughly rhetorical and merits further scholarly attention.

184   **Broadhead, Glenn J., and Richard C. Freed.** *The Variables of Composition: Process and Product in a Business Setting.* **Carbondale: Southern Illinois UP, 1986. Bib. 169p.**

This publication, one in the series "Studies in Writing & Rhetoric," was partly sponsored by the Conference on College Composition and Communication and the National Council of Teachers of English. In the foreword, Richard C. Gebhardt states, "This study of effective staged writing in business emphasizes how widely writing can vary from person to person, from writing environment to writing environment" (x). To understand the writing process in a business environment, the authors examine the composing and revising practices of two proposal writers in a management consulting firm.

The four chapters begin with a seven-variable taxonomy for analyzing the composing process—particularly revision. Next, the authors describe their methods of collecting, analyzing, and measuring data. Then, they apply the taxonomy by describing the institutional procedures, values, and constraints characteristic of the firm they selected for the study. Finally, they analyze and compare how the two writers composed their proposals within the framework of this environment.

Although they observed a highly staged writing process in the proposals written by their subjects, and they recognize the pedagogical value of staged processes, the authors conclude that they do not wish to perpetuate a competition between linear and recursive models. They conclude, "From the perspective of our study, the recursive-oriented cognitive process model is clearly superior because it allows for both recursive and staged (linear) writing strategies or behaviors. It is no longer a case of choosing between the models; it is rather a case of recognizing different composing strategies, variant adaptations of a general model to different rhetorical situations" (131).

185   **Charney, Davida H., Jack Rayman, and Linda Ferreira-Buckley. "How Writing Quality Influences Readers' Judgments of Résumés in Business and Engineering."** *Journal of Business and Technical Communication* **6.1 (January 1992): 38–74.**

Using a methodology similar to their earlier study of engineering recruiters (*JBTC* 3.1, 36–53), the authors consider in this study "how writing quality in résumés influenced the assessments of four groups of readers: marketing recruiters, engineering recruiters, business writing students, and technical writing students" (69). The authors include in their article examples of the résumés used in their study as well as graphs illustrating their findings. They confirm several traditional notions, for example, that résumés not following "standard conventions for mechanics will not be taken seriously, even if the candidate has other strong qualifications" (69). However, the "most surprising result of this study was that the business writing students did not distinguish between error-free and error-laden résumés in their ratings" (62). Another significant difference they found was in terms of style: "Verbal style was apparently an important consideration for marketing but not for mechanical engineering" (69). In addition, their results "do not support those textbooks that overemphasize brevity to the exclusion of timely elaboration" (69). Reflecting on these differences, the authors conclude, "The role of writing teachers is to create effective and critical thinkers and communicators, not to enshrine received practices" (71).

186 **Clampitt, Phillip G., and Cal W. Downs. "Employee Perceptions of the Relationship between Communication and Productivity: A Field Study." *Journal of Business Communication* 30.1 (1993): 5–28.**

This study had two aims: "(a) to determine employee perceptions of the impact of eight dimensions of communication satisfaction on productivity, and (b) to understand how the type of organization may moderate the link between communication and productivity" (5). The organizations studied were a savings and loan with 65 employees and a chair manufacturer with 110 employees. The authors' findings suggest that employees perceive the impact of communication on productivity in ways that vary in kind and magnitude. For example, in the savings and loan, which represented a service industry, employees emphasized "how the relational aspects of communication affected their productivity" (22). In both organizations, feedback from supervisors had a greater impact on productivity than did other forms of communication. The authors conclude, among other things, that "the link between communication and productivity is more complex than previously assumed" (5).

187 **David, Carol, and Margaret Ann Baker. "Rereading Bad News: Compliance-Gaining Features in Management Memos." *Journal of Business Communication* 31.4 (October 1994): 267–90.**

Studying actual memos, the authors attempt to understand the content and style of memos written by managers to their subordinates using "compliance-gaining theory." Compliance-gaining research "has addressed the use of power in persuasion" (269) and has "described persuasion as a reciprocal process, where writers and readers negotiate meanings based on their past experiences and the context of the immediate message" (271). Although they acknowledge that letters between companies and customers may differ, the authors state, "Our memos support research findings that indicate the indirect organizational pattern is not common in business writing. All of the memos begin by announcing the topic. None use a buffer" (284). "Also, the you-viewpoint, which is generally prescribed for written business communication, is absent in these memos"; according to the authors, "'We,' 'our,' and 'us' reinforce the common goals shared by managers and employees to promote the company" (285). They conclude, "Our findings confirm that the writing situation is much more complex than envisioned by traditional business communication advice" (287).

188 **Davis, Richard M. "How Important Is Technical Writing? A Survey of the Opinions of Successful Engineers." *Technical Writing Teacher* 4.3 (Spring 1977): 83–88.**

Although the importance of effective written communication is "obvious to just about anyone who has ever been in industry, business, or government," according to the author of this early study, "a good many people in academia do not seem to be aware of it" (83). The author's purpose is to convince both advisers and students that "technical writing is important to an engineering career—the ability to write effectively really does make a difference" (83). To seek an answer to the question in his title, Davis selected the names of "successful" engineers through the 1973 edition of *Engineers of Distinction*, which was published by the Engineers Joint Council. Of the 348 questionnaires distributed, 245 were returned to the author. The author reports, "The results indicate that the respondents spend a substantial portion of their time (24%) writing; that the writing that they do is very important, often critical, to their positions; and that their ability to write effectively has helped them in their own advancement. Further, a substantial proportion of their time (31%) is spent working with material that others have written" (87). In addition to these results, the author quotes revealing passages from the respondents' written comments.

189 **Doheny-Farina, Stephen.** *Rhetoric, Innovation, Technology: Case Studies of Technical Communication in Technology Transfers*. **Cambridge, MA: MIT P, 1992. Index. Bib. 279p.**

This book, according to the author, "explores the rhetorical nature of the phenomena commonly labeled *technology transfers* and in the process uncovers some of the rhetorical barriers to successful technology transfers" (ix). The author defines technology transfer as an "umbrella term that refers to an entire range of activities involved in developing new technologies and their applications for the marketplace" (3). Chapter 1 critically reviews the communication theory that underpins much research on technology transfer.

Chapters 2 and 3 describe two cases—the formation of an entrepreneurial start-up company and the development of an artificial heart—and the rhetorical elements that spelled success and failure. Chapter 4 presents two cases, "each arguing that expert practical rhetoricians—technical writers—need to become participants in new product development processes from the design stage onward" (x). Chapter 5 considers the pedagogical implications of technology transfers. An appendix offers cases, complete with dialogues of participants, assignments for students, and suggestions for instructors. One way to help technical communication students learn about the relationship of rhetoric to technology, the author concludes, is by allowing them to participate "in projects that simulate the development of new products" (231).

190 **Doheny-Farina, Stephen. "Writing in an Emerging Organization: An Ethnographic Study."** *Written Communication* **3.2 (April 1986): 158–85.**

This study examined the collaborative writing processes of a group of computer software executives during a year-long process as they wrote a business plan. As the author investigated the social and organizational contexts that influenced the writing, a number of implications for theory building and pedagogy emerged. First, the author demonstrates how the writing of "a brief passage of the company's 1983 Business

Plan involved a complex social process" (178). Thus, among other observations, he suggests that the definition of writing in nonacademic settings should "include social interaction as a part of the process" (179). More specifically, the author finds "a reciprocal relationship between writing and the development of an organization" (180). For example, the writing process itself played a role in the development of the organization or social group. He connects this finding to pedagogy by suggesting, "Teachers would do well to recognize this reciprocal relationship when integrating collaborative team projects into their technical, business, and professional writing courses" (180). By providing an ethnographic view of the preparation of a single document, this study offers a rich view of the social process the author describes.

191 Faigley, Lester, and Thomas P. Miller. "What We Learn from Writing on the Job." *College English* **44.6 (October 1982): 557–69.**

This article is based on the authors' federally and locally sponsored study of the writing of college-trained people. They find generally, "Although most college trained people do not have an explicit awareness of rhetorical theory, they often talk about writing in terms of subject matter, audience and the image of themselves which they wish to project through their writing" (562). Among their findings, the authors report that those people in their study "wrote 2.9 letters and memos to persons inside their company or agency and 5.2 letters to persons outside in a given week" (560). They also found a high level of collaboration; in fact, "Only 26.5% of the 200 people we surveyed never collaborate in writing" (561). In addition to various statistical results, the authors quote very revealing comments from those in their study. While they find that writing is important on the job and other results that might be expected, they also observe "how diverse and complex writing is . . . [and] that there are processes of composing rather than a composing process, and that these processes differ among writing tasks and media" (569). They come to a view of writing "that incorporates writing among other forms of communication" (569).

192 Freed, Richard C., and Glenn J. Broadhead. "Discourse Communities, Sacred Texts, and Institutional Norms." *College Composition and Communication* **38.2 (May 1987): 154–65.**

The authors begin with a review of how "the speech community" has come to be investigated by composition researchers under the rubric of "discourse communities." The authors then report on their investigation of two specific discourse communities—a large international management consulting firm (referred to as "Omega") and a large accounting firm (referred to as "Alpha"). In their study, they find that many of the behaviors of those who work for these companies are governed in documents. Alpha's *Management Consultant Proposal Guide*, for example, is "like a sacred text, it contains commandments: 'The manager in charge of each engagement shall prepare at its conclusion a brief report'" (158). But institutional norms are also influenced by the cultures of which employees are a part, some professional and some organizational. The authors conclude, "In teaching our students to analyze audiences and rhetorical situations, we help them to anchor a message to a discourse community, to determine how the message acts within and is acted upon the community" (163).

193   **Freed, Richard C., and David D. Roberts. "The Nature, Classification, and Generic Structure of Proposals."** *Journal of Technical Writing and Communication* **19.4 (1989): 317–51.**

The authors study 40 textbooks to determine whether agreement exists on the definition and generic structure of proposals. They find little agreement in textbooks, which they suggest, "makes it difficult for textbook users to internalize a generic structure that will serve for all proposal-writing tasks" (317). After their review of textbook treatments, the authors suggest, "The purpose of all proposals is to propose a method for doing or providing something" (326). They identify two functions: "1. Doing a study to analyze a problem [analytic proposals]; or 2. Providing a service or product to meet a need [service/product proposals]" (326). They include two appendixes: one lists the textbooks examined, and another provides a 12-page summary that outlines the classifications and parts of proposals described in those textbooks. The authors conclude by describing ways in which "the generic structure of proposals allows one more readily to understand, not only the genre's internal logic and the macropropositions demanded by that logic, but the very nature of the genre itself" (335).

194   **Hagge, John. "The Value of Formal Conventions in Disciplinary Writing: An Axiological Analysis of Professional Style Manuals."** *Journal of Business and Technical Communication* **8.4 (October 1994): 408–61.**

This detailed study uses content analysis to examine 12 professional style manuals (e.g., APA and MLA). According to the author, "This article argues that dichotomizations of formal and rhetorical aspects of writing, although prevalent in composition studies, are beset by methodological problems and internal contradictions" (409). The author demonstrates how these manuals, sponsored by professional associations, encode institutional norms. The author discusses 14 categories of formal categories (such as use of nomenclature, graphics, and bibliographic information) and nonformal categories (such as reference lists, writing advice, and ethical and legal information). The article includes several tables that present demographic and generic data concerning the manuals. The author concludes, "The formal writing conventions so greatly valued in disciplinary prose are highly rhetorical, having evolved to meet the needs of disciplinary readers who expect writing in a field to reflect fundamental disciplinary practices" (454). He recommends that "formal disciplinary writing conventions should form the course core, just as they form core principles in actual writing in the working world" (456).

195   **Jablin, Fredric M., and Kathleen Krone. "Characteristics of Rejection Letters and Their Effects on Job Applicants."** *Written Communication* **1.4 (October 1984): 387–406.**

This article presents a study of the structure and content of "bad news" letters, specifically rejection letters to job applicants, and their impact on the recipients. Among other findings, the authors' examination of actual letters reveals that only 42 percent of the letters attempted to praise the applicants but that 67 percent of the letters were "'indirect' in rejecting the applicant" (395). The authors also find that "the typical rejection letter is rather short, generally containing less than 90 words compressed into three paragraphs of text" (401). As for impact on the recipient, they find that "the structural and content characteristics of the letters did not seem to have much impact on applicants' feelings about themselves"; however, "inclusion of a statement of praise, an indirect style of rejection, some form of explanation for the rejection, and a letter at least moderate in length were all associated with perceptions of the letters as clear and personal" (405). They conclude that "indirect styles of rejection are perceived positively by applicants and as socially appropriate" (405).

196 **Locker, Kitty O. "What Do Writers in Industry Write?"** *Technical Writing Teacher* **9.3 (Spring 1982): 122–27.**

The author points out, "One of the biggest factors in motivating students in technical writing classes is simply convincing them that they will need to be able to write in their jobs in business and industry" (122). To help the teacher, the author presents reasons that refute the student assertion that "I'll never have to write," identifies the kinds of documents writers in several fields write, and suggests implications from the author's survey for the classroom. The author provides comprehensive lists of documents, based in part on her consulting work. She first lists 28 categories from a technical communication contest, then a list of 26 types of internal documents, next a list of 22 documents for external use, and finally 31 documents from an R&D organization. These lists provide ample demonstration to students that they will be required to write on the job. She concludes that "in a quarter or a semester, we can't cover every type of writing our students may be called upon to produce. . . . But we can and should give them some idea of the diversity of documents that writers in industry write" (127).

197 **Matchett, Michele, and Mary Louise Ray. "Revising IRS Publications: A Case Study."** *Technical Communication* **36.4 (November 1989): 332–40.**

This article reports on the authors' work in revising the IRS instruction booklet for the 1040EZ and 1040A forms. The audience, in this case, was "just about every United States citizen," and the only common ground among various subgroups was that the majority of them "approach tax returns with negative emotions ranging from irritation to dread" (332). Matchett and Ray focused on four elements in revising the instructions: organizational problems, readability problems, tone, and visual appeal. One telling example of their revision is an example of a change in one heading from "Privacy Act and Paperwork Reduction Act Notice" to "What are my rights as a tax-payer?" (334). The article gives not only such solutions but also samples of parts of the original and revised documents.

198 **McIsaac, Claudia MonPere, and Mary Ann Aschauer. "Proposal Writing at Atherton Jordan, Inc.: An Ethnographic Study."** *Management Communication Quarterly* **3.4 (May 1990): 527–60.**

This article reports the authors' study that analyzed "the proposal-writing environment and the practices of seven engineers at Atherton Jordan, Inc. (a pseudonym), a Silicon Valley engineering firm that does government defense work" (527). The authors observe a high-stress environment in which the writers must work collaboratively and use a highly structured composing process. To help engineers write proposals, this company formed a "Proposal Operations Center" (POC), which produced significant improvements in their first drafts and the final drafts. Two specific writing strategies stressed by the POC are storyboarding as an aid to collaborative writing and "The Red Team," which is "an independent review team that simulates customer evaluation after the proposal writers have finished their first drafts and before they put together their last ones" (544). One conclusion from the authors' study is that "organizations can have a powerful influence over their employees' attitudes toward writing and their writing practices" (551). For teachers of management and technical writing, they advise, "Because engineers appear to have the most difficulty with analytical and persuasive writing, communication courses should incorporate more of this kind of writing, focusing less on process and description, which engineers are usually quite skilled at" (552).

199   **Miller, Carolyn R. "Genre As Social Action."** *Quarterly Journal of Speech* **70 (1984): 151–67.**

In this article, the author proposes that "in rhetoric the term 'genre' be limited to a particular type of discourse classification, a classification based in rhetorical practice and consequently open rather than closed and organized around situated actions (that is, pragmatic, rather than syntactic or semantic)" (155). Miller asserts, "To consider as potential genres such homely discourse as the letter of recommendation, the user manual, the progress report, the ransom note, the lecture, and the white paper, as well as the eulogy, the apologia, the inaugural, the public proceeding, and the sermon, is not to trivialize the study of genres; it is to take seriously the rhetoric in which we are immersed and the situations in which we find ourselves" (155). The article refines her thesis that genres can be seen as "typified rhetorical actions based in recurrent situations" (159). After describing five typical features of the understanding of genre she has proposed (163), she concludes, "genres can serve both as an index to cultural patterns and as tools for exploring the achievements of particular speakers and writers; for the student, genres serve as keys to understanding how to participate in the actions of a community" (165).

200   **Moore, Patrick. "When Politeness Is Fatal: Technical Communication and the** *Challenger* **Accident."** *Journal of Business and Technical Communication* **6.3 (July 1992): 269–92.**

This article uses the politeness strategies enumerated by Penelope Brown and Stephen Levinson (see 316) to examine the communications between Rockwell subordinates and NASA managers before the *Challenger* accident. "Politeness, the author points out, "minimizes the hard feelings that are created when different views of reality clash" (273). When managers and subordinates use politeness "to minimize threats to people's acceptance or freedom so that people in organizations can work efficiently with others toward commonly shared goals" (288), the results are positive. On the other hand, "if the people who wield the power use it selfishly, for purposes that employees do not respect, and they have the power to sanction subordinates, then politeness promotes another goal—self-preservation. In situations like these, politeness can actively impede the flow of information by muffling and blurring communication" (275). The author asserts, using transcripts and published reports, that the latter occurred in the case of the Challenger accident.

201   **Murray, Denise E. "Requests at Work: Negotiating the Conditions for Conversation."** *Management Communication Quarterly* **1.1 (August 1987): 58–83.**

This article is based on a longitudinal study of communication in a business environment; specifically, the author reports her experience as a participant observer in an IBM research facility where she observed a project manager for one year. She focused on the use of the computer as a medium of communication, in the process examining other communications such as memos and in-house documents. She looks specifically at requests and how "computer-mediated communication (CmC)" demonstrates the dynamics of requests in a workplace environment. She finds that "four validity conditions are negotiable: comprehensibility, truth, sincerity, and rightness" (58). The effects of this medium are minimal, but certain responses seem more typical of CmC than of other media, "for example, while many initial requests are made through CmC, negotiations of the conditions are often made on the telephone or face-to-face" (78). The author states, "This study is a first step in understanding both the way interactants negotiate the conditions of conversation in a business environment and how CmC has become incorporated as an additional medium of communication" (81).

202   **Myers, Greg.** *Writing Biology: Texts in the Social Construction of Scientific Knowledge.* **Madison: U of Wisconsin P, 1990. Index. Bib. 304p.**

Through a detailed rhetorical analysis of drafts and published versions of biologists' writing, the author hopes to "provide some interpretations of scientific texts in their social context that will help us understand how texts produce scientific knowledge and reproduce the cultural authority of that knowledge" (ix). Chapter One, "Controversies about Scientific Texts," takes up the question of various approaches to scientific texts, the use of discourse analysis, and the author's methodology in this book. Chapter Two, "Social Construction in Two Biologists' Proposals," describes the writing and revision processes for two proposals. Myers argues that "we can see in these processes how research programs that the researchers themselves believed radically challenged established ideas were incorporated into the mainstream of the discipline" (x). Chapter Three, "Social Construction in Two Biologists' Articles," examines the refereeing and revision of two journal articles.

Chapter Four considers a heated controversy between one of the researchers and other specialists as well as the texts produced in the process. Chapter Five compares three popular science articles with articles for specialized professional audiences, all written by the same authors. Chapter Six views "the construction of scientific expertise in a larger context, in the debate over the uses of scientific knowledge in society" (xi). In a concluding section, "Reading Biology," he discusses the method of "reading" (and studying) scientific texts, and Myers suggests five strategies: Look for the rhetorical, reconstruct the social context, look for related texts, look for the source of authority, and look for any links between scientific language and everyday uses of language.

203   **Pinelli, Thomas E., Virginia M. Cordle, and Raymond F. Vondran. "The Function of Report Components in the Screening and Reading of Technical Reports."** *Journal of Technical Writing and Communication* **14.2 (1984): 87–94.**

This article, similar to another by these authors (*Technical Communication* 31.2), is based on a survey of engineers, scientists, and managers "to determine the opinions of report users and producers concerning the format (organization) of NASA technical reports and the usage of technical report components" (87). They find, for example, that "the most common sequence used . . . was: title page, abstract, summary, introduction, and conclusion" (89). In addition, "The summary, conclusion, abstract, title page, and introduction were the components most often used for reviewing reports. One or more of these components may be the only ones read; therefore, it is important that each of these components or report sections be written so that it can be read and understood independently of the rest of the report. Further, the reading of the entire report may depend on the ability of one or more of these components to hold the reader's/user's interest" (92).

204   **Rymer, Jone. "Scientific Composing Processes: How Eminent Scientists Write Journal Articles."** *Advances in Writing Research, Volume Two: Writing in Academic Disciplines.* **Ed. David A. Joliffe. Norwood, NJ: Ablex, 1988. 211–50.**

This article reports on a study of the composing processes of nine scientists. The author reviews similar studies, describes the scientists examined in the study, describes her methodology, and reports on the various processes used by the scientists to prepare their professional papers. The author states, "This study challenges some of the conventional wisdom about scientific composing. The evidence presented here suggests that eminent scientists use multiple approaches in writing experimental papers, not only a linear model focused on detailed planning, but a full range of strategies, including highly recursive models focused on revision" (244). The author further concludes, "This study also suggests that scientists frequently discover new ideas about their experimental results and what the science means while composing their journal papers" (244).

205   **Selzer, Jack. "The Composing Processes of an Engineer."** *College Composition and Communication* **34.2 (May 1983): 178–87.**

This article reports a landmark study of the composing process of a single engineer. The author discovers practices that run counter to research on composing when the article was published. For example, Selzer observes, "If for academic and professional writers revision is a messy, recursive matter of discovering and shaping what one wants to say, for Nelson [the engineer] revising is a rather clean matter of polishing a rough draft that already approximates his intentions" (184). Selzer also observes that the engineer analyzes his audience's needs carefully when he wants to generate content, not when he is making stylistic choices later in his writing process (180). Further, "Nelson relies on an impressive array of invention procedures—analyzing audiences, reading, consulting colleagues, brainstorming, and reviewing previously written documents" (181). Based on these and other observations, Selzer concludes, "it may be appropriate to describe the writing process of engineers as more linear than recursive. It may also be appropriate in teaching prospective engineers to emphasize principles and techniques of arrangement and, by contrast, to regard revision as the least important activity in the engineer's writing process" (185).

206   Swales, John M. *Genre Analysis: English in Academic and Research Settings*. Cambridge: Cambridge UP, 1990. Index. Bib. 260p.

This book focuses on the teaching of academic and research English; the book also "attempts to demonstrate the general value of genre analysis as a means of studying spoken and written discourse for applied ends" (1). Swales also points out, for example, that his concern for "advanced English" is shared with business and technical communication. In a brief opening section, Part I, "Preliminaries," he describes his aims as well as outlines the plan of the book. Part II, "Key Concepts," contains four chapters: "The Concept of Discourse Community"; "The Concept of Genre"; "The Concept of Task"; and "Genres, Schemata, and Acquisition." Part III, "Research-Process Genres," includes three chapters: "The Role of English in Research," "Research Articles in English," and "Observations on Other Research-Process Genres" (e.g., abstracts, research presentations, and grant proposals). Part IV, "Applications," contains two chapters with case teaching material and guides for genre analysis and a final chapter ("Epilogue") in which the author states, "The book reflects a long-standing interest in helping those who need to develop further their communicative competence in academic English to achieve that goal" (232).

207   Thralls, Charlotte. "Rites and Ceremonials: Corporate Video and the Construction of Social Realities in Modern Organizations." *Journal of Business and Technical Communication* 6.4 (October 1992): 381–402.

This article "examines corporate videos as cultural texts and develops the claim that videos function as rites and ceremonials in modern organizations, facilitating organizational socialization" (381). Using corporate videos produced by a major national financial services firm, the author demonstrates how videos can function as rites and ceremonials. Specifically, she finds that videos function as four types of rites: integration, passage, renewal, and enhancement. As rites of integration, videos instill and sometimes renew shared feelings that "bind members together and commit them to the larger system" (387). As rites of passage they assist employees in making transitions from one role to another, and as rites of renewal they strengthen existing structures. Finally, as rites of enhancement they "generate and maintain social reality in organizations by drawing favorable attention to the personal status and social identities of group members" (396). The author suggests that one value of corporate videos for researchers studying written communication is that they can be valuable tools in communication ethnographies.

208   Tyler, Lisa. "Ecological Disaster and Rhetorical Response: Exxon's Communications in the Wake of the *Valdez* Spill." *Journal of Business and Technical Communication* 6.2 (April 1992): 149–71.

According to the author, "This study examines Exxon's communication efforts in the wake of [the *Valdez*] disaster and identifies communication practices on Exxon's part that damaged the corporation's credibility, antagonized the public, and contributed to the public perception of its corporate arrogance" (149). Although the author was not able to obtain original company documents, she used many news accounts, including the Sierra Club Books' *In the Wake of the Exxon Valdez: The Devastating Impact of the Alaska Oil Spill* (1990) by Art Davidson (which was also recommended by Exxon). The author cites and discusses 11 damaging communication practices employed by Exxon. The author concludes, "Put on the defensive from the beginning by the very fact of the spill, Exxon officials felt threatened and launched into an escalating spiral of 'defensive communication'" (167). She also recommends some basic, ethical business communication practices which her study suggests. She concludes that this incident makes for an excellent classroom study because of its interest and complexity.

209 **Winsor, Dorothy A. "The Construction of Knowledge in Organizations: Asking the Right Questions about the *Challenger.*" *Journal of Business and Technical Communication* 4.2 (September 1990): 7–20.**

The author states that previous research into the *Challenger* explosion tends "to ask why it happened that various people in the organizations involved knew about the faulty O-rings but failed to pass on the information to decision makers" (7). Winsor sees this question as faulty because it assumes that knowledge exists apart from social forces and that we can simply "pass on" information: "The passing on of information is a misleading concept because it is part of what might be called the *conduit model of communication*" (13).

She offers two questions that address the social context of communication. First she asks, "Given that there were two alternative views of the O-rings' safety available, what factors made one view more acceptable than the other?" (16). She continues, "While it is a commonplace maxim that knowledge is power, it is also true that power is knowledge in the sense that people with power decide what counts as knowledge" (16). Her second question is "How could the advocates of the view that the O-rings were not safe have affected communal knowledge so that this view became the more widely accepted of the two alternative views?" (17) She suggests a pedagogical application: "We might also teach about the necessity for picking battles carefully, since a writer who is critical too often will create the ethos of being constantly at odds with the organization" (17). She concludes that the logical positivist conception of knowledge and the conduit model of communication "work against a dissenting writer acting to gather evidence and build a consensus" (18). Thus she asks a final question: "What advice can we, as scholars of rhetoric, offer to those who struggle to construct knowledge so that we might lessen their chances of experiencing regret when the truth finally becomes known?" (18)

210 **Winsor, Dorothy A. "An Engineer's Writing and the Corporate Construction of Knowledge." *Written Communication* 6.3 (July 1989): 270–85.**

The author states, "Previous research on the writing process in the workplace has given inadequate attention to the collaborative nature of work in an organization" (270). She sees collaborative writing, in part, as meaning that "any individual's writing is called forth and shaped by the needs and aims of the organization, and that to be understood it must draw on vocabulary, knowledge, and beliefs other organization members share" (271). In her study, Winsor follows an engineer as he writes a routine document (a progress report) and a nonroutine document (a technical paper given at a professional meeting) and finds that his processes "are strongly affected by the degree to which his company has previously accepted the claims he makes as given or as knowledge" (270).

She also draws on the notion of the "inscribing process . . . by which groups come to agreement on what symbols should be assigned to reality" (271). She concludes that the inscribing process "helps us understand some of the seeming contradictions between observations made of successful writers in and out of the workplace" (283). Thus, while successful writers at work appear to work less recursively than successful writers in academe, "this difference may be more apparent than real" (283–84).

211   **Winsor, Dorothy A. "Engineering Writing/Writing Engineering."** *College Composition and Communication* **41.1 (February 1990): 58–70.**

As she did in an earlier article ("An Engineer's Writing"; see 210), Winsor examines a professional conference paper and a progress report written by an engineer. Following arguments and documents parallel to the earlier paper, she demonstrates a premise: "Knowledge is not found ready-made in nature. Instead, knowledge is constructed in the interplay between nature and the symbol systems we use to structure and interpret it" (58). In her conclusion, the author reflects on her own writing, "As I worked on this paper, I was uncomfortably aware that I, too, was attempting to exert power" (69). She admits, "As a scholar of writing, it is great fun to say that engineers are actually writing about other writing, a field I presumably know more about than they do. . . . Unmediated knowledge . . . is not possible for any of us. All writing, including mine, constructs the world which the writer can bear to inhabit" (69).

212   **Winsor, Dorothy A. "Owning Corporate Texts."** *Journal of Business and Technical Communication* **7.2 (April 1993): 179–95.**

This article reports through an ethnographic study how the ownership of texts is viewed by writers and engineers at a large manufacturing company. The author spent three months in the PR department of one of this company's divisions where writers must work with engineers to produce documents for public release. The author states, "In theory, an engineer provides technical content, a writer adapts that material for the audience, and the engineer checks to make sure that the adaptation has not altered the technical accuracy of the piece. As I will show, however, the division of labor is not always so clean" (183). She gives one example in which the PR department "sometimes lists an engineer as the author, even if the engineer has had nothing to do with writing it" (188). She points out how an engineer she interviewed found this practice "highly inappropriate" (189). She concludes that for professional writing, "a satisfactory representation of self is achieved only with struggle. Because language and the writing context always precede us, perhaps a struggle is always necessary for a satisfactory relationship to the text to be formed. Neither our native tongue nor our professional language is ever entirely our own. We must constitute ourselves in texts that we do not wholly control" (194).

WRITING, READABILITY, AND LANGUAGE

213 **Allen, Nancy, and Deborah S. Bosley. "Technical Texts/Personal Voice: Intersections and Crossed Purposes."** *Voices on Voice*. **Ed. Kathleen Blake Yancey. Urbana, IL: NCTE: 1994.**

In this chapter, the authors "explore the various elements that work to suppress voice in technical writing, and the ways writers have found to subvert those forces and integrate their own voices into their writing" (81). They argue that the "constraints operating against voice . . . come principally from three areas: (1) the traditions of technical writing; (2) the control exerted by corporations within which so much technical writing occurs; and (3) the power of particular communities within the technical writing world" (81). Following a discussion of these constraints, the authors use excerpts from interviews with a scientist, a manager, a contract writer, a computer industries writer, and a freelance technical writer to illustrate "how writers work within the constraints and freedoms of the technical communications world—sometimes submerging their own voices, and sometimes subverting conventions in order to express a personal voice" (81).

214 **Blyler, Nancy Roundy. "Reading Theory and Persuasive Business Communications: Guidelines for Writers."** *Journal of Technical Writing and Communication* **21.4 (1991): 383–96.**

"In this article, reading theory has been used to derive guidelines for the tacit arguments present in persuasive business communications—guidelines that can supplement reading-based guidelines already derived by specialists in rhetoric and professional communication" (395). The author first gives background "on reading theory and on guidelines that have already been formulated" (383). Next, she demonstrates the "inability of current guidelines to account for the reader impact of one type of persuasive business communication," the solicitation letter. Next, the author discusses "three aspects of reading—inferring, reasoning analogically, and learning" (383). Using sample texts, the author demonstrates the role these aspects play "in building consensual meaning" (383). The author expects "that the supplementary guidelines derived will assist researchers, teachers, and practitioners as they continue to study, teach, and compose persuasive business communications" (395).

215 **Brusaw, Charles T., Gerald J. Alred, and Walter E. Oliu.** *The Business Writer's Handbook*, **4th ed.; and** *Handbook of Technical Writing*, **4th ed. New York: St. Martin's, 1993. Index. 784p. 803p.**

These handbooks present material in encyclopedia format with explanatory entries in alphabetical order. Designed as reference guides both for students and for those on the job, each book includes an introduction discussing the writing process; a topical key grouping entries in categories (e.g., "finding a job"); entries about document types (e.g., internal proposals); usage items (e.g., *affect/effect*); style items (e.g., tone); grammar issues (e.g., dangling modifier); writing-related topics (e.g., layout and design); and a fully cross-referenced index. Samples of document types and graphics are included. The books differ by featuring specific items either for the business writer or for the technical writer. *The Business Writer's Handbook*, for example, covers all letter types—e.g., credit letters, form letters, and collection letters. *Handbook of Technical Writing* includes entries about technical manuals; specifications; and style for mathematical equations, measurements, and other technical data.

216 **Campbell, Kim Sydow. "Structural Cohesion in Technical Texts."** *Journal of Technical Writing and Communication* **21.3 (1991): 221–37.**

The author suggests that "cohesion may be better understood as a general perceptual phenomenon instead of a purely semantic one" (222). She proposes that "cohesion is the result of repeating semantic and structural elements. This repetition, in turn, appears to provide a uniform background against which semantic distinctions are foregrounded (much the same as repeated visual patterns form a background against which visual distinctions are foregrounded)" (222). The article "supplements Halliday and Hasan's categories of cohesive devices by discussing three types of structural cohesion based on an analysis of technical texts. First, cohesion produced through *thematic progression* (i.e., the repetition of topics and comments) is demonstrated; second, cohesion produced through *parallelism* (i.e., the repetition of syntactic structure) is illustrated; and finally cohesion produced with *graphic devices* (i.e., the repetition of typography, enumerators, and chart elements) is discussed" (221). This article, the author argues, demonstrates the theoretical link among these types of structural cohesion "and also provides teachers with a theoretical justification for considering them important in the classroom" (225).

217 **Couture, Barbara, ed.** *Functional Approaches to Writing: Research Perspectives.* **Norwood, NJ: Ablex, 1986. Index. 271p.**

According to the author, "The essays here are united in their investigation of language as social action—an approach to textual study that crosses traditional boundaries of discipline and method to uncover what written language is, how it works, how it affects readers, and what it demands of authors" (1). Among the collection of 14 articles are a number related to business and technical writing. In "An Ethnographic Study of Corporate Writing: Job Status as Reflected in Written Text," for example, Robert L. Brown, Jr., and Carl G. Herndl examine why writers in workplace settings continue to use ineffective techniques, such as nominalization, despite advice and instruction to the contrary. The authors find that job status and anxiety are more influential in this regard than are the precepts of "good writing." In "Thematic Distribution as a Heuristic for Written Discourse Function," Mary Ann Eiler studies how language choice in a physics textbook is based on social interaction. Barbara Couture, in "Effective Ideation in Written Text: A Functional Approach to Clarity and Exigence," examines how registers (like bureaucratic and poetic language) and genres (like business reports and poetry) are related to explicitness and expression. In a final example, Stephen A. Bernhardt uses instructions to demonstrate how texts are directly influenced by the relationship of the writer to the audience in "Applying a Functional Model of Language in the Writing Classroom."

218   **Di Pietro, Robert J., ed.** *Linguistics and the Professions: Proceedings of the Second Annual Delaware Symposium on Language Studies.* **Norwood: Ablex, 1982.**

With the exception of two of the studies in this collection, all were originally presented at the second annual Delaware Symposium on Language Studies held in October, 1980, at the University of Delaware. The editor states, "What the reader will find in these pages . . . is not a catalog of potential applications but the reporting of real and current projects in medicine, law, bureaucracy, and business in which linguists play major roles" (xi). The editor groups the articles in this collection under these "four major headings, each reflecting an area of great public concern: 'language and the medical professions,' 'language and the law,' 'language in commercial and official uses,' and 'language in employment and public services'" (xii). Of special note is an oft-cited work by Veda R. Charrow, "Language in the Bureaucracy," which discusses the work at the Document Design Center.

219   **Freed, Richard C. "This Is a Pedagogical Essay on Voice."** *Journal of Business and Technical Communication* **7.4 (October 1993): 472–81.**

This article explores voice in business and professional communications—in particular, why voice is important, where it comes from, and how it's constructed. These questions are considered in the form of a dialogue. There is, the article asserts, a strategic importance in "projecting the right voice for a given situation" (476). The author provides a transcript of an interview with a writer who offers a chart for "constructing your voice" that can be useful for helping students ask questions when writing proposals (478). Through the dialogue, the author avoids "vaguely asserting that voice is conditioned by a writer's relationship to readers," noting that the "heuristic for determining and constructing voice" provided in the article "specifies that relationship" in terms of "the writer's possible roles" and "how those roles need to be modified both by considerations of competitors' claims" as well as by those "desires of readers" (480).

220   **Freisinger, Randall R., and Bruce T. Petersen. "Toward Defining 'Good' Writing: A Rhetorical Analysis of the Words, Sentences, and Paragraphs in 16 Industrial Scripts."** *Technical Communication: Perspectives for the Eighties* **(NASA Conference Publication 2203, Part 1). Ed. J. C. Mathes and Thomas E. Pinelli. 291–304.**

This report on research, according to the authors, "addresses a significant problem of technical and scientific writing and, in particular, of recent theory and practice in writing across the curriculum programs. These programs and the theory which informs them have proceeded as if teachers . . . of writing in all disciplines agreed on a definition of 'good' writing" (291). Based on their experience that faculty from various disciplines could not agree on a definition of "good writing," the authors examined 16 documents gathered from a wide variety of major corporations. The authors analyzed five factors in the samples: "1) word level, 2) sentence level, 3) paragraph level, 4) discourse level, and 5) readability" (293). After discussing and illustrating their findings, they conclude that many writing elements considered "good" are at odds with what they expected; they comment particularly on pronoun reference, repetition, transitional words and phrases, consistency of grammatical subject, and graphic and typographic features (303).

221 **Gopnick, Myrna.** *Linguistic Structures in Scientific Texts.* **The Hague: Mouton, 1972.**

This seminal study investigates, according to the author, "certain formal properties of short discourses in order to establish for these discourses a computable underlying form" (9). Its final goal "is rather to provide a theoretical framework in which problems of the analysis of texts can be formulated than to establish a particular set of rules to be used in this analysis" (9). Chapter One acts as an introduction to the study; terms are defined, and methodology is explained. Chapter Two gives the "theoretical background for the treatment of the text and [reports] on the general patterns found in the texts" (18). Chapter Three "discuss[es] certain patterns of syntactic structures which appeared in the scientific texts" used in the study (46). Chapter Four, the final chapter, investigates the semantic analysis of texts through the creation of "a new linguistic text which is semantically equivalent to the original text [through paraphrase]" (98). Appendixes found at the end of the study contain "the empirical data: texts used, detailed decompositions, structures of comparatives, patterns of word reoccurrence, patterns of interreference, etc." (18).

222 **Hagge, John, and Charles Kostelnick. "Linguistic Politeness in Professional Prose: A Discourse Analysis of Auditors' Suggestion Letters, with Implications for Business Communication Pedagogy."** *Written Communication* **6.3 (July 1989): 312–39.**

The authors argue that their study, "one of comparatively few to focus on *written* communication, substantiates claims for the universality of politeness strategies by showing that these play a seminal role in the composition of professional documents" (313). In Section One of the article, the authors describe how auditors in a large accounting firm "adhere to the 'institutional norms' of their organization and how they must cope with the uncertainties of producing professional prose in their field" (313). In Section Two, the authors use "discourse-analytical techniques to show that [the] auditors' seemingly peculiar stylistic choices can be explained by the theory of linguistic politeness" (313). In Section Three, the authors compare "the frequency of negative politeness locutions in the [suggestion letters]" with those found in "leading business communication textbooks" (313). Finally, in Section Four, the authors argue that "although [they] do not condone the unthinking overuse of passives, expletives, nominalizations, and hedging particles, [they] believe that business communication pedagogy should demonstrate a more flexible attitude toward these and other locutions that instantiate linguistic politeness strategies" (313).

223   **Harris, John S. "The Naming of Parts: An Examination of the Origins of Technical and Scientific Vocabulary."** *Journal of Technical Writing and Communication* **14.3 (1984): 183–91.**

In this article, the author "examine[s] how various names have been applied in the past and from those practices attempt[s] to formulate some principles that will lead to more effective naming" (184). He first looks at the "common sources for names in the sciences and technology" (184): "Foreign Language Sources," "Naming for Inventor, Discoverer, Maker, or Place," "Naming for Shape," "Naming for Function," "Acronyms," and "Arbitrary Terms and Pressagentry." Then he presents examples of each and explains their effectiveness. It is argued in Harris's article that "although such effects are not entirely predictable or controllable, attention to them can nonetheless lead to more effective naming in science and technology" (183).

224   **Jordan, Michael P. "Toward Plain Language: A Guide to Paraphrasing Complex Noun Phrases."** *Journal of Technical Writing and Communication* **24.1 (1994): 77–96.**

Complex noun phrases, according to the author, are "necessary not only to provide a suitable style for mature readers, but also as means of combining complex thoughts in a clear, concise manner" (77). However, as he also suggests, they can pose problems of readability in technical writing. The author describes the linguistic features of various noun phrases and suggests ways of rephrasing them into simpler structures. He provides 27 examples and identifies the differences in meaning, style, tone, and emphasis when noun phrases are revised. He also provides several cross-reference lists at the end of the article in addition to an appendix listing types of restrictive and nonrestrictive clauses.

225   **Killingsworth, M. Jimmie, and Preston Lynn Waller. "A Grammar of Person for Technical Writing."** *Technical Writing Teacher* **17.1 (Winter 1990): 26–40.**

Noting the recent interest in *ethos* and a "humanized" persona in technical writing literature, the authors warn that technical writing teachers should "beware of introducing their students to the use of such personae without providing a clear understanding of how authors relate to audiences in the various genres of technical writing" (26). One way to understand (and to teach) persona is through the use of a "kernel sentence" applied to three major genres of the field—the proposal, the manual, and the report. First, the authors provide a taxonomy demonstrating the use of a kernel sentence with each genre: "proposal (*I will do this*), manual (*Do this*), and report (*I did this*)" (29). Next, they provide a table showing transformations and additions for the kernel sentences in each genre (31). Finally, they show three continua that demonstrate the relationships of author to audience and invocation to evocation as they involve the three genres. The authors conclude that the grammar of person provides students with "a conceptual framework that they can quickly grasp and use in the analysis of examples" (39).

226   **Manning, Alan D. "Abstracts in Relation to Larger and Smaller Discourse Structures."** *Journal of Technical Writing and Communication* **20.4 (1990): 369–90.**

The author states, "In this article, I propose a unified theory of discourse form to explain, 1) why textbooks consistently recognize just two polar types of abstract, even though in practice the distinction is not always clearly made, 2) why students often produce adequate descriptive abstracts, but not adequate summary abstracts, and 3) how a short paraphrase differs formally and conceptually from a summary abstract" (369). Using the work of C. S. Peirce, T. A. van Dijk, and Stephen Toulmin, Manning describes in detail how "in all levels of discourse, from sentences to extended texts, general and specific components conserve the 'shape' of information. Intermediate discourse components (e.g., sentential tense, the syllogistic middle term, or the body of a text) may be deleted to create a smaller equivalent discourse structure" (388). The article includes five figures which demonstrate the positions of various smaller units of discourse to larger ones. He concludes that students' poor performance on summary-abstracting assignments partly reflects their lack of "topical knowledge" and understanding of the conventions of the discourse community (388).

227   **Markel, Mike. "Techniques of Developing Forecasting Statements."** *Journal of Business and Technical Communication* **7.3 (July 1993): 360–66.**

The author notes that "the effectiveness of a message is enhanced if the writer has forecasted it" (360). Forecasting, the author explains, helps the "reader create a context, a mental framework that makes it easier to understand right away where the writer is going and therefore better able to concentrate on the journey" (361). Listing topics—the most common method of forecasting used in technical documents—can, however, be boring, thereby negating its effectiveness as a forecasting method. In this article, the author "describes techniques, based on four of the journalistic prompts (What? Where? Why? How?), that can help writers create contexts for their readers" (360). In addition to helping the reader "concentrate on the writer's message," use of these techniques "also helps define the writer's ethos: The writer is intelligent, trustworthy, and concerned about the readers' needs" (365).

228   **Pixton, William H. "Technical Writing and Terminal Modification."** *Journal of Technical Writing and Communication* **22.2 (1992): 159–78.**

This article argues for an increased attention to terminal modifiers in order to "significantly increase the options for effective expression by technical writers" (159). The author first "provide[s] explanations and examples of ten nonrestrictive terminal modifiers" (160): absolute, restating appositive, summarizing appositive, participial phrase, nonparticipial adjective plus modifier, adjectival prepositional phrase, adjective clause, adverbial clause, adverbial infinitive phrase, and adverbial prepositional phrase. Then, the author "examines the texts of representative technical reports to determine the extent to which terminal modifiers are currently used" (159). From his study the author concludes, "An emphasis on the absolute, the summarizing appositive, and the nonparticipial adjective plus modifier may give technical writers valuable options in expression" (176).

229   **Popken, Randall. "A Study of Topic Sentence Use in Technical Writing."**
       Technical Writing Teacher **18.1 (Winter 1991): 49–58.**

In this study, the author sought to discover "how conventions for topic sentence use
in technical writing compare with those in other types of writing, particularly in the
academic discourse that most students have already acquired in freshman composition" (50). The author also "hoped to extend understanding of the code constraining
topic sentence use" (50). From his findings, the author concludes that topic sentences are used significantly less than in the four other types of writing with which
technical writing is compared (academic research articles, college textbooks, popular journalism, and scientific writing). The author also found that "the issue of constraints on topic sentence choice involves not just genre and paragraph length but a
more complex three-way interaction between genre, length, and topic sentences"
(54). As a result of his study, the author states, "Instead of giving them rules, we
could give our students strategies, based on principles such as the genre/length/topic
sentence interplay" (57).

230   **Redish, Janice C., and Jack Selzer. "The Place of Readability Formulas in**
       Technical Communication." *Technical Communication* **32.4 (1985): 46–52.**

The authors point to a number of serious problems with readability formulas: (1)
They have been applied without valid research; (2) they are not valid predictors of
how understandable technical material may be to adults; (3) readability formulas
value short words and sentences, which do not necessarily make documents easier
to understand; (4) the underlying assumption of readability formulas that they work
universally is not valid; and (5) they ignore many factors that are essential for people's understanding and ability to use documents. The best method, the authors
explain, to determine the effectiveness of documents is through usability testing in
which users perform tasks with documents, which are then evaluated for their effectiveness. The authors provide a number of reasons why such usability testing is cost
effective even though it may seem more expensive than using readability formulas.

231   **Rentz, Kathryn C. "The Value of Narrative in Business Writing."** *Journal of*
       Business and Technical Communication **6.3 (July 1992): 293–315.**

In order to make documents as accessible as possible, the author states, "Writing
that presents the most important information first and that visually announces its
pattern of organization is the kind promoted by our [business writing] textbooks"
(293). Rentz suggests, "I think we have gone overboard in our rejection of narrative
in favor of more contrived formats for business writing" (294). The author then
details how various types of research suggest that narrative is a useful method in
some business writing situations. She finds that narrative can help writers in a number of ways: "1. to use the past to explain the present and anticipate the future; 2.
to capture readers' attention and influence their behavior; 3. to keep precise records
of events, for legal and other purposes; and 4. to enable a company to be more
responsive to its customers and its employees" (308). Two appendixes include a
sample of a trip report written as a narrative and as a contrasting form that segments
the information.

232   Schriver, Karen A. "Evaluating Text Quality: The Continuum from Text-Focused to Reader-Focused Methods." *IEEE Transactions on Professional Communication* 32.4 (December 1989): 238–55.

The author reviews in detail three general categories of methods used to evaluate text quality: text-focused, expert-judgment-focused, and reader-focused approaches. She states, "My aim is to give an overview of popular methods and to identify their strengths and weaknesses within the context of what is known about text evaluation" (238). She presents a number of criteria by which to judge the value of the methods, and she illustrates their relationship graphically along a continuum. She concludes, "Earlier I argued that an optimal text evaluation method should provide writers with two sorts of information: (1) information about whole-text or global aspects of text quality, and (2) information about how the audience may respond to the text. Clearly, research and experience show us that reader-focused testing methods have the advantage on both counts" (252). She further suggests that reader-focused methods can help in planning and revising texts.

233   Spyridakis, Jan H. "Signaling Effects: A Review of the Research—Part I"; and "Signaling Effects: Increased Content Retention and New Answers—Part II." *Journal of Technical Writing and Communication* 19.3 and 19.4 (1989): 227–40 and 395–415.

Part I of this article reviews previous research on "signals": such devices as headings, topic sentences, and text titles that affect the reader's comprehension of expository prose. This essay includes a five-page appendix that charts 25 studies and graphically displays their various features, such as the type of texts examined and the results. The author finds that inconsistent results among the previous studies "may be due to inadequate methodologies that have failed to control for confounding variables, such as text length and difficulty, reader familiarity with the topic, and timing of comprehension tests" (227). Part II reports the results of the author's own study, which attempts to remedy the shortcomings of the previous studies reviewed in Part I. This study was "constructed to assess the individual and combined effects of headings, previews, and logical connectives" (395). Among a number of other findings, "The results showed that signals do improve a reader's comprehension, particularly . . . of superordinate and superordinate inferential information" (395).

234   Suchan, James, and Ronald Dulek. "A Reassessment of Clarity in Written Managerial Communications." *Management Communication Quarterly* 4.1 (August 1990): 87–99.

After noting that clarity is "sacrosanct" in business communication, the authors state, "This article strongly encourages business and managerial communication instructors to reassess their assumptions about communication clarity" (88). To demonstrate their thesis that what is "clear writing" depends on an organization's language custom, they show two examples—an academic sample and a sample from one Navy electronic communications specialist to another. Reviewed by outsiders, both samples were judged to be unclear; reviewed by insiders, the examples were judged to be not only clear but also appropriate (90, 91). Based on a "contingency view" of communication clarity, the authors conclude that "writing on the job serves more than merely a task or a utility function—transmitting information accurately and efficiently. The language, style, and even formats that a discourse community evolves help determine the linguistic shared vision of the organization" (96).

235   Thompson, Isabelle. "Readability beyond the Sentence: Global Coherence and Ease of Comprehension." *Journal of Technical Writing and Communication* **16.1/2 (1986): 131–40.**

The author argues that readability should be judged in part on "the features that make a piece of writing more or less coherent for an audience" (132). Coherence, the author states, "is affected by three factors: the writer's intentions, the way she represents those intentions, and the reader's understanding of her intended message" (133). Citing an article from *Scientific American*, the author points to the differences in readability and coherence of this article to a mechanical engineer, an undergraduate student studying mechanical engineering, and a professor of English. After looking at various components of coherence, the author concludes, "Among other things, reading speed and recall depend on an audience's ability to make accurate predictions about general meaning and organization" (138). Such "global" issues should be addressed both in research and in pedagogy, the author suggests.

236   Williams, Joseph M. *Style: Ten Lessons in Clarity and Grace*. **3rd ed. Glenview, IL: Scott Foresman, 1989. Index. 241p.**

In his preface entitled "To Those Who Write on the Job," Williams states, "The kind of confused writing that most of us have to live with fails for reasons that don't yield to well-meant but empty generalities or to any list of particular dos and don'ts. To understand why anyone—including ourselves—writes badly, we have to be able to look at a sentence and understand how it works, how the ideas have been distributed through its different parts, and then decide how to write it better" (i). He further tells teachers, this "short book focuses on the single more serious problem that *mature* writers face: a wordy, tangled, too-complex prose style" (iii). Using his own knowledge of language and his experience teaching in organizations, Williams demonstrates in 10 "lessons" various features of clarity and grace, such as cohesion, emphasis, and concision. At the end of the book are exercises with "possible revisions."

INTERNATIONAL AND CROSS-CULTURAL STUDIES

237   Beamer, Linda. "Learning Intercultural Communication Competence." *Journal of Business Communication* **29.3 (1992): 285–303.**

This article contends that "the process by which intercultural communication competence is learned is not well understood," leaving "business communicators" to "flounder," and "business communication educators" without a basis for effective pedagogy (285). Therefore, the article proposes to clarify "what constitutes competence" and to present "a learning process model" for "intercultural communication" (289). *Intercultural communication* is defined in terms of semiotic theory as "the encoding and decoding of attributed signifieds to signifiers in matches that correspond to signs held in the other communicator's repository"; the authors explain that this essentially means that "the personality of the communicator . . . is less important for business communicators than a cognitive understanding of another culture" (289). The "intercultural learning model" that the article offers is broken up into five components: "acknowledging diversity," "organizing information according to stereotypes," "posing questions to challenge the stereotypes," "analyzing communication episodes," and "generating 'other-culture' messages" (291–301). Observing that "if the process by which one acquires intercultural communication competence can be identified, the process for intercultural communication instruction will also have been identified," the authors conclude that "educators can use the model as a rational basis for courses to develop intercultural communication competence in students" (302).

238   **Bosley, Deborah S. "Cross-Cultural Collaboration: Whose Culture Is It, Anyway?"** *Technical Communication Quarterly* **2.1 (Winter 1993): 51–62.**

Because the "criteria by which students are assessed" and the way teachers "tend to structure collaborative projects" may "represent a Western cultural bias that reflects our universalist assumptions about how people should behave in group situations" (51), this article "offers suggestions" which will "prepare students for collaborating with students from many cultures" (53). These suggestions include helping students become sensitized to "cultural characteristics that directly influence group behavior," including "group or individual emphasis," "achievement and responsibility," "decision-making," and "thinking and communication styles" (53–56). The author observes that "collaborative writing projects are often assigned not only for the experience that students gain writing together, but for the experience students gain working together," and so concludes that "only through learning about and respecting the paradigms of others can more effective collaboration be achieved" (60).

239   **Fine, Marlene G. "New Voices in the Workplace: Research Directions in Multicultural Communication."** *Journal of Business Communication* **23.3 (Summer 1991): 259–75.**

This article uses postmodern theories of "resistance" and feminist theories of "harmony" to develop a framework for a model of multicultural communication. The author argues that "even when people of different racial and cultural backgrounds speak the same language, they have difficulty communicating with one another" (259). She maintains that current organizational communication theories are based on the assumption of homogeneity. However, "recognizing the 'assumption of difference'" rather than the norm (263) provides a model for people from diverse cultural backgrounds to work together. The author examines theories that resist "privileged discourse" and create "harmonic discourse." She concludes that these approaches provide a framework for a model of communication that offers "organizations and their members possibilities for creating an organizational discourse that empowers all" (271).

240   **Krone, Kathleen, Mary Garrett, and Ling Chen. "Managerial Communication Practices in Chinese Factories: A Preliminary Investigation."** *Journal of Business Communication* **29.3 (1992): 229–52.**

These authors state that their purpose in this article is to "contribute to the growing body of knowledge on work-related communication in China," and they note that two central questions guided their research: first, "to what extent do Chinese manufacturing organizations conform to a bureaucratic model of organization" and, second, "how does conformity to or divergence from this model relate to managers' communication practices with their employees?" (230) The study briefly considers "how managerial communication both affects and is affected by" Chinese cultural context, defined in terms of "group-centered culture," "Confucianism," "Chinese communism," and "family and modern work life" (231-32). The article outlines the study's procedures and method, in addition to discussing the results. The authors note that the results of the study not only "reveal a distinctive form of bureaucracy operating within [Chinese] factories," but "describe patterns of managerial communication practices that can be traced to cultural context, Chinese ideology, and organizational structure of the state-owned factory in mainland China" (229).

241   **Graham, John L., and J. Douglas Andrews. "A Holistic Analysis of Japanese and American Business Negotiations."** *Journal of Business Communication* **24.4 (Fall 1987): 63–77.**

This article contends that "a critical aspect" of international business relationships is "face-to-face, cross-cultural negotiations" (63). The article investigates Japanese and American business negotiations "using a more inductive or holistic approach" instead of what the author sees as the more traditional means of "preselecting a theoretical perspective and associated methods" (63). The essay is divided into three sections: a discussion of the methods used in the study, a description of the results, and a brief discussion of the "findings and implications for further research" (63). Essentially, the study consisted of 12 simulated negotiations between Japanese and American businessmen, which were videotaped and analyzed in depth for "focal points" or "difficulties in communication" (63). Identifying their "principle theoretical perspective" as "one adapted from social psychology and exchange theory," the authors note that the "outcome of sales negotiations" is generally "a function of three classes of variables—process measures, situational constraints, and individual characteristics" (75). However, the authors argue that it is only "through the use of the holistic analysis [that] some of the difficulties caused by cultural variation of the parties" can be determined (76). "Without question," the authors conclude, the most serious difficulties uncovered in the study were "a consequence of language and other communication problems" (76).

242   **Lee, Jaesub, and Frederick M. Jablin. "A Cross-Cultural Investigation of Exit, Voice, Loyalty and Neglect as Responses to Dissatisfying Job Conditions."** *Journal of Business Communication* **29.3 (1992): 203–28.**

The purpose of this article is twofold: The authors are interested not only in "elaborating the organizational communication characteristics of companies located in South Korea" but also in comparing "the communicative responses of Koreans to dissatisfying work conditions with those of natives of the United States and Japan," in order to "dispel some of the myths that non-Koreans often hold about the communication norms and practices of Korean organizations" (204). The article analyzes the "generalizability of the theory of exit, voice, loyalty and neglect to Koreans (n = 100), and made multiple cross-cultural comparisons between Korean respondents and natives of the United States (n = 80) and Japan (n = 45) with respect to their communicative responses to dissatisfying work conditions" (203). The article furnishes detailed descriptions of the study's methodology and results. The authors observe that "the results of this research provide initial support for the generalizability of the theory of exit, voice, loyalty and neglect as responses to problematic work situations to Korean workers" and that their "findings clearly bring into question the notion that because East Asian countries share some elements of a common sociocultural heritage, the communication behaviors of workers in these countries will be the same" (226).

243   **Limaye, Mohan R. "Responding to Work-Force Diversity: Conceptualization and Search for Paradigms."** *Journal of Business and Technical Communication* **8.3 (July 1994): 353–72.**

"The basic thesis of this article," the author states, "is that the approaches to workforce diversity have so far been dominated by individual-level cognitive and affective models that are inadequate for several reasons" (354). He reviews the changing U.S. demographics, the published material from several areas on the subject, and the current paradigms about managing diversity. He finds three reasons why diversity workshops, though laudable, are problematic. First, he suggests, "They have not faced the real problem, namely, the clustering of women and minority at the bottom levels of U.S. corporate hierarchy" (361). Second, he finds that "diversity training programs proceed from the implicit assumption that difference is deficient" (362). Finally, he asserts, "Diversity workshops have to depend for their success on the goodwill of the top management who may not themselves be really committed to change" (362). He recommends "a two-pronged program for responding to diversity—train the individual and simultaneously change organizational structures and processes" (368). Limaye concludes with suggestions for directions that further research might take.

244   **Limaye, Mohan R., and David A. Victor. "Cross-Cultural Business Communication Research: State of the Art and Hypotheses for the 1990s."** *Journal of Business Communication* **28.3 (Summer 1991): 277–99.**

This article reviews the state of cross-cultural business communication through an examination of scholarly literature and points out conceptual and theoretical shortcomings in existing research. The authors locate the need for such research in the "direct immigration, national multicultural divisions, or guest workers relations" and argue that "employers are increasingly facing the need for cross-cultural business communication even in their own domestic workplace" (279). They evaluate current cognitive and affective paradigms and demonstrate by posing a series of eight hypotheses "the limitations of the Western, linear paradigms" (277). The authors suggest that such paradigms leave some unresolved important questions which have been inadequately researched. They conclude that future research should focus on "new paradigms and redefinitions" of communication concepts and should "include non-Western world views and effectiveness criteria" (293).

245   **Munter, Mary. "Cross-Cultural Communication for Managers."** *Business Horizons* **36.3 (May–June 1993): 69–78.**

The stated purpose of this article is to "synthesize multiple insights—from fields as diverse as anthropology, psychology, communication, linguistics, and organizational behavior—and apply them specifically to managerial communication" (69). Defining *managerial communication* as "communication in a management context to achieve a desired result" (69) (e.g., writing a memo or preparing a presentation), the article discusses several relevant issues, including setting communication objectives, choosing a communication style, assessing and enhancing credibility, selecting and motivating audience members, setting a message strategy, overcoming language difficulties, and using effective nonverbal behaviors. Detailed tables and charts are included.

246   **Pearson, Sheryl. "The Challenge of Mai Chung: Teaching Technical Writing to the Foreign-Born Professional in Industry."** *TESOL Quarterly* **17.3 (September 1983): 383–99.**

This article identifies the most important differences in "what the working professional needs from a course in writing EST [English of Science and Technology]" and what "the university student in a technical degree program needs" (383). "Mai Chung" is the name the author gives to an exemplary representative of a working professional, nonnative speaker of English. The article argues that "recent research on the dynamics of reading technical English can be used to inform the teaching of the technical writing skills that non-native speakers of English require in industry settings" (383). The article considers the case of Mai Chung in its analysis and discussion of the lines of investigation in recent research, the industry professional as EST learner, and the implications for teaching. The author notes that the "growing presence of Mai Chungs in the American workplace invites an educational response," and she argues that the "challenge to teachers of technical writing will be to adapt to teaching methods," while the challenge to researchers will be to "further illuminate the cognitive processes that go into composing and comprehending technical discourse," as well as "to identify more precisely the structures and rhetorical patterns that are characteristic of the genre" (398).

247   **Stevenson, Dwight. "Audience Analysis across Cultures."** *Journal of Technical Writing and Communication* **13.4 (1983): 319–30.**

In this article, the author makes an observation which lies at the heart of this argument: "I am aware of no text in which there is anything more than a passing reference to the fact that English technical discourse is produced by and read by nonnative speakers" (320). Appealing to an audience of "researchers and teachers of technical communication," the article states its purpose as examining the implications of this observation, and it notes that such implications "may influence not only how we deal with whatever nonnative speakers we do have in our classes but may influence also how we deal with native English-speaking students" (320). Employing "research conducted during a series of consulting trips in Japanese industries," the article identifies and discusses such issues as the "assumption of short-range use" (i.e., the assumption that nonnative students will use English technical discourse only as long as they are students here), the "failure to require diversity" in writing tasks, and the "failure to introduce internationalism." (319) In conclusion, the author argues that "in looking at both our students and at their audiences we must adopt an international perspective; in our research, in our texts, and in our classroom method we must learn to look at technical communication across cultures" (330).

248   **Swales, John. "Discourse Communities, Genres, and English as an International Language."** *World Englishes* **7.2 (1988): 211–20.**

In this article, the author not only "propose[s] a particular conceptualization of the term *discourse community*" but also "examine[s] that concept's potential for developing insight into the relationships between texts, text-roles, and text-environments in the modern professional world" (211). *Discourse community* is conceived in this article as "a more functional and goal-directed grouping than either speech community or speech fellowship" (211) and six "characteristics of discourse communities" are established (212–13). The article tests its assertion that "genres are properties of discourse communities" (211) through an examination of the "reprint request" (RR) genre, where an RR is defined as a "request for a reprint (or copy) of a publication mailed to that publication's author" (215). The article concludes that since the RR is "a prototypic exemplar of EIL [English as an International Language]," it is "an established vehicle of communicative traffic in those discourse communities that have come to accept the RR as part of their networking practices" (219). Therefore, "by means of RRs, isolated non-native speakers of English [can] establish and begin to develop the contacts they so badly need" (220).

249   **Thrush, Emily A. "Bridging the Gaps: Technical Communication in an International and Multicultural Society."** *Technical Communication Quarterly* **2.3 (Summer 1993): 271–83.**

After demonstrating how cultural differences affect the interpretation of even graphics, the author describes why technical communication should be concerned with international and multicultural communication. She then discusses five factors that affect the way various cultures read and interpret text: world experience, the amount of common knowledge shared within a culture, the hierarchical structure of society and workplace, culturally specific rhetorical strategies, and cultural differences in processing graphics (274). Thrush concludes with a three-pronged approach to dealing with this subject in the classroom: "raising awareness of the problem, introducing students to sources of information, and providing practice in communicating with people of other cultures" (280).

250   **Tippens, Dora. "Interculturalizing the Technical or Business Communications Course."** *Journal of Technical Writing and Communication* **23.4 (1993): 389–412.**

Tippens writes that technical and business communication courses must be interculturalized "to prepare students for effective productivity and humanity in the new global workplace" (389). After discussing ethnocentrism, language barriers, and cultural differences, the author suggests strategies and specific exercises to sensitize students to such problems. She contends that traditional assignments can be easily updated to provide intercultural content and to accommodate intercultural audiences. She includes an "audience-and-use profile sheet," for example, and discusses specific cultural differences, using Japan as one specific case. Ultimately, however, "the scale of interculturalizing depends on the creativity of the educator, and the partnership within the institution and with business (412)." She lists key books as well as other resources that may be useful to instructors and students.

251   **Victor, David A.** *International Business Communication.* **New York: HarperCollins, 1992. Indexes. Bib. 280p.**

This first text wholly devoted to its subject provides, as the author states, "a framework for asking the right questions for a starting point" (xiv). Its nine chapters survey factors related to communicating across cultures: language, temporal conceptions, environment, technology, social organization, contexting, face-saving, authority, and nonverbal communication. With its abundant citations and detailed bibliography, this book could serve as a useful resource for teaching and advanced study. Numerous and vivid examples of cross-cultural issues appear throughout the book, which concludes with a name index, a subject index, and a culture and nation index.

252   **Weiss, Timothy. "'The Gods Must Be Crazy': The Challenge of the Intercultural."** *Journal of Business and Technical Communication* **7.2 (1993): 196–217.**

The author discusses the film *The Gods Must Be Crazy* and suggests the film's fallen Coca-Cola¨ bottle "presents both the predicament and the challenge of the intercultural: (a) the instability of signifiers outside of their usual contexts and the equivocality of those signifiers that cross cultures; (b) the ineluctability of cross-cultural interactions in our pluralistic, global society and the need to build bridges between ourselves and others" (197). He suggests that with its "creativity and adaptiveness, culture . . . closely resembles human language" (199).He turns to Bakhtin and his dialogic model to assess culture. He also critically examines an ABC publication which, he suggests, views culture as an obstacle to communication. He responds by offering five key topics which he believes can be used more productively in the classroom: "1. the local and the global; 2. culture and nation; 3. modes of communication and types of miscommunication; 4. individuals as carriers and constructors of their culture; and 5. the necessity of second-language training and cross-cultural experience" (212).

TECHNOLOGY AND VISUAL THEORY

TECHNOLOGY IN THEORY AND PEDAGOGY

253 **Barrett, Edward, ed.** *Sociomedia: Multimedia, Hypermedia, and the Social Construction of Knowledge.* **Cambridge: MIT P, 1992. Index. 580p.**

This book is part of a series, "Technical Communication and Information Systems," which examines technical communication: "one of the most rapidly expanding fields of study in the United States" (ix). (See also 287 [Carroll] and 289 [Doheny-Farina].) This volume of 25 separately authored chapters examines "hypertext, hypermedia, and multimedia applications of computational technology in the university" (1). The editor has coined the word sociomedia to signify "that when we design computer media we are hardwiring a mechanism for the social construction of knowledge" (1). The first 10 chapters (Part I, "Perspectives") examine such issues as "Cognitive Architecture in Hypermedia Instruction" by Henrietta Nickels Shirk and similar studies of the impact of computers on university education. The next 15 chapters, Part II, "Practices," look at specific applications, such as "Computer Integrated Documentation" by Guy Boy and the computer's use in medicine and engineering.

254 **Duin, Ann Hill, and Craig J. Hansen, eds.** *Nonacademic Writing: Social Theory and Technology.* **Mahwah, NJ: Erlbaum, 1996. Indexes. 376p.**

In the foreword to this collection of 14 essays, Marilyn M. Cooper defines *nonacademic writing* in part as "writing that gets something done, as opposed to writing that serves an aesthetic, cognitive, or affective function" (x). In the preface, the editors suggest that each chapter is intended to challenge current theory, research, and pedagogy as well as provoke additional inquiry about nonacademic writing (xiv). The chapters cover a broad range of issues in such essays as "Setting a Sociotechnological Agenda in Nonacademic Writing" by Ann Hill Duin and Craig J. Hansen; "The Computer Culture, Gender, and Nonacademic Writing: An Interdisciplinary Critique" by Mary M. Lay; and "Writing as Democratic Social Action in a Technological World: Politicizing and Inhabiting Virtual Landscapes" by Cynthia L. Selfe and Richard J. Selfe, Jr. Other contributors include Carl G. Herndl; Elizabeth Tebeaux; John Ackerman and Scott Oates; Rebecca E. Burnett; Dorothy Winsor; Jo Allen and Carol Thompson; Catherine F. Smith; Sandra Stotsky; Stuart A. Selber, Dan McGavin, William Klein, and Johndan Johnson-Eilola; Curtis Jay Bonk, Thomas H. Reynolds, and Padma V. Medury; and Craig J. Hansen. Both author and subject indexes are provided.

255 **Fulk, Janet, and Charles W. Steinfield, eds.** *Organizations and Communication Technology.* **Newbury Park, CA: Sage, 1990. Indexes. 328p.**

According to the editors, the 13 theoretical essays in this collection address a number of questions: "What forces shape the articulation of organizational and technological systems? What organizational, political and social processes constrain technological possibilities? How do technology and organization interact to shape organizational structures and processes? How do technology and organization interact to shape organizational structures and processes? How do organization and information technology co-determine each other?" (7) In their opening essay, "The Theory Imperative," Steinfield and Fulk assert that theory is critical to the study of new information technologies because, for example, it "provides a framework for synthesis and integration of empirical findings" and "offers guidance as to where to direct future empirical attention" (13). The remaining essays cover such topics as information technology and collective behaviors and information technology and organizational design. All the articles provide references to diverse resources on communication, technology, and organizational theory.

256   **Gerrard, Lisa, ed. *Writing at Century's End: Essays on Computer-Assisted Composition*. New York: Random House, 1987. Index. Bib. 152p.**

In the preface to this collection of 13 essays, the editor states, "Like the contributors to this collection, we may not always agree on the benefits of computer-assisted composition or on the solutions to its problems, but as computer users, software developers, and curriculum designers, we can decide what these benefits and solutions will be. This is both a responsibility and an opportunity" (7). The first eight essays focus on pedagogical issues in such articles as "Processing Words and Writing Instructions: Revising and Testing Word Processing Instructions in an Advanced Technical Writing Class" by Erna Kelly and "Engineers Become Writers: Computers and Creativity in Technical Writing Classes" by Valarie Meliotes Arms. The final five chapters focus on theoretical and political issues in such articles as "Some Ideas about Idea Processors" by David N. Dobrin and "The Politics of CAI and Word Processing: Some Issues for Faculty and Administrators" by Deborah H. Holdstein.

257   **Hawisher, Gail E., and Cynthia L. Selfe, eds. *Evolving Perspectives on Computers and Composition Studies: Questions for the 1990s*. Urbana, IL: NCTE, 1991. Index. 383p.**

The editors state that the purpose of this volume is "to help us, as scholars and teachers, to understand how learning and, more specifically, writing, are changed by electronic environments and to question future directions in computers and composition studies" (4). The 15 chapters are divided into four parts. Part 1 examines research and scholarship and includes "Taking Control of the Page: Electronic Writing and Word Publishing" by Patricia Sullivan. Part 2 treats classroom issues such as evaluation and teacher education, and Part 3 examines the instructional use of hypertext and includes "Hypertext and Composition Studies" by Henrietta Nickels Shirk. Part 4 examines the politics of computers and writing program administration.

258   **Johnson, Robert R. "The Unfortunate Human Factor: A Selective History of Human Factors for Technical Communicators." *Technical Communication Quarterly* 3.2 (Spring 1994): 195–212.**

This article argues that "technical communicators have much to gain by applying human factors methods to the processes of documentation development" (195), defining human factors research as historically "focusing on the needs of humans when they are involved in technology interaction" (196). Important to the purpose of this article is the demonstration of "how an emphasis on technological systems in human factors is historically embedded, and how this emphasis on technology has operated to the detriment of the human user" (196). Employing a historical perspective, the article surveys the various subfields of human factors relevant to technical communicators. The article concludes that since "the active state of users should be a primary concern of documentation writers," the two schools of interface design represented by human activity designers and participatory designers "could very possibly set the stage for important research in future documentation theory and practice" (209).

259 **Levine, Linda, Linda H. Pesante, and Susan B. Dunkle. "Implementing the Writing Plan: Heuristics from Software Development."** *Technical Writing Teacher* **18.2 (Spring 1991): 116–25.**

This article surveys the various ways that instructors of technical writing can "use analogy to efficiently exploit correspondences between the models and processes of composing and software development" (117). "In considering approaches to software development and software life cycle models," the authors observe, "we have gained insight into the problems of writers and the teaching of technical communication" (123). Thus, the authors conclude that the field of software engineering is a useful source of information about "navigating the crucial area between planning and revising that is conventionally called writing" (124).

260 **Markel, Mike. "The Effect of the Word Processor and the Style Checker on Revision in Technical Writing: What Do We Know, and What Do We Need to Find Out?"** *Journal of Technical Writing and Communication* **20.4 (1990): 329–42.**

Surveying the "literature on using style checkers and the text-editing capabilities of the computer to assist in revising technical writing," this article finds that such literature is flawed and inconclusive (329). The article argues that instructors of writing "need to examine the basic premise of the research on revising and word processing," ensure that "our evaluative techniques for measuring writing improvement are valid," and examine "the differences among word processors and among the different style checkers to determine their effects on writing behavior and writing quality" (337). The article makes several recommendations to accomplish these goals, including continuing the study of relationships between revising and quality and between error recognition and writing quality, studying a wide range of computers and software, and considering the special characteristics of the different populations under study.

261 **Norman, Rose, and Daryl Grider. "Structured Document Processors: Implications for Technical Writing."** *Technical Communication Quarterly* **1.3 (Summer 1992): 5–21.**

The focus of this article is structural document processing (SDPs), "a technology that intentionally reduces the individual writer's control over format in order to give the writer greater power over content" (6). The article "describes a range of SDPs now used in industry, and explores their implications for the practice and teaching of technical writing" (5). The article is divided into three parts: first an explanation of "the nature and uses of SDPs" is presented, then the authors relate their own "experience with some SDPs to illustrate how they are changing the way technical writing is done in industry," and finally the authors "explore how these changes in technical writing practice may lead to changes in the teaching of technical writing" (6). The authors conclude that "the most striking effect of SDPs on writing in the workplace is the way they force a convergence of writing and technology, blurring the distinctions" between concepts like writing and engineering (19).

262   **Reynolds, John Frederick. "Desktop Publishing and Technical Writing: Problems and Strategies."** *Computer-Assisted Composition Journal* **5 (1990): 18–22.**

The author recognizes the rapid growth of technical writing and the importance of the "electronic word-production technologies [which] have revolutionized composing" (18). Desktop publishing, the author cites, is the technology which has had the greatest impact on technical writing. This short article catalogs the logistical and pedagogical problems associated with the integration of desktop publishing technology into technical writing courses and writing programs. While the author's strategies for addressing problems of "logistics" (higher costs, learning time, faculty inexperience, hardware/software uncertainties, keeping updated) are like solutions to similar problems in the integration of word processing into composition programs, the author recommends three specific strategies for teaching technical writing: "subverting the textbooks," "making presentation central," and "maximizing materials available" (20–21).

263   **Rice, Ronald E., Shan-Ju Chang, and Jack Torobin. "Communication Style, Media Use, Organizational Level, and Use and Evaluation of Electronic Messaging."** *Management Communication Quarterly* **6.1 (August 1992): 3–33.**

This article presents research which considers "the roles of media characteristics, communicator style, and traditional organizational level in influencing the adoption, use, and evaluation of computer-mediated communication (CMC) systems" (3). The authors argue that "various characteristics associated with different media have implications for choice and outcomes" (3–4). The article provides a detailed description of the study's theoretical framework, method, and multivariate results. The discussion analyzes the implications both for constructs like communicator style, organizational level, media use, direct influence of system usage, and for related research. The authors conclude that "people with varying communicator styles will come to use [CMC] for a wide variety of purposes and accept it as just one of many possibilities for communicating with other people" (28).

264   Selber, Stuart A. "Beyond Skill Building: Challenges Facing Technical Communication Teachers in the Computer Age." *Technical Communication Quarterly* 3.4 (Fall 1994): 365–90.

This article examines pedagogical issues that accompany increased computer use in technical communication classrooms and the limits this causes in moving beyond skill building. The author argues that technical communication teachers should "encourage computer literacies in our classrooms that consider the rhetorical, social, and political implications of computer-mediated communication and work" (366). Through a survey of college and university course descriptions and Internet discussion groups, the author examines "common approaches to integrating computers in technical communication curricula and in what ways these approaches may or may not move beyond skill building to include broader literacy and humanistic issues" (366). The author poses three pedagogical challenges to move beyond skill building, including "Balancing technological with literacy and humanistic concerns," "Re-Envisioning our computer-related curricula," and "Educating teachers who use computers in their classrooms."

265   Selber, Stuart A. "Metaphorical Perspectives on Hypertext." *IEEE Transactions on Professional Communication* 38.2 (June 1995): 59–67.

This article "examines the dominant metaphors that define and describe three basic components of hypertext (texts, nodes, and links), arguing that they contribute in central ways to the current treatment of this technology in technical communication" (59). The author contends that, while hypertext is an increasingly important area of technical communication instruction, the "overwhelming mechanical task of creating applications," for example, "may discourage teachers and students from discussing the ways in which this technology is constituted culturally and discursively and how that constitution contributes to the current treatment of hypertext in technical communication" (59). By tracing some discursive factors that influence the development and use of hypertext in technical communication, the author reveals how the metaphors work to "naturalize certain cultural perspectives on how information might be best designed and used in online environments" (65). Selber contends that "hypertext design choices are both productively and unproductively shaped by social as well as technological forces" (60). The author concludes that "teachers concerned with the ethical and social dimensions of technical communication might help students become critical readers of the maps and metaphors we commonly employ to represent virtual spaces" (65).

266   Smith, Douglas C., and Sandra J. Nelson. "Hypertext: An Emerging and Important Medium of Business and Technical Communication." *Journal of Business and Technical Communication* 8.2 (April 1994): 231–43.

This article focuses on the pedagogical uses and advantages of hypertext, defined as "a structure for information that is available through computer systems," which is organized by interrelated topics (232). The article also briefly discusses terminology, theoretical bases, and the structure of hypertext, as well as several problems that authors and instructors of business and technical communication face with hypertext. The article concludes that while "preparing students to learn to use hypertext requires first teaching them what hypertext is, how knowledge is represented in it," as well as the various problems associated with it, "guidelines for hypertext project selection and for encouraging hypertext authorship will foster a smooth transition to successful and appropriate hypertext use" (242).

267   **Sproull, Lee, and Sara Kiesler.** *Connections: New Ways of Working in the Networked Organization.* **Cambridge: MIT P, 1991. Index. Bib. 212p.**

Based on their research on communication and organizations, the authors find that "new computer-based communication technology—electronic mail, distribution lists, bulletin boards, conferences—is changing how people work" (ix). These technologies, the authors suggest, "do not simply cross space and time; they also can cross hierarchical and departmental barriers, change standard operating procedures, and reshape organizational norms" (xi). These changes form the subject of this book. The nine chapters, some based on earlier essays in various academic journals, can be read independently, according to the authors. They state, "Chapter 1 draws on the social history of the nineteenth century technologies, such as the railroad, typewriter, and telephone, to introduce a two-level framework for thinking about technology changes in organizations" (xi). Their methodology is to examine the "first-level, or efficiency, effects and second-level, or social system, effects" (15). They follow this methodology in the remaining chapters, which examine such issues as "electronic etiquette," crossing social barriers, managerial practices, and how computers will pose problems as well as offer solutions in the future. The authors include a particularly abundant list of references.

268   **Van Pelt, William V. "Teaching Technical Writing for the Computer Sciences."** *Technical Writing Teacher* **10.2/3 (Winter/Spring 1983): 189–94.**

This article contends that university and college writing programs have only begun to respond to the "increasing demand for technical writers who can address the specialized problems of computer documentation" (i.e., developing adequate courses) (189). The author then analyzes two factors which exacerbate that problem: first, "writing for computer systems places the writer in a rigorously specialized context," and, second, there is "the rapid advance of computer technology itself" (189). The article presents an example of a technical writing course which addresses these problems. The article concludes that a computer is not really a single machine, but "an intricate hierarchy of machines, languages, and systematic interfaces"; therefore, "writing for computers requires a constant effort at determining what level of knowledge you are addressing" (194).

269   **Williams, Al, ed.** *Communication and Technology: Today and Tomorrow.* **Denton, TX: ABC, 1994. 226p.**

This collection of articles is a product of the efforts of a committee of the Association for Business Communication originally charged with providing "the ABC membership with an awareness of the impact information systems was having on the communication process" (xi). This publication represents a continuation of that effort. The 13 chapters are divided into five parts. Part One, "Communicating Today," contains a single overview essay, "Communication and Technology" by William H. Baker. Part Two, "Collecting, Storing, and Analyzing Information," includes "Databases: Valuable Information Sources for Business Communicators" by Marie E. Flatley and "Analytical Software Programs and Integrated Packages: Their Place in Business Communication" by Herb Smith. Part Three, "Presenting Information," includes "Word Processing" by Pat Duffy; "Graphics" by John M. Penrose, Jr.; and "Hypermedia" by Rebecca B. Worley. Part Four, "Exchanging Information," includes "Electronic Mail" by JoAnne Yates, "Electronic Conferencing" by Joel P. Bowman, "Voicemail" by Raymond W. Beswick, "Teleconferencing" by John C. Sherblom, and "Local Area Networks" by Douglas A. Goings and Al Williams. Part Five, "Communicating Tomorrow," includes "Artificial Intelligence and Expert Systems" by Henrietta Nickels Shirk and "The Future of Business Communication Technology: Where Are We Headed, Captain?" by Ross Figgins. A glossary of communication technology terms follows the chapters. A summary, a set of questions, and references or a bibliography conclude each chapter, which suggests that this publication could also be useful as readings for students.

TECHNICAL PUBLICATIONS AND EDITING

270   **Allen, O. Jane, and Lynn H. Deming, eds.** *Publications Management: Essays for Professional Communicators*. **Amityville, NY: Baywood, 1994. Index. 251p.**

The editors state, "We have collected these essays for students in academic programs in technical and professional communication and for communication professionals in the workplace" (ix). The focus of the 18 separately authored chapters is on managing projects, people, and technical communication programs. Part I, "Communication and the Manager," includes three articles on the process of project management, personnel issues, and meetings. Part II, "Management and Supervision," includes four articles concerning such issues as hiring freelancers and managing internships. Part III, "Project Management and the Information Development Cycle," contains six articles on such topics as developing timetables, document standards, and estimating costs. Part IV, "Legal and Ethical Issues," contains two articles; and Part V, "Pedagogy," includes three articles in program and course development for professional communicators. Many of the articles include both references and selected readings.

271   **Alred, Gerald J., Walter E. Oliu, and Charles T. Brusaw.** *The Professional Writer: A Guide for Advanced Technical Writing*. **New York: St. Martin's, 1992. Index. 426p.**

This text is specifically designed as a resource and guide for "undergraduate and graduate students who are preparing for writing careers in business, industry, and government" (vii). The authors state that they wish to balance theory and practice: "Throughout this book, we present the concepts and research findings that under-

pin the practices of the professional writer" (vii). The 15 chapters cover such topics as the document process, special audience needs and reading theory, collaborative work, computer graphics, layout and typography, electronic publishing, review
and evaluation, document standards, and online documentation. The professional
writing process is demonstrated with a case history of a professional writer that
includes interviews, parts of the document, and the finished manual intended for
international bankers.

272   **Beene, Lynn, and Peter White, eds.** *Solving Problems in Technical Writing.*
New York and Oxford: Oxford UP, 1988. Index. 241p.

Although this anthology is directed toward different readers, "all of whom face similar problems in communicating information effectively," it is particularly intended
for the education of professional technical writers (i). According to the editors, the
articles present a broad perspective that reflects both theoretical and practical
approaches to professional writing that "neither overwhelms students or beginning
writers nor condescends to professional technical writers" (i). Nevertheless, the
authors suggest this collection's value lies in graduate education, and they hope that
the essays provide students with "a sense of the major goals of research and technical documentation" (i).

Among the articles are "How Can Problem-Solution Structures Help Writers
Plan and Write Technical Documents?" by Michael P. Jordan, "How Can Technical
Writing Be Persuasive?" by Scott P. Sanders, "How Can Rhetorical Theory Help
Writers Create Readable Documents?" by Robert De Beaugrande, "How Can Text
and Graphics Be Integrated Effectively?" by M. Jimmie Killingsworth and Michael
Gilbertson, "How Can Technical Writers Give Effective Oral Presentations?" by
Peter White, and "How Can Technical Writers Further Their Professional
Development?" by Sandra Whipple Spanier.

273   **Bresko, Laura L. "The Need for Technical Communicators on the Software
Development Team."** *Technical Communication* **36.1 (April 1991): 214–20.**

This article "analyzes the current status of technical communicators in the software development field and presents research that supports a new, expanded role
for the technical communicator" (214). The article contends that this new role
may solve many of the communication problems in software development. The
method and results of a survey of software development managers are presented
(detailed tables are included); the survey "shows that most [software development
managers] use technical writers, but only at the end of the process," even though
"most think that English or technical writing training is critical" (214). The article concludes that a "technical communicator needs a thorough understanding of
software development techniques and must master the tools used to implement
those techniques" (219).

274   **Buchholz, William J. "The Boston Study: Analysis of a Major Metropolitan
Business- and Technical-Communication Market."** *Journal of Business and
Technical Communication* **3.1 (1989): 3–35.**

This article offers a sense of the breadth and depth of communication in business, industrial, governmental, and nonprofit settings by examining a single, metropolitan communication-employment market. The author focuses on the business and technical communication market in Boston, Massachusetts, identifying "the abundance of professional titles, duties, attitudes, responsibilities, aptitudes, and skills in business and technical communication" (5). He discusses six communication categories: technical communication, publishing, public relations, marketing, development, and training. While this is not a definitive analysis of the entire professional outlook, the author suggests that a single-market focus "can contribute to a growing understanding of the professions often grouped under the rubric business and technical communication" (30). He contends that "probes into other metropolitan communication markets would no doubt reveal equally abundant, though certainly different, occupational types and driving forces" (30). The author concludes that communication practitioners can expect healthy growth in the profession.

275   **Buehler, Mary Fran. "Defining Terms in Technical Editing: The Levels of Edit as a Model."** *Technical Communication* **28.4 (1981): 10–15.**

The author states that "when we—as technical editors—try to communicate clearly about technical editing, we find that we have not yet agreed on standard meanings for our own terms" (10). After demonstrating the confusion over the term *copy editing* as an example, she describes the "levels-of-edit" concept, which was also described in a book she published by the Jet Propulsion Laboratory (JPL), *The Levels of Edit* (1980), with Robert Van Buren. As reported in that book, nine types of edit are performed with documents at JPL: "Coordination, Policy, Integrity, Screening, Copy Clarification, Format, Mechanical Style, Language, and Substantive" (11). After brief descriptions of each edit, she suggests how these terms can be used to define other terms of editing, such as *copy editing*. "Whether we in technical communication use the terminology of the types and levels of edit or not," she concludes, "we must find some commonly understood terms with which we can communicate, if we are to prevent or remove our misunderstandings—unless we are content to struggle with misunderstandings for all our days" (14).

276   **Dragga, Sam, and Gwendolyn Gong.** *Editing: The Design of Rhetoric*. **Amityville, NY: Baywood, 1989. Index. Bib. 231p.**

The authors state that the purpose of this book is "to familiarize readers with the theoretical basis and practical applications of the editing process. This involves the examination of the rhetorical canons—invention, arrangement, style, and delivery—and the corresponding rhetorical objectives of editing—accuracy, clarity, propriety, and artistry" (9). Correspondingly, the chapters are divided according to the rhetorical canons, which are described in Chapter 1. Chapter 2, "Invention," discusses such issues as audience analysis, information gathering, and editing for accuracy. Chapter 3, "Arrangement," includes discussions of such topics as verbal-visual orientation, organization, and coherence. Chapter 4, "Style," covers both visual and verbal style; and Chapter 5, "Delivery," covers typography, page design, and "editing for artistry" among other topics. Each chapter is divided into two parts: rhetorical theory and practice, which illustrates the theory with specific examples from technical, news, and promotional publications.

277 **Duffy, Thomas M., Theodore Post, and Gregory Smith. "Technical Manual Production: An Examination of Five Systems."** *Written Communication* **4.4 (October 1987): 370–93.**

This article presents a study whose objective was "to begin an analysis of the technical manual production process" and "identify those factors contributing to the difficulties in producing a usable manual"; specifically, the article focuses on "the strategies through which technical, rhetorical, and design expertise were utilized in the production process" (373). The article describes in detail the study's method and results, and a flowchart of the typical technical information development process is provided. The article concludes that the research indicates the process model of writing "may be usefully applied in interpreting group, functional writing tasks"; that "guidelines are an inadequate mechanism for bridging the gap between expert and novice"; and that "the planning process is critical to the design of effective documents" (389–90).

278 **Farkas, David K. "The Concept of Consistency in Writing and Editing."** *Journal of Technical Writing and Communication* **15.4 (1985): 353–64.**

The author believes that "the concept of consistency should be recognized as a necessary component of any comprehensive rhetoric of technical and professional writing" (363). In this article, the author states that his aim is "to analyze consistency as a communication concept and to set forth useful guidelines for establishing the most desirable patterns of consistency" (354). Following a discussion of five major categories of consistency (semantic, syntactic, stylistic, spatial, and mechanical as well as instances of unnecessary consistency), the author defines guidelines for consistency which he believes will lead to the establishment of patterns of consistency that are logical, evident, functional, resource efficient, and stable (359).

279 **Hackos, JoAnn T.** *Managing Your Documentation Projects***. New York: Wiley, 1994. Index. Bib. 629p.**

The author states, "Few books or training programs exist that deal with the specific requirements of publications-project management" (xvii). This book, part of the "Wiley Technical Communication Library," is intended to fill that gap. The author has written this book not only for publications project managers and independent project contributors but also for instructors of future technical communicators and publications project managers. The 29 chapters are divided into six parts: "Managing for Quality—An Introduction to Publications Project Management," "Starting the Project—The Information-Planning Phase," "Establishing the Specifics—The Content-Specification Phase," "Keeping the Project Running—The Implementation Phase," "Managing the Production Phase," and "Ending the Project—The Evaluation Phase." Five appendixes provide various checklists and guides intended to help managers maintain high-quality technical publications. A substantial bibliography on project management is also provided.

280 **Helyar, Pamela S. "Products Liability: Meeting Legal Standards for**

Adequate Instructions." *Journal of Technical Writing and Communication* **22.2 (1992): 125–47.**

"This article," the author proposes, "defines the legal standards for adequacy and illustrates how the courts interpret them. It also defines how technical communicators can meet those standards" (126). The author provides and explains in detail a list of 10 guidelines which, she argues, should result in "safer products" and "legally adequate instructions." In conclusion, she states, "With these precautions and a paper trail in hand, manufacturers can slay the snake while it sleeps and successfully defend against claims of legally inadequate instructions" (143).

281   Jordan, Stello, Joseph M. Kleinman, and H. Lee Shimberg, eds. *Handbook of Technical Writing Practices*. 2 vols. New York: Wiley-Interscience, 1971. Index. Bib. 1374p.

This two-volume publication was designed to help professional technical writers with every possible publication task. In fact, it is a collection of articles written by leaders in the field of technical writing on subjects ranging from writing reports and parts catalogs to managing technical publication departments.

The two volumes are divided into four parts. Part I, "Documents and Publications," is the largest and comprises the first volume entirely. Part II, "Supporting Services for Technical Writing," discusses illustrations, production, and editing. Part III, "Management of Technical Writing," covers numerous aspects of the technical publication department, including the role of technical writing activities and supervision. Part IV, "Guides and References," serves as a literature review for the field of technical writing up to 1970 and includes "Basic Recommended Reference Shelf: A Selected Bibliography of Technical and Scientific Writing" by John A. Walter. Each volume has its own index.

282   Kemnitz, Charles. "How to Write Effective Hazard Alert Messages." *Technical Communication* **38.1 (1991): 68–73.**

This article focuses on writing hazard alert messages that meet the guidelines set forth by the American National Standards Institute (ANSI). To help technical writers develop systems that meet ANSI standards, the author provides an interpretation of the standard as well as some practical advice on writing hazard alert messages. The article defines a *hazard* as "any *source* of danger presented by a product either through use or foreseeable misuse" (69) of a product. The author outlines the three levels of a hazard alert message and discusses the appropriate use of signal words: *danger*, *warning*, and *caution*. He details the seven basic elements defined by the ANSI standard and offers practical advice on how to effectively convey hazard alert messages. The author concludes with an analysis of a sample hazard alert message.

283   Killingsworth, M. Jimmie, and Betsy G. Jones. "Division of Labor or Integrated Teams: A Crux in the Management of Technical Communication?" *Technical Communication* **36.3 (August 1989): 210–21.**

The authors state, "Two models of collaboration predominate in the process by which technical documents are produced . . . *the division of labor model* and the *integrated team model*" (210). In this article the authors report on a survey "that suggests the prevalence of each model and that gives insights into how the choice of a management model affects the practice of technical communication and the attitudes of technical communicators" (210). In the first section of the article, the authors provide a historical and theoretical perspective of the two organizational models and a brief literature review. In the second section of the article, the authors discuss the methodology and results of a survey of technical writers which they conducted. Included is a sample of the questionnaire used.

284   **Lutz, Jean A. "Attitude toward the Editing Process: Theory, Research, and Pedagogy."** *Journal of Technical Writing and Communication* **16.1/2 (1986): 157–65.**

"Drawing on rhetoric and cognitive psychology," in this article the author argues for "the complexity of the editing process and that of the writer-editor relationship" (158). "This perspective," the author explains, "is tentatively supported by a study of the revising and editing patterns of professional and experienced writers. The study suggests that revising and editing may be equally complex tasks. Further, the complexity increases if editors and authors discuss their changes as opposed to legislating them. Several methods for imparting this perspective and related knowledge to students are discussed" (157). The author concludes: "If we accept and acknowledge complexity in the editing process, we will take more seriously our own need as teachers of the process to explain and negotiate the changes we advise in our students' work. They, in turn, may come to look upon our *editing* as negotiation for meaning in their texts" (164).

COMPUTER DOCUMENTATION

285   **Barker, Thomas T., ed.** *Perspectives on Software Documentation: Inquiries and Innovations.* **Amityville, NY: Baywood, 1991. Index. 279p.**

In the introduction to this collection of essays, the editor proposes "a broad working definition of software documentation and [looks] at the kinds of professionals who create it" (8). The editor also reviews a number of fields—linguistics, cognitive science, learning psychology, ergonomics/human factors, and reading—that contribute to an understanding of software documentation. The book is divided into two parts. Part 1, "Inquiries," is further divided into three sections, each of which contains two or three essays by various authors. In the first of these sections, "Education and Research," the essays address "instructional methods appropriate for teaching software documentation" (26) and survey "the traditional advice on style" (46). Section 2, "The Influence of Cognitive Science," contains essays which examine the benefits of both cognitive writing techniques (i.e., parallelism, hierarchies, sequences, etc.) and a schematic approach to the production of software documentation. Essays in Section 3, "Issues of Design," consider various aspects—human factors, computer engineering, and problems of form—which impact the production of software documentation. The essays in Part 2, "Innovations," offer practical applications and models for the successful production of software documentation. The seven essays in this part are divided into three sections: "Managing Software Documentation," "Improving the Quality of Software Documentation," and "Software Documentation of the Future—Online." A subject index is included.

286   **Brockmann, R. John.** *Writing Better Computer User Documentation: From Paper to Hypertext Version 2.0.* **New York: Wiley, 1990. Index. Bib. 365p.**

According to its author, this book, written in the format of a software user's manual, "is designed to help you write accurate, clear computer documentation for users—documentation beyond systems and programming documentation. This book presents a systematic approach to writing paper and on-line documents, and follows the process of creating materials from the inception of the documentation project to updating after publication" (1). The author further states, "This book assumes no prior knowledge of either software or documentation" (5). Its intended audience includes technical communicators, human-factors engineers, documentation specialists, programmers, students, systems analysts, and managers of information services. The book is divided into two parts. In Part One, "The Documentation Problem," the author "describes the problems of user documentation, what the possible consequences of inadequate documentation may be, and why these problems have occurred" (6). Problems, both on paper and online, are addressed. In Part Two, "The Standard Documentation Process," the author "outlines a solution to user documentation problems—the Standard Documentation Process (SDP)" (6). Each of the nine chapters in Part Two covers one step in the process from "Developing the Document Specifications" to "Maintaining the Document." The book includes an extensive list of references, a glossary, and an index. A tear-out reference card to the SDP is also included.

287   **Carroll, John M.** *The Nurnberg Funnel: Designing Minimalist Instruction for Practical Computer Skill.* **Cambridge, MA: MIT P, 1990. Index. Bib. 340p.**

The *Nurnberg Funnel* refers to a legendary funnel, into which someone might pour knowledge to make people wise very quickly. "The very idea of 'pouring' material into the mind seems ill-conceived," the author states, yet in trying to make instruction efficient, "designers have frequently lapsed into trying to pour information into the learner's mind" (10).

This book gathers together "two dozen or so separate empirical projects and theoretical discussions" (xviii) about the way "people learn to use computer application systems by self-instruction, that is, in the absence of human coaches or teachers" (xvii), which were published over the preceding decade by Carroll, Robert Mack, and Clayton Lewis. The author says that their "analysis of specific learner problems exposed fundamental flaws in the standard systems approach to instruction and suggested an alternate instructional model, which [they] call the minimalist model" (xvii). This book consists of nine chapters, each of which is further divided by headings into one- or two-page sections. Following Chapter 1, an introductory chapter, Chapters 2 and 3 "describe qualitative analyses of the learning problems of new users of computer systems" (10). Chapter 4 acts as a "bridge between learner problems and the instructional approach they impel" (xviii). The author cites this chapter as "the pivotal chapter in the book. It presents a unifying analysis of the learner problems and develops the minimalist training model" (11). Chapters 5 through 8 develop "the minimalist approach through the review of design case studies. Each discusses specific projects in which [the author, Mack, and Lewis] designed, built, and evaluated an instructional tool, guided by the minimalist model" (11). In the final chapter of the book, the author "examines implications and further challenges for minimalist instruction" (15).

288   **Chisholm, Richard M. "Selecting Metaphoric Terminology for the Computer Industry."** *Journal of Technical Writing and Communication* **16.3 (1986): 195–220.**

The author argues that new computer users find the terminology used to describe computers and their functions "difficult to interpret because we continue to employ terms and phrases that naïve users find obscure" (197). In an effort to combat this problem, the author proposes seven criteria which act as "tools for predicting the effect of individual terms upon certain groups of users. They help us," the author believes, "to select the terms that communicate best rather than to use the term nearest at hand or the current vogue word" (217). These criteria are: "1) Is a metaphoric term needed? 2) Is the old word familiar? 3) Is the metaphoric relation close? 4) Is the usage of the word consistent? 5) Is the metaphoric word brief? 6) Is the metaphoric usage acceptable? 7) Is the metaphoric word memorable?" (195)

289   **Doheny-Farina, Stephen, ed.** *Effective Documentation: What We Have Learned from Research.* **Cambridge, MA: MIT P, 1988. Index. 354p.**

This collection of 16 essays, according to its editor, offers "a range of useful information for technical writers, document designers, managers of technical writing departments, technical communication researchers, and teachers and students of technical communication" (1–2). In the essays, some authors report on their own research projects. Others "review the implications of a wide variety of empirical research on a given topic or topics" (2). Still others "discuss how technical communicators may incorporate research activities within the documentation cycles of their organizations" (2). In-depth discussion is provided on "Research into User Learning and Performance, Research into Format and Graphic Design, Research into the Management of Documentation Processes, and Analyses of Research Methods for Technical Communication" (2). In the essay which begins the book, Mary Beth Debs reviews "other publications that offer technical communication guidelines based on research" (7).

290   **Duffy, Thomas M., James E. Palmer, and Brad Mehlenbacher.** *Online Help: Design and Evaluation.* **Norwood, NJ: Ablex, 1992. Indexes. Bib. 260p.**

The authors of this book begin by answering the question "What is online help?" in Chapters 1 through 3. "Chapters 4 and 5," they state, "emphasize the design of online help systems, and Chapters 6, 7, and 8 focus on the evaluation of online help systems" (20). The authors believe that researchers will be particularly interested in Chapters 3, 7, and 8. In Chapter 3 they "outline [their] model of the users of online help systems and in Chapters 7 and 8 [they] show how that model can be used to design an evaluation tool for rating the effectiveness of help systems that support a variety of software applications across different computer platforms" (20). Chapters 2, 4, 5, and 6 will be of special interest to practitioners. In Chapters 2 and 4 the authors "summarize research relevant to designing online help systems and provide advice on how to apply this knowledge to different design situations; Chapters 5 and 6 present the concerns of actual online help designers and outline strategies for effectively evaluating online help systems" (20). An appendix contains a "Help Design Evaluation Questionnaire (HDEQ)" to be used "to evaluate the design of any online help system" (217).

291   **Horton, William K.** *Designing and Writing Online Documentation: Hypermedia for Self-Supporting Products*. **2nd ed. New York: Wiley, 1994. Index. 439p.**

The author states that online documentation "requires a rapid and convenient way of retrieving and displaying that information" and that this book "explains how to design and write such documents" (iii). He calls this book a "style guide," which "tells what to do, but does not present system-specific details of how to do it" (iii). The overall organization of the book breaks down into 14 chapters which are divided among eight categories: overview, managing, access, architecture, user-interface, media, specific forms, and conclusion (iv–v). The chapters are further divided into small sections of one to six pages. Some of the questions the book answers are: "Why should I put my document online?" "How do I plan and manage an online documentation project?" "How do I make information accessible?" "How do I design documents to help users at work?" and "How will online documentation change my job?" (iv–v).

292   **Mirel, Barbara. "Cognitive Processing, Text Linguistics, and Documentation Writing."** *Journal of Technical Writing and Communication* **18.2 (1988): 111–33.**

In this article, the author provides a set of "guiding principles that account for the multidimensional functions of language in the communication act of a user's manual" (111). The author derives these principles from a review of "findings from research in cognitive processing and text linguistics" (111). The author then demonstrates "how one would apply these principles to a widely used manual" (112). "For too long," the author believes, "documentation has been regarded as referential prose, the consequent assumption being that information in manuals is static and a direct reflection of the external reality it describes. With our growing awareness of reader's schema and multidimensional strategies for processing information to create meaning, we can no longer rest confident that so long as information is just given, readers will be informed. How information is given makes all the difference" (130).

293 **Price, Jonathan, and Henry Korman.** *How to Communicate Technical Information: A Handbook of Software and Hardware Documentation*. **Redwood City, CA: Benjamin/Cummings, 1993. Index. Bib. 402p.**

The authors' goal with this book is to show new and experienced technical writers how to create "convivial" software or hardware manuals, manuals which "empower people to do what they want" (viii). The 21 chapters are divided into three parts. In Part 1, "Planning," the authors move the reader through the prewriting stage. The reader learns how to study the subject and audience and to plan what documents to write, schedule, and budget. In Part 2, "Writing," some of the topics discussed are tables of contents and introductions, tutorials, computer-based training, reference materials, indexes and glossaries, and online help. Part 3, "Revising," covers the process of revision and includes advice about feedback, rewriting, refining style, updating manuals, and reviewing other manuals. At the end of each chapter, the authors provide a checklist that covers the chapter's main points. The bibliography is organized to correspond to individual chapters. This book is a revision of Jonathan Price's earlier book, *How to Write a Computer Manual* (Benjamin, 1984), which dealt specifically with software documentation.

294 **Weiss, Edmond H.** *How to Write Usable User Documentation*. **2nd ed. Phoenix: Oryx, 1991. Index. 267p.**

The author states, "The purpose of this book is to enhance the power and professionalism of everyone who plans, designs, or writes user documentation" (viii). The book is divided into three parts. Part 1, "Toward a Science of User Documentation," provides an overview of user documentation, explains ways user documentation succeeds and fails, and discusses the criterion of usability in user documentation. Part 2, "A Structured Approach to User Documentation," moves the reader through the "life cycle" of user documentation: analysis, outline, storyboard, assembly, editing, testing, and maintenance. Part 3, "Online Documentation and Internal Support," covers "User Documentation without Books," "Strategies for Online Documentation," and, in an afterword, looks "Into the Next Century." Appendixes include "Excerpt from the User Support Plan," "Illustrative Modular Outlines for User Manuals," Illustrative Module Specs," "Illustrative 2-Page Modules," "Glossary of Selected Terms," and "Books and Periodicals for Documenters."

295 **Woolever, Kristin R., and Helen M. Loeb.** *Writing for the Computer Industry*. **Englewood Cliffs, NJ: Prentice-Hall, 1994. Index. 208p.**

This book, the author states, "is designed to help new technical writers and technical writing students understand the basics of writing computer documentation" (ix–x). Chapter 1 provides an overview of the types of computer documentation. Chapters 2 and 3 cover analysis of audience and purpose. Beginning with Chapter 4, the author "takes writers through the documentation process, from the preliminary planning to the final edits" (x). Each chapter contains exercises so that, the author suggests, in addition to acting as a reference, the book can be used as a classroom text, a company training manual, or a self-paced tutorial.

Visual and Graphic Design

296   **Barton, Ben F., and Marthalee S. Barton. "Ideology and the Map: Toward a Postmodern Visual Design Practice."** *Studies in Technical Communication: Selected Papers from the 1991 CCCC and NCTE Meeting.* **Ed. Brenda R. Sims. Denton, TX: U of North Texas, 1991. 35–71.**

This article examines how maps illustrate that visuals are not simply neutral representations but are "complicit with social-control mechanisms inextricably linked to power and authority" (39). Barton and Barton discuss, in particular, how "Rules of inclusion determine whether something is mapped, what aspects of a thing are mapped, and what representational strategies and devices are used to map those aspects" (40). They also show how "rules of exclusion" repress ideas and interests. Moreover, they point out how differences can be repressed by naming practices, particularly in the use of proper names. To demonstrate how representational strategies attempt to manipulate the viewer, they show two maps of the London Underground, one from 1924 and the more recent London Underground Diagram (LUD). The original map demonstrated how "central London is seriously congested" (52), while the more recent one gives the "overall impression of a rather homogeneous structure" (53).

What is needed, the authors assert, "is a new politics of design, one authorizing heterodoxy—a politics where difference is not excluded or repressed, as before, but valorized" (57). They describe in some detail their own proposal for a postmodern visual design practice that involves collage and palimpsest: "Clearly, the governing aesthetic of the visual as collage-palimpsest is not the modernist 'less is more' but rather the postmodernist 'less is a bore'—an aesthetic that privileges complexity over simplicity and eclecticism over homogeneity, an aesthetic that tends toward the fragmentary and the local, an aesthetic that renounces the driving ambition toward Unity with a capital 'U' and 'disperses itself among discreet claims and observations'" (66).

297   **Barton, Ben F., and Marthalee S. Barton. "Simplicity in Visual Representation: A Semiotic Approach."** *Iowa State Journal of Business and Technical Communication* **1.1 (January 1987): 9–26.**

Stating that simplicity, "as an ideal in the design of visual representations, has not received systematic attention" (9), the authors review and analyze various concepts of visual simplicity. Using Charles Morris's communication model, they divide their discussion into his trichotomy of communication levels: "the syntactic, the semantic, and the pragmatic" (9). They then discuss methods of limiting visual clutter and enhancing element compatibility as well as matters of referents and representations. After presenting an analysis of the incompatibilities that threaten visual simplicity, the authors conclude: "Should we discard the notion of simplicity as an ideal in visual design? Our analysis leads us to answer 'No'" (23). An extensive list of references follows the article.

298   **Benson, Philippa J. "Writing Visually: Design Considerations in Technical Publications."** *Technical Communication* **32.4 (1985): 35–39.**

Serving "as a refresher for experienced technical writers and as a primer for those writers who are new to the field of document design," this article discusses "the merging roles of writers and graphic designers, and provides some guidelines that document designers can use to reveal and reinforce the structure of a text" (35). According to the author, "research in cognitive psychology, instructional design, reading, and graphic design indicates that documents are most usable when the information in them is apparent both visually and syntactically" (35). Emphasizing that writers and designers must understand the constraints on document design, Benson provides several guidelines and examples for achieving effective design through the use of fonts, line length, leading, margins, white space, headings, graphs, tables, flowcharts, and diagrams.

299   **Carter, Rob, Ben Day, and Philip Meggs.** *Typographic Design: Form and Communication.* **New York: Van Nostrand Reinhold, 1985. Index. Bib. 262p.**

This richly illustrated book is both commentary and guide for understanding the use of typography in design. It presents a wide variety of semiotic analysis of, for example, photographs and various typefaces. At one point, the authors show a typographic rendering of Edgar Allan Poe's "The Bells," which employs various typefaces and sizes to interpret the sounds of the poem. The authors suggest, "Effective typographic messages result from the combination of logic and intuitive judgment" (70). The book contains eight chapters: "The Evolution of Typography," "The Anatomy of Typography," "Syntax and Communication," "Legibility," "Typographic Technology," "Typographic Design Education," "Case Studies in Typographic Design," and "Type Specimens." The authors also include a glossary and various other sections related to using typography.

300   **Cross, Anita. "Design Intelligence: The Use of Codes and Language Systems in Design."** *Design Studies* **7.1 (January 1986): 14–19.**

This article contends that "designerly" thought is essentially nonverbal and "differs from abstract thinking, but can be engaged, externalized and progressed by 'modeling' language systems, e.g. drawings, diagrams and constructions" (15). Therefore, the article focuses on examining the relationships between designerly thought (i.e., design intelligence) and appropriate language systems. The article addresses the issue of a biological component in design intelligence, as well as its relationship to various symbolic code systems. The article concludes that "the ways of thinking peculiar to design are inextricably linked to non-verbal codes or languages which designers acquire and use" (18).

301   **Dragga, Sam. "Evaluating Pictorial Illustrations."** *Technical Communication Quarterly* **1.2 (Spring 1992): 47–62.**

According to the author, "Technical writing teachers . . . often have a solid grounding in the theory of verbal composition, but little experience or familiarity with visual communication" (47). He contends that this lack of expertise comes at increasing cost given "the increasingly common substitution of pictures for words in a wide variety of promotional and instructional materials" (48). Using a theory of pictorial images presented by Evelyn Goldsmith in her book *Research into Illustration,* Dragga presents a 12-cell matrix that incorporates three levels of visual communication (syntactic, semantic, and pragmatic), each of which is affected by four factors (unity, location, emphasis, and text parallels). He suggests that the questions raised by the matrix may be used as a heuristic to address "issues of aim and audience and thus [give] technical writers a rhetorical orientation to visual information, corresponding to their orientation to verbal information" (60–61). Dragga writes, "Focusing on the composition of pictorial illustrations allows inexperienced communicators to improve their visual skills, develop their vocabulary, and ultimately advance to a universal theory that assesses the merits of their illustrations relative to accompanying illustrations, the design of the page, the typography, the binding, and so on" (48).

302   Duffy, Thomas M., and Robert Waller, eds. *Designing Usable Texts*. **Orlando: Academic P, 1985. Indexes. 423p.**

In this collection, *text* is defined broadly; in fact, the range of subject matter examined in terms of design is quite broad within the 14 articles. The book is divided into four parts. Part I contains a single article, "On the Designing and Understanding of Written Texts" by David R. Olson, who places text in a "general theoretical framework of communications in which text is an utterance" (xiv). He concludes that design is "in relatively good hands" considering the tradition of publishing and illustrating together with the growing body of research (14).

Part II, "Authoring, Editing, and the Production Process," contains six chapters that include "Training Authors of Informative Documents" by Daniel B. Felker, Janice C. Redish, and Jane Peterson; "Readability Formulas: What's the Use?" by Thomas M. Duffy; and "Lessons in Text Design from an Instructional Perspective" by John F. Carter. Part III, "Graphics and Design Alternatives," contains four chapters that include "Studying Strategies and Their Implications for Textbook Design" by Thomas H. Anderson and Bonnie B. Armbruster and "Using Pictorial Language: A Discussion of the Dimensions of the Problem" by Michael Twyman. Part IV, "Identifying Information Requirements," contains three chapters: "Understanding Readers and Their Uses of Text" by T. Sticht, "Modeling Users and Their Use of Technical Manuals" by Richard P. Kern, and "Testing Design Alternatives: A Comparison of Procedures" by Gary M. Schumacher and Robert Waller. This collection blends well the work of design practitioners and researchers.

303   Hartley, James. *Designing Instructional Text*. **2nd ed. London, Kogan Page; New York: Nichols, 1985. Index. Bib. 175p.**

The author states that this book is "intended to give some general guidelines for producers of instructional materials. The guidelines are based upon current practice—particularly as employed by typographers—and upon a critical reading of relevant research. This research has increased dramatically in the interval between the first edition (1978) and the second one (1985)" (7). The first 12 chapters cover various specific topics, such as page size, typefaces, and illustrations, as well as discussion of more general issues, such as basic planning decisions, theory into practice, and alternatives to prose. The last three chapters cover listing information, designing electronic text, and evaluating instructional text. The chapters are followed by an annotated bibliography as well as subject and author indexes. The chapters are generously illustrated with examples of the principles the author presents.

304   **Jonassen, David H., ed.** *The Technology of Text: Principles for Structuring, Designing, and Displaying Text.* **2 vols. Englewood Cliffs, NJ: Educational Technology, 1982/1985. Index. 478p./442p.**

This two-volume collection of essays examines, as the editor states in Volume One, "the technology of sequencing, structuring, designing, and laying-out of the printed page, whether that text is reproduced on paper or in electronic signals on a cathode ray tube" (ix). Three years later, in Volume Two, the editor suggests, "The expansion of computer applications in all facets of our existence will eventually make *computer-based text* as common [as] or even more common than paper-based text" (xiii).

Volume One is composed of 22 essays divided into four sections: "Implicit Structures in Text," "Explicit Techniques for Structuring Text," "Electronic Text," and "Individual Differences and Learning from Text." Volume Two contains 18 essays which are divided into seven sections: "Learner Processing of Text," "Signaling the Structure of Content," "Controlling the Processing of Text," "Providing Access to Information in Text," "Electronic Display of Text," "Designing Special Purpose Text," and "Evaluating Textual Materials." Most essays in both volumes are well illustrated and include references to a wide variety of interdisciplinary sources in such areas as visual design, educational technology, human factors, computer design, and learning theory.

305   **Killingsworth, M. Jimmie, and Scott P. Sanders. "Complementarity and Compensation: Bridging the Gap between Writing and Design."** *Technical Writing Teacher* **17.3 (Fall 1990): 204–21.**

Citing the trend toward "semiotically diverse ('iconic-mosaic')" texts commonly produced through desktop publishing and similar means, the authors note the growing need "to develop special principles and procedures for rhetorical analysis to help student writers reconcile the often competitive demands of prose and graphical features within the same text" (204). They suggest that two especially useful principles for developing such a reconciliation are complementarity and compensation. They define *complementarity* as a descriptive principle asserting that "the introduction of any textual feature cues readers to a deep structural change" and *compensation* as "an instrumental principle asserting the need for choices among different textual elements [meaning] . . . in every revision . . . something is lost and something is gained" (204). In their study of three cases of student work, they find that "because of compensation, the gap between writing and design is never completely closed, but can be effectively bridged by a rhetoric of complementarity" (204). They conclude by offering professional writing teachers suggestions to "improve the chances of harmony between writing and design" (220).

306   **Kostelnick, Charles. "The Rhetoric of Text Design in Professional Communication."** *Technical Writing Teacher* **17.3 (Fall 1990): 189–202.**

Because the rhetoric of text design is "shaped by contextual variables, such as the purpose of the communication and the proximity of visual cues within the document, as well as by the reader's familiarity with visual conventions," the author underscores the need for technical communicators to consider the importance of these factors in the production of documents (189). He divides the remainder of the article into "Visual Rhetoric and Contextual Variables," "Visual Language as a Structural Tool," "Visual Language as a Stylistic Tool," and "Visual Conventions and Reader Expectations" and includes several figures to illustrate various rhetorical strategies. He concludes, "Because desktop publishing fosters typographical variety, technical communicators need to consider the rhetorical aspects of visual language if they intend to design reader-oriented documents. To use visual language effectively, technical communicators must respond to immediate contextual variables, just as they do when they write" (201).

307 Margolin, Victor, ed. *Design Discourse: History, Theory, Criticism*. Chicago: U of Chicago P, 1989. 291p.

This book is an anthology of essays which attempt "to ground design studies in some of the recent theories that are opening up new directions in research" (9–10). The essays are organized into three sections: "After the Modernists," "The Interpretation of Design," and "Writing Design History." The essays in the first section "are united only in their departure from or opposition to modernist conceptions of design"; in the second section, "the focus is on how we give meaning to design"; in the third section, the essays are grouped separately "to emphasize the importance of understanding how the study of design's past depends on assumptions of what it currently is" (10). The author observes that the valuable research in current design studies is fragmented, with "a fairly sharp bifurcation" existing "between theories of design, and studies of design as a part of culture" (286). Numerous photographs and other illustrations are included.

308 Moore, Patrick, and Chad Fitz. "Using Gestalt Theory to Teach Document Design and Graphics." *Technical Communication Quarterly* 2.4 (Fall 1993): 389–410.

This article develops Ben Barton and Marthalee Barton's suggestion that "we apply principles from Gestalt psychology to improve the visual literacy of students" (389). According to Moore and Fitz, Gestalt "psychology principles of figure-ground segregation, symmetry, closure, proximity, good continuation, and similarity provide a simple yet powerful analytic vocabulary for discussing page layout and graphics" (389). In addition, these principles "explain many difficulties that readers have in processing texts and graphics, and they explain why well-designed pages and graphics are effective" (389). The authors begin with an overview of Gestalt theory and use several illustrations to discuss the six principles mentioned above. After presenting classroom exercises that students can use to develop document design skills, the authors conclude with a comparison of Gestalt theory and rhetoric.

309 Pinelli, Thomas E., Virginia M. Cordle, and Robert McCullough. "A Survey of Typography, Graphic Design, and Physical Media in Technical Reports." *Technical Communication* 33.2 (1986): 75–80.

Basing their investigation on a study of the NASA technical report, the authors analyzed 50 technical reports gathered from industry, research institutions, and government agencies "to determine current practice with regard to (1) typography, including composition method, type style, type size, and margin treatment; (2) graphic design, including layout and imposition of material on the page; and (3) physical media, including paper, ink, and binding methods" (75). Comparing their results with the "experimental/theoretical literature and . . . the results of a reader preference survey," they conclude, among other things, that "Ragged right margins promote greater legibility and are preferred by readers over justified right margins, illustrative material (e.g., tables and figures) should be aligned with the text, and text printed in black ink on white or off-white paper promotes greater legibility and is preferred by readers" (75). Pointing out that the factors affecting the design, layout, and production of a technical report are dynamic rather than static, they conclude that their "'snapshot' of typical technical report publication practices . . . should not be viewed as the ideal or epitome, but rather as the product of the tradeoffs among these factors" (79).

310   **Porter, James E., and Sullivan, Patricia A. "Repetition and the Rhetoric of Visual Design."** *Repetition in Discourse: Interdisciplinary Perspectives*, Vol. 2. **Ed. Barbara Johnstone. Norwood, NJ: Ablex, 1994. 114–29.**

Examining the role repetition plays in professional writing, this chapter reports "on a longitudinal study of a developing professional writer who wrote, tested, and revised a tutorial for using the page layout program Aldus Pagemaker" (114). According to the authors, "Repetition is a vital element in the design of professional documents— but . . . its use has to be guided by rhetorical considerations" (114). In the first portion of the chapter, the authors discuss theoretical aspects of rhetoric and professional writing, as well as those of rhetoric and visual design theory. They then present the methodology, results, and discussion of the portion of their study in which the subject anticipates what users will do with his tutorial. They conclude, "Repetition can help establish a common order and/or familiar framework for the audience, but in some situations familiarity can also undermine the aims of the discourse" (127–28).

311   **Rubens, Phillip M. "A Reader's View of Text and Graphics: Implications for Transactional Text."** *Journal of Technical Writing and Communication* **16.1/2 (1986): 73–86.**

According to the author, this article surveys "the major directions of theory and research applied to the creation of a *visual grammar*" and considers "three significant areas of graphic activities—*layout, typography*, and *illustrations*" (74). The author also assesses "the importance of major studies and ways in which they could prove useful for both teachers and practitioners" (74). He concludes that despite what is known about this subject, "It is still impossible to account for everything that happens when a reader encounters either a text or a visual. The transaction that flows from page to eye to brain to action is still, in some vague and indefinable way, touched with an element of mystery" (84).

312   **Schriver, Karen A. "Document Design from 1980 to 1989: Challenges That Remain."** *Technical Communication* **36.4 (November 1989): 316–31.**

According to the author, "This article provides a snapshot of the evolution of document design, includes a comprehensive list of research references, and stresses the need to integrate theory and research with practice" (316). Defining *document design* as "the theory and practice of creating comprehensible, usable, and persuasive texts," she provides diagrams to depict and discuss the evolving areas of theory and research that influenced document design in 1980 and those that influenced it a decade later (316). She concludes with "an agenda of research questions for document design in the 1990s" (325). Her extensive list of references reflects the various research that has been conducted on document design.

313   **Tufte, Edward R.** *Envisioning Information.* **Cheshire, CT: Graphics P, 1990. Index. 126p.**

"The world is complex, dynamic, multidimensional; the paper is static, flat. How are we to represent the rich visual world of experience and measurement on mere flatland?" (9). To help answer that question, the author presents principles "that have specific visual consequences, governing the design, editing, analysis, and critique of data representations. These principles help to identify and to explain design excellence—why some displays are better than others" (9). This book itself is lavishly designed with many full-color illustrations. Chapter 1, "Escaping Flatland," presents a variety of design strategies to reproduce dimensions and "data density" (richness). Chapter 2, "Micro/Macro Readings," treats the reduction of clutter and the revision of illustrations that contain too many details. Chapters 3 through 6 treat "Layering and Separation," "Small Multiples," "Color and Information," and "Narrative of Space and Time." Much like a "studio" course, the author's theory is communicated as much through an appreciation of the examples as through his words.

314   **Tufte, Edward R.** *The Visual Display of Quantitative Information.* **Cheshire, CT: Graphics P, 1983. Index. 197p.**

While stressing the integrity of data, the author treats the display of quantitative information as much as a visual enterprise as a mathematical or mechanical exercise. In the first chapter, for example, he provides nine principles for graphic display, including that graphical displays should "induce the viewer to think about the substance rather than about methodology, graphic design, the technology of graphic production, or something else" (13). But displays should also "avoid distorting what the data have to say" and "be closely integrated with the statistical and verbal descriptions" (13). The rest of Part I, "Graphical Practice," examines effective and ineffective graphics. Part II, "Theory of Data Graphics," containing six chapters, "provides a language for discussing graphics and a practical theory of data graphics. Applying to most visual displays of quantitative information, the theory leads to changes and improvements in design, suggests why some graphics might be better than others, and generates new types of graphics" (10). While the author's verbal explanations are useful, his examples are far more eloquent in their ability to teach the reader.

INTERDISCIPLINARY CONNECTIONS

The following lists are intended to serve as starting points, particularly for new instructors, for study and further research in important interdisciplinary areas.

COMMUNICATION AND CULTURE

315 Bakhtin, M. M. *Speech Genres and Other Late Essays*. Trans. Vern M. McGee. Ed. Caryl Emerson and Michael Holquist. Austin: U of Texas P, 1986. Index. 177p.

In the book's title essay, "The Problem of Speech Genres," Bakhtin defines the *utterance* as a unit of speech and distinguishes it from the sentence, which is a unit of language. "We speak only in definite speech genres, that is, all our utterances have definite and relatively stable typical *forms of construction of the whole*" (78). Speech genres are acquired through assimilation in a manner similar to the acquisition of native language abilities. "The better our command of genres, the more freely we employ them, the more fully and clearly we reveal our own individuality in them (where this is possible and necessary), the more flexibly and precisely we reflect the unrepeatable situation of communication—in a word, the more perfectly we implement our free speech plan" (80). Utterance and speech genres are based in context—unlike the units of language (words and sentences), which "lack this quality of being directed or addressed to someone: these units belong to nobody and are addressed to nobody" (99).

The final three essays in this book—"The Problem of the Text in Linguistics, Philology, and the Human Sciences," "From Notes Made in 1970–71," and "Toward a Methodology for the Human Sciences"—are a series of entries taken from Bakhtin's notebooks. The author's fragmented notes cover several topics, including texts, authorship, laughter, and dialogue.

316 Brown, Penelope, and Steven C. Levinson. *Politeness: Some Universals in Language Usage*. Cambridge: Cambridge UP, 1987. Indexes. Bib. 345p.

This book is a close, sociolinguistic analysis of the nature and practice of politeness across different cultures. The authors determine universal principles of politeness in their investigations of human interaction. As Brown and Levinson define it, politeness "is basic to the production of social order, and a precondition of human cooperation, so that any theory which provides an understanding of this phenomenon at the same time goes to the foundations of human social life" (xiii). The work reissues the 1978 edition in order to bring itself up to date on recent theoretical work in anthropology, linguistics, psychology, and studies in ritual. Drawing on the work of Goffman and Durkheim, the authors examine the formal structures of aggression and its control that goes far beyond the niceties of "good manners" or etiquette.

Their research takes them into ethnographic research (e.g., Geertz [318]) as they explore how different kinds of speech acts resonate in different contexts and in different languages. Their updated research also takes into account recent work in language, power, feminism ("genderlects"), and child psychology.

317 **Fisher, Walter R.** *Human Communication as Narration: Toward a Philosophy of Reason, Value, and Action*. Columbia: U of South Carolina P, 1987. Indexes. **201p.**

In this book, Fisher proposes his narrative perspective of human communication. He asserts, for example, that "all forms of human communication need to be seen fundamentally as stories—symbolic interpretations of aspects of the world occurring in time and shaped by history, culture, and character" (xi). Fisher builds on past theory and research to create a comprehensive explanation of human communication and its logic. He believes that human beings draw on known narratives to understand one another and to create new narratives in the process.

Fisher begins in the first two chapters with a discussion of the history and underpinnings of his perspective. Through this discussion, he sets up the basis of his arguments and tenets. In Chapters Three through Six, he explicates his narrative viewpoint. The last few chapters are devoted to applications of Fisher's perspective to different forms of communication. Chapter Seven looks at the political rhetoric of former president Ronald Reagan, and Chapter Eight looks at two famous literary works: *The Great Gatsby* and *Death of a Salesman*. Chapter Nine uses the narrative perspective to discuss and explain the philosophical debate between Socrates and Callicles in *Gorgias*. Fisher rounds out the text with a final chapter reiterating the points of his perspective.

318 **Geertz, Clifford.** *The Interpretation of Cultures: Selected Essays*. New York: Basic Books, 1973. Index. **470p.**

In this work of interpretive anthropology, Geertz rejects, on the one hand, overly cognitive approaches to culture and society and, on the other, overly psychologistic (and behavioristic) approaches. Geertz's own method is borrowed from Gilbert Ryle's idea of "thick description," which—for Geertz—recommends that anthropologists pay attention to the peculiarly rich semiotics of a given culture, its complexly ordered symbolic content. "As interworked systems of construable signs," Geertz writes, "culture is not a power, something to which social events, behaviors, institutions, or processes can be casually attributed; it is a context, something within which they can be intelligibly—that is, thickly—described" (14). Geertz is particularly skeptical of ethnography that transmutes cultures into folklore and collects data without any explicit attempt to interpret its meaning. An ethnography enlivened by Geertz's interpretive principles is nontotalizing and intrinsically incomplete. The book demonstrates these principles as the author offers cultural analyses of a wide variety of subjects: nationalism, revolution, ethnicity, urbanization, status, death, time, and the multitude of concrete, lived contexts in which these things become meaningful. It is in the symbolic realm of culture, therefore, that Geertz finds the most palpable, and deeply interpretable, resources for his anthropological inquiry. Geertz continues and expands his work in literary/semiotic anthropology in *Local Knowledge: Further Essays in Interpretive Anthropology* (Basic Books, 1983).

319 **Hall, Edward T.** *Beyond Culture*. Garden City, NY: Anchor/Doubleday, 1976. Indexes. Bib. **256p.**

This work examines cultural understandings of time and "context." Hall suggests that to varying degrees cultures view time as "monochronic" (M-time) or "polychronic" (P-time). M-time cultures are those which view time as tangible and linear, stressing the completion of tasks. P-time cultures stress the simultaneous occurrence of many things and emphasize the completion of human transactions rather than holding to schedules. By *context*, Hall refers to how much or how little individuals assume others understand about a subject under discussion. In "high-context" communications, the participants already understand the context and thus do not feel a need to exchange much background information. In "low-context" communication, the participants assume little knowledge and communicate in great detail. Two other works, *The Silent Language* (Doubleday, 1959) and *The Dance of Life* (Anchor/Doubleday, 1983), are further explications of Hall's theories of time, context, and culture. In 1990 he published (with Mildred Reed Hall) a book for businesspeople that summarizes his earlier works: *Understanding Cultural Differences: Germans, French, and Americans* (Intercultural Press).

320   **Hirokawa, Randy Y., and Marshall Scott Poole, eds. *Communication and Group Decision-Making*. Beverly Hills, CA: Sage, 1986. 315p.**

Seeing the need to organize work done on the relationship between communication and group decision making, editors Hirokawa and Poole compiled this collection of 12 essays. The group communication studies in this book focus on the group interaction process and how it relates to group outcome, instead of concentrating exclusively on group performance.

This book is divided into four parts. Part I is dedicated to decision development and effectiveness; its essays address the developmental processes, faulty group decision making, and counteractive functions of communication. Part II deals with communication and information processing; these essays address the topics of inferential errors and understanding how decisional choices develop during group interaction. The essays in Part III examine the role of communication in influencing decisional choices, including the issues of influence, argumentation, conflict, and leadership. Part IV, "Innovative Theoretical Perspectives," includes essays that summarize the development of theories related to the relationship between group communication processes and decision making. Specifically, the essays discuss the symbolic convergence theory and the theory of structuration.

This book not only provides an overview of current scholarly work in the area of communication and group decision making but also "aims to stimulate thought, to promote programmatic research, and to produce models for further development" (17).

321   **Hofstede, Geert H. *Cultures and Organizations: Software of the Mind*. New York: McGraw-Hill, 1991.**

Following the publication of *Culture's Consequences: International Differences in Work-Related Values* (Sage, 1984), this "new book," according to the author, "does what should have been done earlier: it addresses itself to any interested reader. It avoids scientific jargon where possible and explains it where necessary; a glossary is added for this purpose" (ix). The book's 10 chapters and an appendix are divided into four parts. In Part I, the author "lays the foundation for a good understanding of the rest of the book by explaining what we mean when we talk about 'culture,' and by providing a small vocabulary of essential terms" (xi). In Part II, the author "deals with differences among cultures at [the] *national level*. The author "deals with *organizational cultural differences*" in Part III and, in Part IV, "with the *practical implications* of culture differences and similarities" covered earlier in the book (xi). A final section, "added as an appendix," is "addressed at research colleagues" and "deals with how to collect reliable information about cultural differences" (xii).

---

322   **Kincaid, D. Lawrence, ed.** *Communication Theory: Eastern and Western Perspectives*. **San Diego, CA: Academic P, 1987. Index. Bib. 364p.**

In this collection of essays, Kincaid examines theoretical approaches to communication according to Eastern and Western experiences and ideologies. Eastern perspectives are derived from China, Korea, Japan, and India. The Western perspectives are predominantly representative of the United States.

The 23 chapters are divided into three sections. Part 1 explains basic Asian perspectives, which Chung-Ying Cheng expands with a detailed summary of important philosophical principles from Chinese literature. Cheng's discussion examines many concepts discussed throughout Part 1, including "indivisible *oneness* and *unity* of reality, how knowledge arises in an *indefinite* and *ever-changing* process, the *dialectical* nature of change, and the *paradoxical* nature of ordinary language" (12). Other articles include the influences of Confucianism and Buddhism on Korean communication; the effects of Taoism as well as Confucianism and Buddhism on Japanese relations; and discussions of the effects of native Indian philosophy on communication.

Part 2 focuses on U.S. communication theory. One author analyzes the three main American paradigms (control, network/convergence, and information seeking) and introduces a new one: the *autopoiesis* paradigm. Among other topics included are cultural elements of communication, constructivist ideas, Aristotelian views, and the possibility of developing a science of human communication. Part 3 is the "synthesis" of the East and West. This section focuses on comparing and contrasting perspectives as a way to encourage combining ideas. One author argues that a common origin for Eastern and Western "ways of thinking" exists.

---

323   **Logan, Robert K.** *The Alphabet Effect: The Impact of the Phonetic Alphabet on the Development of Western Civilization*. **New York: Morrow, 1986. Index. Bib. 272p.**

This book traces the beginnings of Western civilization through the writing system, the phonetic alphabet. As do others, Logan argues that the Western writing system has affected several facets of contemporary life. He asserts that the alphabet "has influenced the development of [Western] thought patterns, [Western] social institutions," and the senses that Westerners have of themselves (18). Furthermore, Logan states, "The alphabet has contributed to the development of codified law, monotheism, abstract science, deductive logic, and individualism," to name a few outcomes (18). Logan's book is an extension of alphabet-effect studies by Harold Innis and Marshall McLuhan. However, this author's theme is based on the notion that "a medium of communication is not merely a passive conduit for the transmission of information but rather an active force in creating new social patterns and new perceptual realities" (24). Much of the book compares the development of Eastern and

Western writing systems with an interesting discussion on the technologizing of the alphabet effect: the printing press. The book ends with a chapter on the "electronic age" of the alphabet, suggesting how the alphabet may function into the future.

324   **Searle, John R.** *Speech Acts: An Essay in the Philosophy of Language.* **Cambridge: Cambridge UP, 1969. Index. 203p.**

Searle's book follows the Wittgensteinian dispensation known as "ordinary language philosophy," which is a way of describing the nature and principles of communication by examining everyday expressions in their contexts. For Searle, the basic unit of linguistic communication is not merely the symbol, word, or sentence but rather "the production or issuance of the symbol or word or sentence in the performance of the speech act" (16). Thus, according to Searle, the study of language and the study of individual speech acts are deeply complementary. The majority of the book is taken up with closely argued analyses of expressions and kinds of speech acts, as the author takes on some of the most difficult problems in modern philosophy of language: the nature of meaning, reference, predication, universals, and how one derives *ought* from *is* (the fact-value distinction). Searle is particularly interested in speech acts he calls "illocutionary"—by which he refers to linguistic utterances where the meaning is explicitly "performed" (as in the cases of a promise). Searle's hypothesis about speech acts is paralleled by "the principle of expressibility"—a principle that closes the distance between meaning, intention, understanding—and by the rules supervising all these elements of the act of communication. Searle believes that speaking a language is to engage in a rule-governed form of behavior and that these performances may be examined according to rules peculiar to their contexts.

325   **Shannon, Claude E., and Warren Weaver.** *The Mathematical Theory of Communication.* **Urbana, IL: U of Illinois P, 1949. 117p.**

This book comprises two technical papers written in the late 1940s that influenced theoretical perspectives of the communication process. In the first paper, "The Mathematical Theory of Communication," Shannon describes the process of communication as an engineering problem, where "the semantic aspects of communication are irrelevant" (3). The concepts are based on the five-part communication system made up of information source, transmitter, channel, receiver, and destination. Shannon uses a mathematical perspective to explain the fundamental principles and the problems involving three categories of communication systems: discrete (i.e., telegraph message), continuous (i.e., radio message), and mixed (i.e., speech message).

In the second paper, "Recent Contributions to the Mathematical Theory of Communication," Weaver explains the role Shannon's technical level of communication plays in understanding the communication process. This paper is divided into three sections that describe three levels of communication problems: technical (accuracy of transmitting symbols), semantic (preciseness of transmitting meaning), and effectiveness (meaning's affect on desired conduct). The second section reviews Shannon's main ideas, while minimizing his mathematical terminology. The third section examines the interrelationship of the three levels of communication problems. Weaver closes his paper asserting that a complete understanding of the communication process integrates technical, semantic, and effectiveness aspects.

326 **Terpstra, Vern, and Kenneth David.** *The Cultural Environment of International Business*. **3rd ed. Cincinnati: Southwestern, 1991. Index. Bib. 252p.**

This textbook attempts to "aid the reader in understanding the complexities of operating in foreign environments" by providing "an introduction to cultural anthropology adapted for business use" (v). The book's eight chapters are organized into three parts and are followed by an epilogue, appendix, and bibliography. The individual chapters are structured as follows: first, "the cultural system is defined"; next, the authors "sketch major ways in which the cultural system differs in various societies and world regions"; finally, the authors "draw attention to policy implications (for countries as well as companies) of the cultural system" (v). Exercises and minicases are also included in each chapter.

COMPOSITION AND RHETORIC

This list does not contain items included in *The Bedford Bibliography for Teachers of Writing*, Fourth Edition.

327 **Bizzell, Patricia, and Bruce Herzberg.** *The Bedford Bibliography for Teachers of Writing*. **4th ed. Boston: Bedford, 1996. Index. 149p.**

This bibliography "is intended as a guide for those who wish to extend their knowledge in this prospering discipline, knowledge that is essential for teaching English in colleges today" (vi). Following a section titled "A Brief History of Rhetoric and Composition," the authors group the 455 entries under five major headings: "Resources," "History and Theory," "Composing Processes," "Curriculum Development," and "Writing Programs." These major groupings are further divided into 26 subheadings. The authors state: "In the annotations of articles and single-author books we attempt to summarize the thesis and main points of the work. In annotations of edited collections . . . we characterize the central theme of the collection and then list several of the authors and essays included" (viii). In this edition, the authors have "included citations for works of history, theory, and research that are not, strictly speaking, 'immediately applicable to classroom practice' but which engage pressing issues for the discipline" (vi). The authors provide an index of authors cited.

328 **Ede, Lisa, and Andrea Lunsford.** *Singular Texts/Plural Authors: Perspectives on Collaborative Writing*. **Carbondale: Southern Illinois UP, 1990. Indexes. Bib. 284p.**

Citing their own long-standing collaborative relationship, Ede and Lunsford challenge the idea of writing as a solitary act of authorship and explore historical and theoretical aspects of collaborative writing. The book contains five chapters. "Old Beginnings" gives a background for this project. "Collaborative Writers at Work" describes in detail the collaborative practices of several writers in varied fields and presents survey results of seven major professional organizations' memberships regarding writing in the workplace. "The Concept of Authorship" reviews the history of "authorship" and discusses challenges to the traditional concept in contemporary literary criticism and in practices such as corporate authorship, honorary authorship in the sciences, and electronic media. "The Pedagogy of Collaboration" offers historical perspectives, provides a context for collaboration within composition studies, and suggests a pedagogy consistent with theories of plural authorship. "New Beginnings" notes that "we have only begun to scratch the surface of what it means to describe writing as a social or collaborative process. Every aspect we have touched on—in the work world and in technological practices, in theory, in pedagogy—calls for further investigation, exploration, elaboration" (141).

329   **Lanham, Richard A.** *The Electronic Word: Democracy, Technology, and the Arts*. **Chicago: U of Chicago P, 1993. Index. 285p.**

In this collection of essays, the author explores the impact of the computer on literacy and literacy's future in an electronic world. In the first six essays, Lanham presents "a case for traditional rhetorical education in a new form" (138). He argues that "electronic expression has come not to destroy the Western arts and letters, but to fulfill them" (xiii). Chapter One examines the effects, both current and future, of digitization on literature and other arts. Chapter Two suggests that, "in practice, the computer often turns out to be a rhetorical device as well as a logical one" and argues that our "fixation on logic has so bemused us that we have failed to notice the extraordinary way in which the computer has fulfilled the expressive agenda of twentieth-century art" (31). In Chapter Three, the author makes "some tentative readings in rhetoric's expanded domain and venture[s] a few preliminary observations on their relation to the electronic word" (55). In Chapter Four, he suggests that "three new conditions, or clusters of conditions have emerged [since the "Yale Faculty Report of 1828"]—social, technological, and theoretical—and [he believes] their convergence suggests a new kind of 'core' for the liberal arts" (102). Chapter Five takes a look at the electronic "textbook" and at the impact of electronic text. In Chapter Six, Lanham argues for the usefulness of the computer as a nonlinear tool to reestablish "traditional rhetorical education," and in Chapter Seven he confronts "the 'Q' question": "Can we really argue that the arts and letters make us better?" (xii). Chapters Eight and Nine are devoted to the examination of "a cluster of books . . . which, taken together, debate the convergence [the author has] sought to describe": "an interplay between democracy, technology, and the arts" (195). In Chapter Ten, the author concludes "by interiorizing . . . grave reservations about, and bright hopes for, the electronic word, putting them into an internal dialogue" with himself (258). "For if I feel optimistic," the author concludes, "about how we might use digital technology to sustain our public and private discourse, I also share the fears and longings for the book" (258).

330   **Lauer, Janice M., and J. William Asher.** *Composition Research: Empirical Designs*. **New York: Oxford UP, 1988. Indexes. 302p.**

Lauer and Asher provide composition researchers with chapter-long basic introductions of eight empirical methods: case studies, ethnographies, sampling and surveys, quantitative descriptive studies, prediction and classification studies, measurement, true experiments, and quasi-experiments. They leave out the statistical details, choosing instead to emphasize the theoretical bases of each design method while illustrating them with specific models from composition research. Throughout, they note the strengths and weaknesses of each design and emphasize that the field of composition benefits from a variety of research methods. They conclude by discussing how these methods might be applied to program evaluation.

331   **Nystrand, Martin.** *The Structure of Written Communication: Studies in Reciprocity between Writers and Readers*. Orlando: Academic P, 1986. Index. Bib. 234p.

The author notes that this book "presents a series of inquiries exploring the implications" of the principle of reciprocity for written communication, focusing in particular on "how the character of discourse is shaped by the premise of reciprocity between writer and reader" (ix). The volume's eight chapters are organized into two parts: "Writing" and "Learning to Write." Part I comprises five chapters that examine the writing process by addressing such topics as the "reader expectations as an essential factor in the writer's task," reciprocity as a principle of discourse, the doctrine of autonomous texts, and the differences "between topic-level elaborations and commentary-level elaborations" (x). Chapters Six through Eight make up Part II, which examines various issues involved with the process of learning to write, including the "process of socialization which learning to write represents" and the role of discourse communities and the importance of readers in the process of learning to write (x). As the author notes, overall Part II examines "the social foundations of text functionality" (x). The author warns, however, that readers "should not expect to find the sequential development of a single argument" in this book, but rather a "set of explorations—some theoretical in character, others empirical," noting that the book "reads more like spokes on a conceptual hub than episodes in a thematic narrative" (ix).

332   **Phelps, Louise Wetherbee.** *Composition as a Human Science: Contributions to the Self-Understanding of a Discipline*. New York: Oxford UP, 1988. Indexes. Bib. 268p.

The author suggests that this collection of essays "will be taken as 'theoretical,' part of the scholarly effort to define, locate, and legitimize composition studies as a discipline" (vii). However, as she argues, since "theory is autobiography," these essays, in addition to recording the story of "the development of composition from an adolescent stage in the 1970s toward self-reflective maturity," also chart her own "personal growth as a writer trying to help bring about that maturation" (vii–viii). In Part 1, "Constructing an Ecology of Composition," the author makes "explicit the project of theory as autobiography in terms of two concepts: context and change" (x). The six essays which make up Part 2, "The Process of Reconstruction" are a "set of philosophical sketches" which begin by addressing practical problems. In Chapters 6 and 7, the author takes her discussion to the level of metatheory in order to construct a "framework of frameworks, as an instrument for understanding acts of framing and the selves that enact them" (ix). The author concludes Part 2 by raising "the question of method in composition at this metalevel of analysis" (183). In Part 3, "Application," the author argues for a praxis which begins without assuming "an inherent, single, abstract, fixed relationship between theory and practice, or no relationship at all," but instead begins "with the hypothesis that this relationship is contextually defined and varies from one situation to another" (207). The author concludes: "Theory, disciplined by our own freedom to reflect and to experience, is for composition praxis an enabling fiction, and science and art are not, after all, so far apart" (241). Name and subject indexes are included.

333   **Rafoth, Bennett A., and Donald L. Rubin, eds.** *The Social Construction of Written Communication.* **Norwood, NJ: Ablex, 1988. Indexes. 330p.**

Editor Donald Rubin observes that this anthology is about both how "written discourse is shaped by the social context in which it takes place," and how "writing (and the activities surrounding it) shape social contexts" (1). The contributors' essays are organized thematically according to "four interrelated perspectives on the ways people socially construct written communication," including representing social contexts, creating social context through writing, creating texts collectively, and assigning social values to writing (2). The anthology in general "treats social accounts and cognitive accounts of written communication as fundamentally complementary" because "neither a social nor a cognitive focus provides by itself an adequate picture" (26). Rubin concludes, "the works in this volume testify to the essential interconnectedness, the unity, of these dimensions of the social construction of written communication" (29).

334   **Selfe, Cynthia L., and Richard J. Selfe, Jr. "The Politics of the Interface: Power and Its Exercise in Electronic Contact Zones."** *College Composition and Communication* **45.4 (December 1994): 480–504.**

After reflecting on the nature of computer design as culturally defined, the authors conclude, "In general, computer interfaces present reality as framed in the perspective of modern capitalism, thus, orienting technology along an existing axis of class privilege" (486). They describe, for example, how the computer's "desktop" contains objects that are most familiar to "the white-collar inhabitants of that corporate culture: manila folders, files, documents, telephones, fax machines, clocks and watches, and desk calendars" (486). They propose three general tactics to address this issue. They state, "one tactic of responding to the interested nature of computer interfaces has to do with encouraging a general level of critical awareness about technology issues on the part of both pre-service and in-service teachers" (496). A second tactic is "focused on the efforts of those faculty who are computers and composition specialists" (497), such as recommending they have greater access to software design. Their third suggestion is "to involve composition teachers and students in composition classes in an ongoing project to revise interfaces as texts. The purpose of these . . . sessions would be to come up with ideas for changing the interface to reflect a range of cultural, linguistic, and ideological perspectives" (499).

335   **Welch, Kathleen E.** *The Contemporary Reception of Classical Rhetoric:*

Appropriations of Ancient Discourse. **Hillsdale, NJ: Erlbaum, 1990. Index. Bib. 186p.**

"This book," the author states, "presents a version of how classical rhetoric has been studied since 1965 when Edward P. J. Corbett published *Classical Rhetoric for the Modern Student* and suggestions for those appropriations that are the most productive for current rhetoric and composition studies" (vii). The book is divided into two parts: "A Critique of Contemporary Appropriations of Classical Rhetoric," which contains two chapters; and "Rehistoricizing Classical Rhetoric," which covers the remaining four chapters. The author states that "the issues raised in [Chapter 1] include the 'interpretive options' not only of the contemporary reception of classical rhetoric but of the ways that language study in general in the United States promotes certain values and epistemologies over other ones" (33). In Chapter 2 "a version of thought frequently called 'logic,' but in fact not connected to traditional logic, provides the focus of concern" (37). "The 'logic' analyzed in this chapter," the author continues, "refers to the common idea of logic as exaggerated reason, hyperationalism, and a procedural way of thinking that not only excludes emotion but in fact looks down on it" (37). In Chapter 3, which marks the beginning of Part II, the author concludes that "Recognizing the subjective while giving up nostalgia and elitism in the study of classical rhetoric as well as of traditional literary studies offers many intellectual/pedagogical possibilities" (92). In the final three chapters—"Appropriating Plato's Rhetoric and Writing into Contemporary Rhetoric and Composition Studies," "Appropriating Competing Systems of Classical Greek Rhetoric: Considering Isocrates and Gorgias with Plato in the New Rhetoric of the Fourth Century B.C.," and "Classical Rhetoric and Contemporary Rhetoric and Composition Studies: Electrifying Classical Rhetoric"—the author presents some of those possibilities. A glossary of keywords is included.

MANAGEMENT AND ORGANIZATIONAL THEORY

336 **Alvesson, Matt, and Hugh Wilmott, eds. *Critical Management Studies*. London: Sage, 1992. Index. 230p.**

According to the editors, this collection of 10 essays is "directly informed by the tradition of Critical Theory"; they contribute to a growing literature that is "responsive to management as a social phenomenon meriting serious critical examination" (1). The present volume, they state, "arises from a two-day meeting, convened in Spring 1990," where "[t]wo kinds of contributions were invited" (2). The first are essays on accounting, information systems, marketing, operational research, and personnel/human resource management. "The second group of papers ranges more widely over the terrains of management and organization to explore how its theory and practice may be advanced by the emancipatory impulse of Critical Theory" (2). The editors say that in "each of the chapters, Critical Theory provides a point of reference for advancing critical studies of management," but they caution the reader that "although the emancipatory intent of Critical Theory provides a common thread upon which to string this collection, its contributors are more attracted to its emancipatory spirit than to the authoritative letter of any particular Critical Theorist" (3).

337   **Autry, James A. *Love and Profit: The Art of Caring Leadership*. New York: Morrow, 1991. 213p.**

This book is an unusual blend of management principles and poetry about the workplace by an author with strong credentials in both areas. Autry begins with some principles about work and management he considers essential. He states, for example, "Good management is largely a matter of love. Or if you're uncomfortable with that word, call it caring, because proper management involves caring for people, not manipulating them" (13). The book is divided into five parts, which are further divided into many small sections that serve as lessons. These lessons are interspersed with moving and remarkably accurate poems about office relationships, retirements, death, and the struggles of keeping life and work in balance. At one point, Autry (president and CEO of a publishing conglomerate) states, "It's easy to forget what the measurements are measuring. Every number—from productivity rates to salaries—is just a device contrived by people to measure the results of the enterprise of other people. For managers, the most important job is not measurement but motivation. And you can't motivate numbers" (39).

338   **Bell, Daniel. *The Coming of Post-Industrial Society: A Venture in Social Forecasting*. New York: Basic Books, 1973. Indexes. 507p.**

The thesis of this book, according to the author, "is that in the next thirty to fifty years we will see the emergence of what [he calls] 'the post-industrialist society'" (x). The author identifies this as "primarily a change in the social structure" and notes "its consequences will vary in societies with different political and cultural configurations" (x). In Chapter 1, "From Industrial to Post-Industrial Society: Theories of Social Development," the author discusses the theories of Karl Marx, Werner Sombart, Max Weber, Emil Lederer, Joseph Schumpeter, and Raymond Aron. In Chapter 2, "From Goods to Services: The Changing Shape of the Economy," the author "explores, within the framework of the United States, two of the five major dimensions of the post-industrialist society: the change from a goods-producing to a service economy, and the changes in the occupational slopes, wherein the professional and technical class emerges as the predominant occupational group in the post-industrial society" (41). In the first half of Chapter 3, "The Dimensions of Knowledge and Technology: The New Class Structure of Post-Industrial Society," the author seeks to define *knowledge* and *technology*. The latter half, according to the author, "is a detailed statistical effort to sketch the structure of the knowledge class . . . and the allocation of resources for a technical society" (42). In Chapter 4, "The Subordination of the Corporation: The Tension between the Economizing and Socializing Modes," the author "scrutinizes the logic of these two modes and argues that the balance between the two is a primary question for post-industrial society" (43). In Chapter 5, "Social Choice and Social Planning: The Adequacy of Our Concepts and Tools," the author sets forth "some propositions which question the older formulations and, in part, [proposes] a number of new ones which may be more adequate in understanding some perplexities about American life" (301). Finally, in Chapter 6, "'Who Will Rule?' Politicians and Technocrats in the Post-Industrial Society," the author "deals primarily with the relationship between technocratic and political decision-making" (43). The author concludes with a "forty-thousand-word Coda" which explores "the major questions that a post-industrial society will have to confront in the decades ahead" (xi).

339   **Daft, Richard L.** *Management*. **3rd ed. Fort Worth, TX: Dryden, 1994. Indexes. 824p.**

As in the first two editions of this textbook, this third edition attempts to capture "the excitement and adventure of organizational management" by offering "the most recent management thinking and research as well as the contemporary application of management ideas in organizations" (vii). However, this edition "is especially focused on shaping the future of management education by identifying and describing emerging management trends" (vii). These include international issues; employee participation and empowerment; a discussion of network, modular and team-based organization structures; and the impact of new information systems and production technologies. The book's 23 chapters are organized into six parts around the topics of planning, organizing, leading, and controlling. Part I introduces management, Part II examines planning, Part III considers organizing processes, Part IV focuses on leadership, Part V examines the controlling functions of management, and Part VI describes entrepreneurship and career management. The two appendixes "include supplementary material on organizational behavior and management science aids for decision making" (ix). The book also includes photo essays, i.e., "the use of photographs accompanied by detailed captions that describe management events and how they relate to chapter material" (ix).

340   **Drucker, Peter F.** *Post-Capitalist Society*. **New York: HarperCollins, 1993. Index. 232p.**

This account of the shift from capitalism to a knowledge society by Drucker, long-time educator and management philosopher, points to various trends in the global economy. The 12 chapters lead to his understanding of a *post-capitalist society* as "both a knowledge society and a society of organizations, each dependent on the other and yet each very different in its concepts, views, and values" (215). He suggests that the educated person in this society will need "to live and work simultaneously in two cultures—that of the 'intellectual,' who focuses on words and ideas, and that of the 'manager,' who focuses on people and work" (215). Under these circumstances, he suggests, communication is important because "All educated persons in the post-capitalist society will have to be prepared to *understand* both cultures" (216).

341   **Eccles, Robert G. and Nitin Nohria.** *Beyond the Hype: Rediscovering the Essence of Management*. **Cambridge, MA: Harvard Business School P, 1992. Index. Bib. 278p.**

"This book," the authors state, "is addressed to the thoughtful manager" (x). Thoughtful managers, the authors believe, are "eager for and open to new ideas," but "also have a healthy skepticism about the latest sure-fire solutions to what they realize are eternal problems that must be constantly managed" (xi). In this book, the authors "turn [their] attention to the triadic relation of rhetoric, action, and identity in managerial practice" (x). Following an introductory chapter, the book is divided into three parts: "Building an Action Perspective," "Rethinking Management Basics," and "Lessons for the Present." Each of these parts contains three chapters. In the introduction, the authors explain the concepts of rhetoric and identity "in as

plain a language as possible," and "build a case for why [they] think managers need
. . . to adopt the perspective that [they] are advocating" (2). Part I devotes a chapter
each to the concepts of rhetoric, action, and identity and, as the authors state, "sets
up an alternative way of thinking about management" (13). In Part II the authors
"apply the insights of the first section to the traditional organizational trio of strategy, structure, and performance measurement" (13). In Part III they explore "some
broader themes—knowledge, change, and finally, individual practice," in order to
"give managers a fresh way of thinking about their situation in general, and to suggest how certain issues might be approached differently" (13). Also included is a
bibliography that is divided into five parts: Humanities; Social, Cognitive, and
Physical Sciences; Management; Business Press; and Case Studies.

342 **Gibson, James L., John M. Ivancevich, and James H. Donnelly, Jr.**
     Organizations: Behavior, Structure, Processes. **8th ed. Burr Ridge, IL: Irwin,
     1994. Indexes. 802p.**

This textbook "seeks to present a realistic view of people working in organizations
throughout the world," according to its authors (vii). It "presents theories, research
results, and applications that focus on managing organizational behavior in local,
national, and worldwide organizations" (vii). The book's organization is based on
"three . . . characteristics common to all organizations: behavior, structure, and
processes" (viii). Part I constitutes an introduction to the topic and contains three
chapters. Part II and Part III focus on behavior (individual and group, respectively).
Part IV focuses on the "anatomy of organizations." Part V discusses processes such
as communication, decision making, and career and social processes. Part VI "presents the theory of organizational development in the context of an integrated model
and then describes and evaluates the more widely used OD [organizational devel-
opment] techniques" (ix). Two appendixes are included. The first "reviews research
procedures and techniques used in studying organizations" (ix). The second contains three "comprehensive" case studies.

343 **Helgesen, Sally. *The Female Advantage: Women's Ways of Leadership*. New
     York: Doubleday, 1990. 263p.**

According to the author, "the female advantage" is the edge gained from the
viewpoint of "an outsider unfamiliar with the corporate game" (xvi). The author
explains that this book is about "what business can learn from women" and, more
specifically, that the book attempts to "define and reaffirm the values that women
recognize as a source of their strength—values that have for too long been dis-
missed as signs of weakness" (xx). Those values include an attention to process,
a willingness to consider how personal actions affect others, a concern for the
needs of a community, and a willingness to forgo counterproductive rituals and
symbols of status.
    The book is organized in three parts. Part One considers women's ways of
leading and "how women structure things differently from men" (45). Part Two
consists of "diary studies" (i.e., case studies) of "women who were strongly conscious of their management styles" (65). In Part Three, the author presents her
conclusions and attempts to articulate the various differences between women's

and men's leadership styles. The author claims that the "splitting off [of] values for human connection and interdependence and assigning them to the female sphere has left the public world a hostile place" (254), and she therefore concludes that the entry of women into the public sphere can be seen "as a profound evolutionary response to a pervasive cultural crisis" (255).

344 **Nunamaker, J. F., Jr., et al. "Information Technology for Negotiating Groups: Generating Options for Mutual Gain."** *Management Science* **37.10 (October 1991): 1325–46.**

"This paper," the authors state, "presents an integrated series of laboratory experiments and field studies investigating the effects of EMS [Electronic Meeting System] support for option generation by groups that meet face-to-face in the same room at the same time. [Their] objective was to investigate the impacts of different EMS configurations, group characteristics and meeting processes on EMS-supported option generation" (1326). In section two of the article, the authors review "prior research and theory," and in section 3, using tables to illustrate, they present the results from their various research experiments (1326). In the final section, the authors "present several implications for theory development and system design and use, as well as a tentative model for computer-supported group option generation" (1324).

345 **Quinn, Robert E.** *Beyond Rational Management: Mastering the Paradoxes and Competing Demands of High Performance.* **San Francisco: Jossey-Bass, 1989. Index. Bib. 199p.**

The author notes that "administrative theory, the prescriptions of consultants, and even the explanations of successful managers" fail to reflect the dynamics of management (xiv). Quinn states, "In order to understand managerial effectiveness, we must move beyond the theories of rational management and begin to better understand the dynamic, paradoxical, and competing forces that block us from creating high-performance systems" (xiv). One purpose of this book, then, is "to provide the practitioner with a conscious understanding of what he or she has felt intuitively about management," and another purpose is "to affect the thinking of scholars in the field of management and organization" (xvi). One method of achieving those purposes is to discuss and critique in the 10 chapters various philosophical roles generally proposed for managers. In fact, at the end of the book, Quinn provides a bibliography that arranges works according to the various managerial roles, such as "facilitator," "mentor," "director," and "coordinator." Throughout the book, he provides many graphic illustrations to situate those roles within larger frameworks. He concludes, "Moving beyond rational management means moving to a metalevel that allows one to tolerate, consider, and employ both purposive and holistic frames. It means simultaneously using multiple frames to more effectively function in a world of paradox and competing demands" (165).

346 **Peters, Tom.** *Liberation Management: Necessary Disorganization for the Nanosecond Nineties.* **New York: Knopf, 1992. Index. 834p.**

The author claims that after coauthoring *In Search of Excellence* (Harper, 1982) and after writing *Thriving on Chaos* (Knopf, 1987), he has "finally shaken off the vestiges of 30 years of traditional thinking" with the writing of this book (xxxiv). This book is divided into six sections which encompass 47 chapters, each of which is subdivided into short sections. In Part I, "Necessary Disorganization: The New Exemplars," the author introduces the concept of fashion as the driving force in today's business and examines several corporations (EDS, CNN, and ABB Asea Brown Boveri) in order to demonstrate how the concept of disorganization is necessary to success in today's business world.

In Part II, "Learning to Hustle," the author presents case studies which "describe firms learning to hustle" (60). In Part III, "Information Technology: More, and Less, Than Promised," the author acknowledges the impact of information technology and presents examples of "information technology's stunning organizational implications" (121). The largest section of this book is Part IV, "Beyond Hierarchy," where the author shows how "Listening harder to employees, getting them involved in improvement processes, turning the organization into a collection of projects" (121), and getting beyond hierarchy do not mean "committing to anarchy" (132). Again, the author uses cases to explain. In Part V, "Markets and Innovation: The Case for Disorganization," the author argues that "giving the market free rein, inside and outside the firm, is the best—perhaps the only—satisfactory answer" concerning how to satisfy the unprecedented need for innovation (480). In Part VI, "Fashion!" the author notes that his "primary objective in this section . . . is to draw you a step away from the rational, the logical" (677). He argues that we "must learn to revel in the irrational, cotton to it, take it to our bosom, smile at it, grin at it. It's not enough to 'cope with it' or 'deal with it,' though that's more than most of us, trained as administrators, engineers, or scientists, do" (677). In an afterword the author emphasizes education as the key to success and concludes with the thought that "freedom to fail and try again is the essence of liberation, in America or elsewhere" (763).

347   Schein, Edgar H. *Organizational Culture and Leadership*. 2nd ed. San Francisco: Jossey-Bass, 1992. Index. Bib. 418p.

This book attempts to reveal "what the content of culture is and how leadership [is] intertwined with it" (xii). In addition, a "number of practical suggestions for dealing with cultural issues in organizations" are offered (xii). The book is organized into six parts: what culture is and does, the dimensions of culture, how to study and interpret culture, the role of leadership in building culture, the evolution of culture and leadership, and learning cultures and learning leaders. The author contends that cultural analysis is necessary in organizational studies because it "illuminates subcultural dynamics within organizations," promotes the understanding of "how new technologies influence and are influenced by organizations" (xii), and is an important component of "management across national and ethnic boundaries" (xiii). The author also argues that "organizational learning, development, and planned change cannot be understood without considering culture as a primary source of resistance to change" (xiv).

348   **Tannen, Deborah.** *Talking from 9 to 5: How Women's and Men's Conversational Styles Affect Who Gets Heard, Who Gets Credit, and What Gets Done at Work.* **New York: Morrow, 1994. Index. Bib. 368p.**

This book is the third of a series in which sociolinguist Deborah Tannen explores differences in conversational styles. Her trilogy began with *That's Not What I Meant!* (Morrow, 1986), a broad examination of conversational differences across race, class, region, and ethnicity in addition to gender. Her second book, *You Just Don't Understand* (Morrow, 1990) focuses on the differences between men and women in conversation. Over four years on the *New York Times* bestseller list, this book focuses on gender-based conversational differences in the private sphere. Tannen stresses that neither male nor female conversational styles are superior and that they are "different but equally valid styles" (15). Labeling these differences "Asymmetries," Tannen uses many examples to illustrate her points. Major topics include power paradigms, conversational intimacy, patterns of interruption, and conflict resolution.

Building on her second work, Tannen examines conversational differences among men and women in the workplace in *Talking from 9 to 5.* In this book, she suggests that talk at work is public and "what we say as we do our work can become evidence on which we are judged" (12). Included in the nine chapters are discussions of indirectness, status, and influence. Rather than call for people to change their ways of speaking, which she sees as "risky," she writes that "understanding what goes on when people talk to each other is the best way to improve communication—and get more work done—in the workplace as in all aspects of our lives" (309).

349   *Zuboff, Shoshana. In the Age of the Smart Machine: The Future of Work and Power.* **New York: Basic Books, 1988. Index. 468p.**

This book is a blending of empirical, historical, and theoretical forms of inquiry to explore the shift to a computerized workplace and a historical moment the author identifies as "the edge of a historical transformation of immense proportions" (xiii). Zuboff states that she "wanted to understand the practical problems that would have to be confronted in order to manage the new computerized workplace in ways that would fulfill the lofty promise of a knowledge-based society and to generate knowledge that would be instructive to those charged with that managerial responsibility" (xiv).

The book is divided into three parts, each focusing on one of three "dilemmas of transformation" to a computerized workplace: "Knowledge and Computer-Mediated Work," "Authority: The Spiritual Dimension of Power," and "Technique: The Material Dimension of Power." Each part blends historical commentary and empirical discussion from Zuboff's studies at eight different sites between 1981 and 1986. The three parts together make up Zuboff's theoretical argument about the management of computerized work processes.

One of Zuboff's key arguments is that information technology has dual capacities to "automate" and "informate." *Automating* "replace[s] the human body with a technology that enables the same processes to be performed with more continuity and control" (9). *Informating* is the technological process whereby information technologies generate "information about the underlying productive and administrative processes through which an organization accomplishes its work" (9).

Zuboff argues that although information technologies open the possibility of fulfilling "the lofty promise of a knowledge-based society," the technology cannot
alone make the change: there must be transformations, also, in the authority and
techniques of management.

PHILOSOPHY AND SCIENCE

350   Baudrillard, Jean. *Simulations*. Trans. Paul Foss, Paul Patton, and Philip
Beitchman. New York: Semiotext(e), 1983. 159p.

Defining *simulation* as "the generation by models of a real without origin or reality: a hyperreal," this book examines the complex theoretical implications of simulation and simulcra (2). The book is divided into two sections: "The Precession
of Simulacra" and "The Orders of Simulcra." The first section focuses on the
observation that "simulation threatens the difference between 'true' and 'false,'
between 'real' and 'imaginary'" and analyzes the implications of this notion for
topics as diverse (perhaps) as ethnology, Disneyland, Watergate, ideology, power,
and nuclear deterrence (5). The second section analyzes what the book identifies
as the three orders of simulcra: counterfeit ("based on the natural law of value"),
product (based "on the commercial law of value"), and simulation (based "on the
structural law of value") (83). These orders are seen as historical and sequential;
the current order of simulation is the "most accomplished form" (104), and its
central construct is "digitality" (115). Again the theoretical implications are analyzed for a range of issues, the sum of which defines a digital space of cultural
control. According to the author, this announces a "completely imaginary con-
tact-world" (140), which is described as "the great Culture of tactile communication, under the sign of the technico-luminous cinematic space of total spatio-
dynamic theatre" (139).

351   De Certeau, Michel. *The Practice of Everyday Life*. Trans. Steven Rendall.
Berkeley: U of California P, 1984. 229p.

De Certeau enters into a dialectic of "making" and "doing" in order to disclose the
modes of representation and power in everyday life. The author assumes that
"Everyday life invents itself by *poaching* in countless ways on the property of others" (xii), and so he is naturally curious about consumer production and the micro-
mechanisms of colonialism. Following the work of Foucault, De Certeau analyzes
cultural activities from the standpoint of those who do not produce culture but rather
"use" it blindly and in exploitative and exploited ways. The precise operations char-
acterizing consumption are implicated in "force-relationships" that are part of political, economic, and scientific arrangements over which consumers would seem to
have no control. The author borrows insights from Wittgenstein's ordinary language
theory to investigate the apparatus of everyday language and signifying practices.
De Certeau also examines the activity of reading as a form of consumption in which
we are trained to "poach" from the world, even as written texts represent the only
way cultures can enjoy longevity.

352   **Foucault, Michel.** *The Order of Things: An Archaeology of the Human* *Sciences.* **New York: Vintage, 1973.**

Foucault's archaeology describes the conditions that made knowledge possible in the three modern disciplines central to the human sciences: philology, biology, and economics. These disciplines make "Man" both the object and subject of study, "a strange empirico-transcendental doublet," which is the term Foucault employs for the reflexivity that takes place within the realms of life, labor, and language. He begins his archaeology of the concept "Man" by describing the philosophical antecedents to these three disciplines, emphasizing the discontinuity between earlier and later models. The seventeenth- and eighteenth-century disciplines depended on Classical, or Enlightenment, philosophies of representation, which saw language's role as a means for pointing out order based on similarities. But recent philosophies of language have considered knowledge as evolving, dynamic, and progressive and therefore fasten on ruptures and discontinuities. Foucault points to the works of Darwin, Marx, and Freud as representative of those who employ this modern view of language. He ends with a caution that the rules of formation that allowed "Man" to exist may shift once again and cause him to disappear.

353   **Gleick, James.** *Chaos: Making a New Science.* **New York: Viking, 1987. Index.** **352p.**

"Chaos theory" is now generally credited as the most revolutionary new idea in the physical sciences since the theory of relativity and quantum mechanics. Gleick's book is a summary of the research that has surrounded this idea in the last 30 years. In its simplest form, *chaos* refers to the science of hitherto unrecognized patterns of dynamic systems. The key assumption of the theory is that everything from cigarette smoke to the stock market is deeply processive rather than static, and that close attention to all phenomena will reveal new kinds of order underlying their manifest irregularities. The first chaos theorists, Gleick writes, "had an eye for pattern, especially pattern that appeared on different scales at the same time. They had a taste for randomness and complexity, for jagged edges and sudden leaps" (5). What may appear chaotic in one frame of reference may contain an order, even a beautiful continuity, when put into a different frame. Chaos concerns the global nature of systems and thus cuts across many disciplines, from particle physics to meteorology to cellular biology to astronomy. What unites these disciplines, according to Gleick and the chaos theorist, is the idea that there may be complexity without randomness.

Despite its rather misleading name, *chaos* actually refers to dynamic systems that do not merely tend toward absolute disorder, as the theory of entropy would have it. Chaos suggests complex patterns within dissipation. As one theorist puts it: "God plays dice with the universe. . . . But they're loaded dice" (314).

354   **Habermas, Jurgen.** *Moral Consciousness and Communicative Action.* **Trans.** **Christian Lenhardt and Shierry Weber Nicholsen. Cambridge, MA: MIT P,** **1990. Index. 225p.**

According to Thomas McCarthy's introduction, Habermas's discourse ethics succeeds in "locating the common core of morality in the normative presuppositions of communicative interaction, it develops a thoroughly intersubjectivist interpretation of the moral point of view: practical discourse as a reflective continuation of communicative interaction preserves that common core" (xi). Emerging like Rorty from the Kantian and Hegelian traditions, Habermas is a pragmatist who believes that the best that philosophy can do is play the role of a "stand-in" and interpreter, rather than presume to settle issues with reason and authority. Habermas assumes that argumentation about questions of justice possesses cognitive meaning and should be treated like truth-claims and that these issues take place in a real discourse that is necessarily dialogic—hence, the importance of participation and "communicative action" in the development of moral consciousness. Discourse ethics postulates the consent of all and yet avoids absolutist and universalist assumptions about moral certainty. Only a sufficiently materialist and dialectical theory of society, for Habermas, can promise this form of consent.

355   **Jameson, Fredric.** *Postmodernism, or, The Cultural Logic of Late Capitalism.* **Durham, NC: Duke UP, 1991. Index. 438p.**

This exploration of the concept of postmodernism involves, the author says, "an experiment, namely, the attempt to see whether by systematizing something that is resolutely unsystematic, and historicizing something that is resolutely ahistorical, one couldn't outflank it and force a historical way at least of thinking about that" (418). The first two essays, "The Cultural Logic of Late Capitalism" and "Theories of the Postmodern," appear here essentially unchanged from their original publication. "The remainder of the volume," the author tells us, "turns essentially on four themes: interpretation, Utopia, survivals of the modern, and 'returns of the repressed' of historicity" (xv). In his attempt to "historicize" postmodernism, the author includes an examination of such topics as video, architecture, reading, space, theory, economics, and film.

356   **Kuhn, Thomas S.** *The Structure of Scientific Revolutions.* **2nd ed. Chicago: U of Chicago P, 1970. 210p.**

Kuhn's book is often referred to as a landmark in intellectual history. It is a landmark because Kuhn effectively practices a metascientific inquiry that calls into question the very nature of scientific method. The object of greatest scrutiny for Kuhn he calls "normal science," which refers to a tradition of research sanctioned by a particular scientific community. To examine this essentially conservative (and unreflective) set of codes, Kuhn proposes the idea of "paradigms." For Kuhn, paradigms "provide models from which spring particular coherent traditions of scientific research" (10). Normal science does not disclose its supervising paradigms, nor does it take seriously the anomalies that always crop up in scientific experiments. When these anomalies come to predominate, then, Kuhn claims, a new paradigm is called for to make sense of them. This is how one tradition supplants another. Most of Kuhn's book is an examination of how and why scientific revolutions occur— why a paradigm shift happens at a certain point in the history of science. Far from being based on objective, foundational facts, this history is permeated by conventions, communities, and intuitions that make it difficult to predict the course of inquiry. Kuhn's book may itself be seen as occasioning a paradigm shift, as the sci-

entific world undergoes another Copernican revolution is recognizing the historicity of its most cherished assumptions.

In an important postscript (written seven years later), Kuhn addresses the criticism of his colleagues, especially regarding his sometimes ambiguous use of the
term *paradigm.*

357   **Latour, Bruno, and Steve Woolgar.** *Laboratory Life: The Social Construction
of Scientific Facts.* **Beverly Hills, CA: Sage, 1979. Bib. 271p.**

This book is the result of Latour's two-year study of a laboratory and the "daily and
intimate processes of scientific work" which took place there (12). "In this book,"
Jonas Salk says, "the authors demonstrate what they call the 'social construction' of
science by the use of honest and valid examples of laboratory science" (12). In
Chapter 1, the authors "focus on two major questions: How are the facts constructed in a laboratory, and how can a sociobiologist account for this construction? What,
if any, are the differences between the construction of facts and the construction of
accounts?" (40) In Chapter 2, the authors "portray the laboratory as seen through the
eyes of a total newcomer" (40). A "close examination of the historical construction
of one particular fact and of the implications for subsequent laboratory work" is
undertaken in Chapter 3 (41). In Chapter 4, the authors consider "the microprocess-
es of negotiation which take place continually in the laboratory" (41). The authors,
in Chapter 5, "look at the series of strategies taken up by members of the laboratory in their decisions to back the construction of one or other fact and in their efforts
to enhance their ability further to invest in the construction of 'new' facts" (41). In
Chapter 6, the authors review, based on their observations, "the essential elements
of the process whereby an ordered account is fabricated from disorder and chaos"
(41). They conclude with a discussion of "the essential similarity between the construction of accounts" in the laboratory and their "own construction of an account
which portrays the laboratory in this way" (41).

358   **Lincoln, Yvonna S., and Egon G. Guba.** *Naturalistic Inquiry.* **Beverly Hills,
CA: Sage, 1985. Index. Bib. 416p**

"This is a book," state the authors, "aimed at helping the reader both to understand and
to do naturalistic inquiry" (9). The first seven chapters "are devoted to laying out the
arguments against the conventional inquiry paradigm, which [the authors] most often
label the 'positivistic,' proposing an alternative paradigm, the 'naturalistic,' and arguing for its adoption" (10). In Chapter 8, the authors move from "the purely theoretical
and toward the practice of naturalistic inquiry" (10); they argue that "loyalty to one or
another paradigm has implications for the methodology that an investigator employs"
(10). The authors state that "Chapters 9 through 13 are the 'doing' chapters" (11),
wherein they address issues of design, implementation, data processing, and reporting.
Appendix A suggests audit trail categories, file types, and sources of evidence.
Appendix B provides a procedure for auditing naturalistic inquiries.

359   **Lyotard, Jean-Francois.** *The Postmodern Condition: A Report on Knowledge.*
**Trans. Geoff Bennington and Brian Massumi. Minneapolis: U of Minnesota
P, 1984. Index. 110p.**

Lyotard develops his ideas about how societies legitimate knowledge by moving through three sets of binaries. First, he contrasts modernity's rationalism with the postmodernity's language games, which locates knowledge within the dynamics of language and culture. Next, he contrasts the empirical methods of scientific knowledge with the metanarratives of cultural knowledge until he blurs the distinction between them, leaving science bound to the rules in its use of metanarratives. Finally, he contrasts the stability of broad, cultural metanarratives with the dynamics of local paralogy, or a "move . . . played in the pragmatics of knowledge" (61). In the end, Lyotard suggests that for resolving human conflict society follow language models rather than scientific models.

360   **Maslow, Abraham H.** *The Psychology of Science: A Reconnaissance.* **New York: Harper & Row, 1966.**

In this book, the author "pursues questions like the following: How adequate are the concepts and methods of classical science for acquiring knowledge about the human person? What are the consequences of the inadequacies? What counterproposals can be offered and tested? What are the implications for those who plan programs to train researchers?" (xii). In Chapter 1, the author states: "This book is not an argument *within* orthodox science; it is a critique of orthodox science and of the ground on which it rests, of its unproved articles of faith, and of its taken-for-granted definitions, axioms, and concepts" (1). Written in the form of a series of lectures, the author tends to be more personal, "to use examples from his own experience, [and] to express his own opinions, doubts, and conjectures" (xvi). The author does not believe this book to be a "divisive effort to oppose one 'wrong' view with another 'right' view, nor to cast out anything" (5). He believes that "The conception of science in general, of which this book is a sample, is *inclusive* of mechanistic science" (5). He also believes, however, that mechanistic science is "too narrow and limited to serve as a *general* or comprehensive philosophy" (5).

361   **Pirsig, Robert M.** *Zen and the Art of Motorcycle Maintenance: An Inquiry into Values.* **New York: Morrow, 1984. 412p.**

Pirsig's novel has become something more than a cult classic since its publication. It is now recognized as an extremely acute analysis of a certain schizoid temperament that must remind one of C. P. Snow's *The Two Cultures* (363). Like Snow, Pirsig wishes to diagnose a tendency in Western society to separate technological expertise from a more holistic, humanistic understanding of the world. The controlling metaphor for this analysis is the motorcycle, which for Pirsig represents a piece of technology one may tinker with in the same way one tinkers with one's own beliefs and desires. The adventure of the tinkering soul Pirsig calls a "Chautauqua"—a way of enlightening the culture by literally and philosophically traversing its geography. Pirsig's main question in the novel is "What is quality?" as he tries to move beyond the platitude of "What's new?" to the far more compelling question "What is best?" This question takes Pirsig back to Greek philosophy and encourages him to make a distinction between two modes of understanding: romantic and classic. Pirsig finds motorcycle riding romantic, while he sees motorcycle maintenance as classic.

An editor and writer of technical manuals before writing his novel, Pirsig struggles to understand how technical writing became so far removed from a sense of caring about both the readers of these manuals and the actual technological device being described. By introducing the Eastern concept of "Zen" into Western rationality, Pirsig hopes to suggest an alternate framework for making sense of our own technology. The novel itself describes his quest to humanize rationality and heal over the schizoid state—actually a form of madness for the narrator—produced by an overanalytical view of life.

362   Rorty, Richard. *Philosophy and the Mirror of Nature*. **Princeton, NJ: Princeton UP, 1979. Index. 401p.**

Rorty's first major book is an interrogation of what he believes is the central, foundational concern of the Western philosophical tradition: a general theory of representation. The governing metaphor of this theory is ocular and inherited from the Greeks—the idea that the mind is a great mirror that contains a variety of more or less accurate representations, the accuracy of which may be determined by nonempirical means. "The aim of the book," Rorty claims, "is to undermine the reader's confidence in 'the mind' as something about which one should have a 'philosophical' view, in 'knowledge' as something about which there ought to be a 'theory' and which has 'foundations,' and in 'philosophy' as it has been conceived since Kant" (7). It was Wittgenstein, Heidegger, and Dewey, Rorty believes, who brought us into a period of revolutionary philosophy by variously "deconstructing" traditional philosophical problems not so much by attacking them directly as by supplying new terms and vocabularies which make these problems irrelevant. Rorty acknowledges that the moral of his book is "historicist," in the sense of situating concepts of "mind," of "knowledge," and of the "philosophical" in the paradigms that once gave them relevance and urgency. Rorty hopes his critique of these governing paradigms (all supervised by the "mirror of nature" metaphor) will have the effect of making them seem "quaint." Only after we are no longer captivated by mirror imagery and the corresponding ideal of objective cognition will we be free to realize Dewey's (and Rorty's) hope that the arts and the sciences will flourish together without anyone's worrying about accuracy of representation. In Rorty's own field, this amounts to practicing "philosophy without mirrors," which is indeed what his book is trying to make possible.

363   Snow, C. P. *The Two Cultures: And a Second Look*. **London: Cambridge UP, 1965. 107p.**

Snow's diagnosis of a growing split in Western culture has become a landmark in social and intellectual history. As a trained scientist and a professional writer, Snow is in a position to see this rift opening and to analyze the reasons for it. Snow sees Western society as being polarized between the "literary intellectuals" and those in the physical sciences. For Snow, "This polarization is a loss to us all. To us as people, and to our society. It is at the same time practical and intellectual and creative loss" (11). Snow's discussion leads him to examine the nature and consequences of the Industrial Revolution, the scientific revolution, increasing distance between the rich and the poor, and the disintegration of the arts and the sciences in higher education. The fact that the West is splitting apart into two cultures is both cause and effect of a complete breakdown in communication in Western society—the inability of two groups to generate any sympathy or tolerance for each other. Worse than this, for Snow, is the basic ignorance that keeps the scientists and the literary intellectuals apart, for it is a willed ignorance, bred of snobbery and condescension. Educational reform at all levels is the only way to begin to bring the two cultures back together again, so that we are "not ignorant of imaginative experience, both in the arts and in science" (100). Without this reform, incomprehension and ignorance will intensify and quite literally tear Western society apart.

TECHNOLOGY STUDIES

364 **Baecker, Ronald M., and William A. S. Buxton, eds.** *Readings in Human–Computer Interaction: A Multidisciplinary Approach.* **San Mateo, CA: Morgan Kaufmann, 1987. Indexes. 738p.**

Noting the "absence of any appropriate text" in the area of user interface design, the authors offer this as a "source book of outstanding papers in the field" (2). Of the book's 14 chapters, 13 are organized into three parts: Part I addresses the historical, sociopolitical, and physical context of human–computer interaction; Part II examines interactive computer systems in terms of both user and usage; and Part III focuses on system design as a process. Each of these three parts presents a specific case study. The final chapter discusses "research frontiers and unsolved problems" (2). Individual chapters and case studies include an introduction as well as "key articles selected and reprinted from the literature" (2). The authors note that the volume can "not only serve as a valuable free-standing collection but as a set of pointers and a guide to the rich and rapidly evolving literature of human-computer interaction" (3). Numerous tables, graphs, and illustrations are included.

365 **Berk, Emily, and Joseph Devlin, eds.** *Hypertext/Hypermedia Handbook.* **New York: McGraw-Hill, 1991. Index. 583p.**

The editors state that their "goal in editing this book was to collect and contrast as many contradictory views about hypertext as we could" (xiv). The book is divided into 10 sections: "Introduction," which includes some definitions and a history of hypertext; "Types of Hypertexts," which features a debate between text-only and multimedia hypertexts; "Conventions for Writers/Readers of Hypertext," a discussion of hypertext as a literary genre with a bit about interactive fiction; "Automatic versus Hand Generation," an explanation of how the new automatic text-to-hypertext conversion systems work and how they can best be applied; "Designing Hypertexts," which provides authors with suggested approaches to take when designing and implementing hypertexts; "Licensing and Protection of Electronically Published Information," which highlights legal issues that hypertext publishers should consider; "Issues for Hypertext Readers," another debate—this one focusing on the dreaded syndrome known to hypertext authors as "Lost in Hyperspace"— plus a suggested cure; "Integrating Hypertext with Other Technologies," in which hypertext is described in the context of other computer-based information management and retrieval techniques; "Industrial-Strength Hypertext," in which three luminaries in the field of hypertext discuss where they think hypertext technology needs to go in order to become truly useful; and "The Future of Hypertext," a discussion of the need for standards and of the future promise and responsibilities that attach to hypertext as a new mass medium. Three appendixes are included, which contain case studies, a glossary, and a list of references.

---

366   **Feenberg, Andrew.** *Critical Theory of Technology.* **New York: Oxford UP, 1991. Index. 235p.**

This book presents a thorough critique of two prevalent approaches to technology, "the neutrality of technology and the related theory of technological determinism," in order to pave the way for an alternative approach (v). The book is divided into three main sections plus an introduction and conclusion. The introduction attempts to situate the critical theory of technology among other theories, especially those coming out of the Frankfurt school and orthodox Marxism. Part I is a critique of Marx's theory of labor in technical society with an emphasis on its lack of a "coherent strategy for change." Part II builds on another critique of Marxist theory, "the idea that States are the primary agents of change in a culture," and discusses the ways humans are implicated in the complex technical systems associated with late capitalism. Part III considers the cultural implications of widespread democratic technological change and his conclusion lays the groundwork for a specific plan encouraging such change.

Feenberg complicates the traditional definition of *technology* as "things," arguing that technology is instead a type of social development that enframes those things we usually think of as "technologies," machines and processes, along with people. As a social process, technology is not a benign push for progress, nor is it the vast, overdetermining and oppressive force that Heidegger imagines. Instead, technology is characterized by its "ambivalence," a system subject to change based on the people who participate in it. Since technologies are designed by people, within the ethical and political spheres of a culture, the values that are manifested in the design, production, and use of technologies are subject to change. Feenberg calls these values "the technical code." It is through a grassroots process of democratic participation in the re-design of the technical code that Feenberg sees possibilities for positive change.

---

367   **Heidegger, Martin.** *The Question Concerning Technology and Other Essays.* **Trans. William Lovitt. New York: Harper & Row, 1977. 182p.**

This book contains five essays that are organized into three parts. The first essay in Part I, "The Question Concerning Technology," interrogates the essence of technology through the Greek concept of *techne*, or artistic knowledge in its "widest sense" interpreted as a "mode of revealing." We understand Greek techne as the activity of "bringing forth" in the classical sense of an artistic craft or the production of goods. Modern technology alters this mode of revealing by setting upon and ordering nature as *Ge-stelle*, or "Enframing," the revelation of the world as "standing-reserve," a resource ready for use and exploitation. A critical danger arises when humans perceive this ordering as "natural" and its technology (Enframing) as "neutral," because we mistakenly see ourselves as masters who control technology when in reality we humans have also become ordered by Enframing into an exploitable resource of standing-reserve. Enframing follows its own destiny and thus conceals the revealing power of *techne*, hiding the truth of our relation to technology. Since the "destining" of modern technology remains incomplete, only questioning our preoccupation with technology will confront its dangers. Thus Heidegger concludes that "questioning is the piety of thought" (35). The second essay in Part I, "The Turning," deals with how Being itself has been disguised by Enframing. Yet Heidegger insists that within the concealment of Being, a "flashing glance" or insight is offered to us, which allows "the turning," or a new coming to presence in which we might reestablish an authentic relationship to Being.

Part II contains an essay on "The Word of Nietzsche: 'God Is Dead,'" which relates Nietzsche's idea of the death of God to Heidegger's notion that Being has disguised itself and withdrawn from human presence. The metaphysics of God give way to a human metaphysics of valuing, based in reason and operating as a techne or enframing principle of nihilism: the-world-as-object swallowed up by human subjectivity, which becomes the adversary of thought. Nietzsche's metaphysics of revaluing values, on the other hand, confronts nihilism as the desire for thinking beyond reason and the death of God. Part III contains the last two essays, "The Age of the World Picture" and "Science and Reflection," which discuss how science and technology have metaphysically positioned the modern subject and its view of the world-as-object so that only that which science allows to be revealed as truth will be so revealed.

368   **Heim, Michael. *The Metaphysics of Virtual Reality*. New York: Oxford UP, 1993. Index. Bib. 175p.**

Continuing the line of thought Heim developed in his previous book, *Electric Language* (Yale UP, 1987), this book traces the recent progress of computing technology as it shifts our information infrastructure from the context of a digital reality to that of a virtual reality. In 10 chapters, Heim describes how the move toward virtual reality involves an "ontological shift" in how we perceive, know, and perform in daily life. Chapters One through Three look at how, in the 1980s, digital computers altered our methods of reading and searching through information, and how the linear logic of computers, Boolean searches, and hypertext continue to transform our habits of thought. Chapter Four focuses on the distinctions between print and computer literacies and how writing software changes writers into idea processors; Chapter Five presents Heidegger and MacLuhan as the first philosophers to assess fully the pervasive changes technology imposes on everyday life. The remaining five chapters deal with questions concerning simulated environments, including video screens as interfaces to cyberspace, the primal and erotic origins of cyberspace in Plato and Leibnitz, definitions of virtual reality, existential distinctions between virtual and real realities, and the fears and fervors evoked by popular visions of virtual reality in the media.

Heim strikes a balance between describing how technology changes our literacy habits and discussing the philosophical implications of such changes. He investigates why virtual reality has excited our imaginations and repeatedly considers the basic question: "How much can humans change and still remain human as they enter the cyberspace of computerized realities?" (xii). Although he looks at both negative and positive effects of technology, he concludes that the sublime and awesome come together in virtual reality, making it ultimately a philosophical experience as well as an unfolding dimension of a new and unifying network of human presence.

The book includes a 15-page glossary entitled "Useful Vocabulary for the Metaphysics of Virtual Reality," relevant Internet addresses, and a list of "Selected Readings."

369   **Helander, Martin, ed.** *Handbook of Human-Computer Interaction.* **Amsterdam: North-Holland, 1988. Indexes. 1167p.**

This book is "concerned with the principles of Human Factors Engineering for design of the Human–Computer Interface"; in addition, it "summarizes the research and provides recommendations for how the information can be used by designers of computer systems" (xi). The book's 52 chapters are divided into seven parts, according to the following topics: models and theories of human–computer interaction, user interface design, individual differences and training, applications of computer technology, tools for design and evaluation, artificial intelligence, and psychological and organizational issues. The author notes that even though computer development is rapidly changing, the information presented in the book will not be quickly outdated, chiefly because much of the information "deals with generic Human Factors problems and principles for systems design" (xii).

370   **Holtzman, Steven R.** *Digital Mantras: The Languages of Abstract and Virtual Worlds.* **Cambridge, MA: MIT P, 1994. Index. Bib. 321p.**

This book examines the aesthetic foundations of computer use in areas of creative expression such as language, music, art, and virtual reality. The book is divided into three parts: "Structures," "Structure Manipulators," and "Vibration." Part I looks at abstract structures in established traditions, including the first concepts of grammar in the Aryan culture of ancient India, Ferdinand de Saussure's development of structuralist linguistics, and Noam Chomsky's work in generative grammars. Holtzman relates the abstract concept of linguistic structures to music and the visual arts, focusing on Arnold Schoenberg's serial music theory; postwar composers such as Berg, Webern, and Boulez; and the abstract art of Wasily Kandinsky. Part II begins with Liebnitz's calculus, a history of calculating machines, and their relationship to natural language. Holtzman then traces the influence of composing machines on musicians Gottfried Koenig and Iannis Xenakis and on the visual artist Harold Cohen. He concludes Part II with a chapter on "virtual worlds," which discusses the advent of virtual reality in cyberspace. Part III explores the creative, aesthetic, and mystical implications of computers as a new means of creative expression, focusing on their idiomatic potential, the relation of structure to meaning, and the place of computers in the mystical tradition.

Wide-ranging and synthetic in his approach, Holtzman argues that computers have ushered in a new age of creative expression but that their essential role as manipulators of abstract structures reveals the aesthetic foundations of a long cultural tradition that equates meaning with form and structure with expression. Although the connections he makes between such diverse areas of knowledge as modern linguistics, music, and Indian mysticism are highly speculative, Holtzman clearly and succinctly sketches the significance of important new ideas in the history of linguistic representation, the aesthetic theories of several modern artistic movements, key events in the history of computing technology, and the impact of these events on the work of musicians and artists. The book contains a five-page bibliography of sources.

371   **Postman, Neil. *Technopoly: The Surrender of Culture to Technology*. New York: Knopf, 1992. Index. Bib. 222p.**

Observing that the culture of technology is separate from human culture, the author argues that these two cultures "are in fierce opposition to each other, and that it is necessary for a great debate to ensue about the matter" (xi–xii). Thus, this book "attempts to describe when, how, and why technology became a particularly dangerous enemy" (xii). The book is organized into eleven chapters. Chapters 1 through 3 argue that technological change is total change and attempt to trace the historical evolution of technocracy into Technopoly in the United States. Chapter 4 examines the causes of the current Technopoly, while Chapter 5 analyzes the effects of Technopoly on American social institutions, including how it "hopes to control information and thereby provide itself with intelligibility and order" (91). However, in Chapters 6 through 11, the author "tells the story of why this cannot work, and of the pain and stupidity that are the consequences" (91). The author concludes that the Technopoly creates a need for "a curriculum in which all subjects are presented as a stage in humanity's historical development; in which the philosophies of science, of history, of language, of technology, and of religion are taught; and in which there is a strong emphasis on classical forms of artistic expression" (199).

372   **Schrage, Michael. *Shared Minds: The New Technologies of Collaboration*. New York: Random House, 1990. Index. Bib. 227p.**

This book analyzes the nature and practice of collaboration as it is related to available and emerging technologies. Organized into 14 chapters, the book examines first "the communications and technical underpinnings of collaboration and explains why collaboration will become a dominant theme of professional relationships"; next, "it defines and explores the dynamics of collaboration and the importance of language and tools in harnessing them"; finally, it "looks at the emerging generation of collaborative tools and examines the challenges of designing collaborative environments for the future" (xxv). The author acknowledges that "collaborative tools don't necessarily lead to better collaborations" (195), but he points out that "collaborative media are designed explicitly to augment the quality of the [collaborative] interaction itself" (196).

373   **Shneiderman, Ben. *Designing the User Interface: Strategies for Effective Human–Computer Interaction*. 2nd ed. Reading, MA: Addison-Wesley, 1992. Indexes. 573p.**

As in the first edition of this book, the author "presents design issues, offers experimental evidence where available, and makes reasonable recommendations where suitable" (iv). Some of the improvements over the first edition include attention to topics like internationalization, the needs of disabled and elderly users, virtual reality, teleoperation, window design, computer-supported cooperative work, and a discussion of ethical and social issues. The book is organized into 14 chapters, to which an afterword is appended. The author notes that while it was important in the second edition to reflect the current state of human factors design research, the goal of this book "is not to record what is happening at every research frontier" but rather "to give a balanced and thorough presentation of our steadily growing discipline" (v). Ample pictures, tables, graphs, and illustrations are included.

374   **Suchman, Lucy A.** *Plans and Situated Actions: The Problem of Human—Machine Communication.* **Cambridge: Cambridge UP, 1987. Indexes. Bib. 203p.**

This book analyzes "the conception of purposeful action, and consequently of interaction, informing the design of interactive machines" (2) by investigating "the basis for beginning to speak of interaction between humans and machines" (3). The book is organized into eight chapters, with Chapter 1 serving as an introduction. Chapter 2 "introduces the notion of interactive artifacts, and its basis in certain properties of computing machines"; Chapter 3 "examines the view of plans as the basis for action and communication held by designers of artificially intelligent, interactive machines"; Chapters 4 and 5 "present the alternative view of action and communication as situated"; Chapters 6 and 7 "offer an analysis of encounters between novice users of a machine and a computer-based system intended to be intelligent and interactive"; Chapter 8 presents the book's overall conclusions (3–4). The author observes that there exists in human–machine communication an essential "asymmetry that substantially limits the scope of interaction between people and machines" (181); moreover, the author concludes that "as long as machine actions are determined by stipulated conditions, machine interaction with the world, and with people in particular, will be limited to the intentions of designers and their ability to anticipate and constrain the user's actions" (189).

375   **Williams, Frederick, and David V. Gibson, eds.** *Technology Transfer: A Communication Perspective.* **Newbury Park, CA: Sage, 1990. Index. 302p.**

Technology transfer, as the editors describe, "reflects all or some of the process of moving ideas from the research laboratory to the marketplace" (10). This book makes a case for the importance of studying technology transfer as a communication process (involving group, organizational, and interpersonal communication research strategies) and provides a comprehensive examination of this concept.

The book has five sections. It opens with an essay that highlights the economic impact of technology transfer in a global marketplace. Part II includes studies that examine the environments or organizational settings of intraorganizational and interorganizational technology transfer. Part III looks at the specific contexts surrounding technology transfer. Part IV consists of essays that describe specific international perspectives from Mexico, Japan, Italy, and India and an essay on how technology transfer is integrated into training programs in multinational corporations. The book closes with a bibliography of additional sources (beyond those cited in the book) considered relevant to the study of technology transfer as a communication process, thus providing a resource for scholarship as well as for the practice of this "communication phenomenon."

376   **Winner, Langdon.** *The Whale and the Reactor: A Search for Limits in an Age of High Technology*. **Chicago: U of Chicago P, 1986. Index. 200p.**

Winner's book is about the meaning and consequences of the vast, transcultural systems of communication and technology that have come to permeate our lives. Winner studies the politics of technical objects in order to move beyond their instrumentality. In the largest sense, Winner proposes a political philosophy of technology whose basic question is: "How can we limit modern technology to match our best sense of who we are and the kind of world we would like to build?" (xi). An important aspect of this question, for Winner, is vocabulary we typically use to address issues about technology, society, and the environment. Winner wants to "open up the conversation" (x) by generating a richer vocabulary for expressing our interests. Unless we begin to generate this more complex and subtle vocabulary, Winner believes we will never be able to set limits on our technological experiments and ambitions, no matter how disastrous the consequences may be. Until we who live in a "technopolis" see the importance of limits on our technological advances, we will be arrogantly committed to excess, which for Winner is often connected to the gigantism of the war industry and its advocates: people who prize reactors over whales.

AUTHOR INDEX

Following the entries are item numbers that appear in the text in the left margin beginning on page 24.

SUBJECT INDEX

Item numbers appear in regular typeface, and page numbers appear in italics. Sections appear in boldface, with page numbers following.